KNOW THE PERSONALITY OF YOUR CHILD

USING THE SCIENCE OF NUMBERS (NUMEROLOGY)

NEIL KOELMEYER

BALBOA.
PRESS

A DIVISION OF HAY HOUSE

Balboa Press books may be ordered through booksellers or by contacting:

Balboa Press
A Division of Hay House
1663 Liberty Drive
Bloomington, IN 47403
www.balboapress.com.au
1 (877) 407-4847

Because of the dynamic nature of the Internet, any web addresses or links contained in this book may have changed since publication and may no longer be valid. The views expressed in this work are solely those of the author and do not necessarily reflect the views of the publisher, and the publisher hereby disclaims any responsibility for them.

The author of this book does not dispense medical advice or prescribe the use of any technique as a form of treatment for physical, emotional, or medical problems without the advice of a physician, either directly or indirectly. The intent of the author is only to offer information of a general nature to help you in your quest for emotional and spiritual well-being. In the event you use any of the information in this book for yourself, which is your constitutional right, the author and the publisher assume no responsibility for your actions.

Any people depicted in stock imagery provided by Thinkstock are models, and such images are being used for illustrative purposes only.
Certain stock imagery © Thinkstock.

Print information available on the last page.

ISBN: 978-1-5043-0580-8 (sc)
ISBN: 978-1-5043-0581-5 (e)

Balboa Press rev. date: 12/21/2016

Introduction

Know the Personality of your Child is an endeavor to help parents, grandparents, guardians, and others to gain a timely understanding of the personalities of children in their charge. Such understanding will inevitably contribute toward knowledgeable upbringing and a mutually beneficial interaction. It should, at the same time, make life easier, enjoyable, and educational for those charged with the responsibility of nurturing a single child or many children.

This book is the result of many consultations I have had over the years with people who have a natural interest in the personalities of their children. Interesting revelations have come to light from time to time. For instance, I have met parents who mistakenly believe they have what they term a "problem child" on their hands. But after some discussion I have found that the "problem" did not necessarily exist with the child but with the parent or parents themselves. There is often a lack of understanding that their children are not the same as themselves, and that they are individuals with personalities of their own. Children may resemble their parents in physical features but not in temperament and potential. The fact that children are perennial contributors to adult education is a truth that some parents do not acknowledge.

The principles of this book are based on the science of numbers, commonly known as Numerology. It has been produced as a quick reference for busy people and not as a comprehensive study or textbook. There are many books available on this topic for anyone interested in acquiring a good working knowledge of Numerology. Readers are welcome to refer to any of the following books written by me: *The Secret Language of your Name* by Neil Koelmeyer and Ursula Kolecki, and *The Complete Numerology of Relationships* by Neil Koelmeyer. This subject is not a recent or newfangled invention but an ancient study practiced for centuries by the Hebrews, Greeks, Indians, and Chinese, each with a system of their own. The most popular one in the western world was introduced by the Greek philosopher and mathematician Pythagoras. This book is based on this system. The numbers of our birth date and to some extent the numbers in our names, particularly the given name, are used to determine the personality and potential of an individual.

The three areas of influence which are more than sufficient to obtain a good knowledge of a child's personality and potential are the birth day, birth month and given name. There are other areas of influence such as the birth year and other names but all these cannot be taken into consideration in a book of this size. That would be a monumental task given the complexity of explaining multiple interacting forces.

I have listed below many pertinent questions that may be asked when a child's birth day and birth month are examined.

- To what degree does a child possess self-confidence and self-sufficiency, or the lack or weakness, of these attributes?
- Will the child be a leader, follower, a strict individualist, a loner, or something in between?
- Is the child extroverted, reserved, shy, or introverted?
- How will the child relate to parents, siblings, cousins, and schoolmates?
- To what extent is the child physically, emotionally, mentally, or spiritually oriented? Is there an emphasis on one or two levels of expression or an even distribution?
- Is the child of a sentimental nature—easily demonstrative of emotion (cries easily), or serene and unflappable, avoiding too much body contact (not always cuddly)? Is the child of a thoughtful and contemplative disposition or active and energetic?
- Will the child be competitive, non-competitive, or something in between? Has the child an assertive, aggressive, defensive, or cooperative nature?
- Will the child be talkative, quietly spoken, taciturn, or with a mixture these?

- How will a particular child react to correction or reprimand? To what degree will a child exhibit rebelliousness or acceptance?
- Will the child need frequent company, or demand constant attention or notice?

To what extent will a child need private time?

- Is the child of a studious nature, intellectual, and imaginative, or practical and down-to-earth? What general direction should a child's education take?
- Will the child grow into a taker, giver, or sharer?
- Could the child become subject to bullying or resort to bullying?

When an examination of a child's birth day and month is made, answers to these questions reveal an amazing accuracy in mostly every case. Accuracy is influenced by various factors in the child's life.

When a baby is born it perceives no difference between itself and its mother. Ideas of a "self" first enter the consciousness of a child when it identifies with bodily feelings and later when it adds emotional feelings; later again, into logical thought and lastly with the realization of its individuality. Many of the personality traits and talents each child is born with emerge gradually during the years of growth and as opportunities are presented for their expression. Many traits may remain dormant until early adulthood or maturity. More often than is realized, children absorb emotional and other cues from parents, older siblings, and other adults. Children are not necessarily born with a clean slate, so to speak. Advantages and encumbrances of parental heritage and various influences of their surroundings often make or mar certain aspects of their personalities to various degrees. Some adults may hold a belief in the possibility of a carry-over of personality traits and talents, positive or negative, from previous incarnations. With some children all these influences may remain as permanent fixtures while in others they may be shed or altered for better or worse as they grow older. The following are some specific conditions that could interfere with an accurate assessment of a child's personality:

- The gestation period and birth itself, during which the baby may have been traumatized for various reasons, such as a medical condition, the mother's physical/emotional turmoil, and/or the mother's neglect of her health
- A dysfunctional or broken family. Confusion arising from divided loyalties in situations of parental divorce early in the child's life. Absence of extended family support
- Adverse socio/economic conditions such as extreme poverty or a violent environment
- Working parents who may be time poor
- Neglectful parents. Parents with poor maternal and paternal skills. Parents not yet ready for parenthood
- Children showered with material goods but deprived of demonstrated love and family togetherness. Such children may develop an unrealistic sense of entitlement. The possibility of children taking over personality quirks and habits from their parents that are not natural to them, not knowing whether they are theirs or their parents
- Possessive, fearful, and fussy parents
- Parents who are uncommunicative, inaccessible, and poor confidants
- Parents who are reluctant or incapable of dealing with conflict
- Unrealistic adult expectations of children who may not have the potential to live up to the expectations of the parent. Failure to accept children for exactly who they are
- Parents projecting their own fears, ambitions, or lost ambitions on their children
- Regular use of negative criticism and derogatory pet names. Belittling children in the presence of others
- Inhibitive or restricting family traditions (cultural and religious), that no longer conform to current conditions
- Indoctrination: never allowing the child to think for themselves as they grow
- Serious long-term upheavals in life such as war, natural disasters, and persecution. Restriction or discrimination suffered by an ethnic or religious minority, or just physical appearance

- Parents who have never resorted to self-examination and self-education. Those with no self-control
- Physical, emotional, sexual, and mental abuse
- Parents who are not capable of coping with a child's physical or mental disability, either from birth or after birth
- Parents adopting or fostering children who have already been negatively influenced
- Parents with an authoritative nature who have never had the opportunity to exercise their authority in public life may do so within the home, often unjustly. Children are often their victims.

These and other likely hazards of babyhood and childhood make it clear that nature as well as nurture affect the child's ability to take advantage of the natural tendencies the birth day and birth month have given them.

The Given Name

The given name is the third factor that could influence an individual's personality. This name can either add a positive influence, or be ineffective, or burdensome, depending on how its vibration interacts with the other two areas. The importance of a child's name should, therefore, be given consideration. The vibration of this name is a special sphere of influence. It could contribute to the success and wellbeing of an individual. A carefully selected name will provide an outlet for self-expression into a field not provided by the birth date. For instance, a birth date such as the twentieth day of the fifth month 1999 is mostly an emotionally oriented structure. A vibration from the physical plane such as a 1, 4, or 7 could greatly assist the individual. Alternatively, the birth date of the tenth day of the fourth month, 2004, is essentially physically oriented with a fair degree of rigidity. A name with an emotional number will soften the personality and provide some degree of flexibility. While a birth date cannot be changed, some assistance can be given to a one-sided or lop-sided birth date such as the sixth day of the sixth month, 2006 (an overload of the 6 vibration) or the eleventh day of the eleventh month 1991 (an overload of the 1 vibration). The idea is to achieve a reasonable balance between physical, emotional, mental, and spiritual realms by introducing another vibration that will enrich the child's potential. For obvious reasons, the repetition of a name with the same number of the birth day and month should be avoided. It would merely cause an overloading of an existing vibration.

Using the following table a name could be converted into a suitable number or vibration. All multiple numbers are reduced to a single digit.

A, J, S = 1
B, K, T = 2
C, L, U = 3
D, M, V = 4
E, N, W = 5
F, O, X = 6
G, P, Y = 7
H, Q, Z = 8
I, R = 9

This book will follow the format used in Australia to express a birth day, for example, when a full birth day is written as follows:

Jane, born on 4.7.2001
The 4 is the day, the 7 is the month.

International readers will need to take note of this in case it is their practice to put the month before the day.

Examples:

Jane, born on 4.7.2001

J   A   N   E

1 + 1 + 5 + 5 = 12
1 + 2 = 3

3 is the vibration of this given name. It will contribute attributes of the 3 vibration to the integral personality, thus expanding characteristics and talents.

Richard, born on 5.6.2008

R I C H A R D
9 + 9 + 3 + 8 + 1 + 9 + 4 = 43
4 + 3 = 7

7 is the vibration of this given name. The integral personality is enriched by the attributes of the 7 vibration operating on the physical plane.

A 3 name will be ideal for Jane while a number 7 name will be good for Richard.

Here is a summary of the meaning of the numbers which you can use for a quick reference:

NUMBER 1

POSITIVE

> Ambition, assertiveness, authority, confidence, courage, creativity, determination, energy, enterprise, independence, individuality, initiative, inventiveness, leadership, originality, perseverance, persistence, self-reliance.

NEGATIVE

> Aggression, arbitrary and autocratic manner, boastfulness, conceit, defiance, dictatorship, dominancy, egotism, materialism, obstinacy, rigidity, self-centeredness, self-indulgence.

Whether positively or negatively inclined all One personalities possess an "I" and "My" mentality and the ability to work alone if necessary.

NUMBER 2

POSITIVE

Adaptability, affability, agreeability, benevolence, compliance, consideration, cooperation, courtesy, diplomacy, emotion, friendliness, harmony, helpfulness, modesty, patience, receptivity, response, sensitivity, support, tact, unpretentiousness.

NEGATIVE

Condescension, dependence, fault-finding, fantasy, fear, impressionability, indecision, lack of self-confidence, malleability, over-sensitivity, shyness, suspicion, subject to flattery, uncertainty.

Whether positively or negatively inclined all Two personalities look for care and consideration from others, and they give the same in return. They also possess a psychic ability whether they are aware of it or not.

NUMBER 3

POSITIVE

Accuracy, animation, courtesy, creativity, enthusiasm, exhilaration, friendship, imagination, joy, leadership, optimism, originality, popularity, self-expression, sociability, sparkle, style, vivacity, wit, youthfulness.

NEGATIVE

Attention seeking, argumentative, boastfulness, condescension, criticism, cynicism, disapproval, envy, extravagance, fear, fussiness, hesitance, pettiness, pomposity, tactlessness, unsociability, verbosity.

Whether positively or negatively inclined all Three personalities seek to be the center of attention. Artistic talents in a variety of fields are also natural features.

NUMBER 4

POSITIVE

Accuracy, attention, caution, compliance, conscientiousness, constancy, conventionality, dedication, deliberation, dependability, determination, discipline, duty, endurance, helpfulness, frugality, loyalty, method, obedience, patience, practicality, prudence, punctuality, reliability, thrift, unflappability.

NEGATIVE

Apathy, bigotry, bluntness, contradiction, discourtesy, dominance, indecision, inflexibility, intransigence, insensitivity, laziness, narrow-mindedness, obstinacy, unfriendliness, unimaginativeness, unyieldingness, vulgarity.

Whether positively or negatively inclined, all Four personalities possess excellent manual skills, and have good business acumen and money management skills.

NUMBER 5

POSITIVE

Activity, adaptability, adjustment, alertness, animation, changeability, charm, charisma, conviviality, curiosity, daring, dynamism, enterprise, enthusiasm, experimentation, exuberance, flexibility, freedom, independence, informality, non-conformity, progress, spontaneity, versatility, wit.

NEGATIVE

Accident-prone, capriciousness, carelessness, deceit, excitability, extravagance, forgetfulness, hysteria, impetuosity, inconsistency, negligence, unpredictability, unreliability, waywardness.

Whether positive or negatively inclined, all Five personalities thrive on change. They are alert, curious, flexible, and adaptable.

NUMBER 6

POSITIVE

Accommodation, accountability, amiability, analysis, balance, benevolence, cooperation, conciliation, consideration, dependability, domesticity, duty, education, exactitude, extroversion, harmony, kindness, loyalty, mentoring, non-competitiveness, peacemaking, resourcefulness, responsibility, sociability, stability, support, tranquillity, trustworthiness, unflappability

NEGATIVE

Anxiety, argument, criticalness, despair, discontent, dramatization, interference, introversion, melancholy, pessimism, pettiness, possessiveness, suspicion, worry, bias, bigotry, greed, self-centeredness, self-serving, unimaginative, unsympathetic.

Whether positively or negatively inclined all Six personalities are family and community-oriented people.

NUMBER 7

POSITIVE

Accuracy, analysis, attentiveness, authority, calm,
concentration, contemplation, creativity, curiosity,
deliberation, diligence, discrimination, enlightenment,
faithfulness, individualism, inspiration, intellectuality,
introspection, logic, individuality, observance, peace,
philosophy, poise, punctuality, reserve, reason,
research, responsibility, scholarship, spirituality.

NEGATIVE

Aloofness, antisocialness, anxiety, cynicism, deceit, despair,
distrust, eccentricity, evasiveness, extremism,
fanaticism, humorlessness, indecision, intransigence,
insensitivity, introversion, melancholy.

Whether positively or negatively inclined all Seven personalities
safeguard their privacy. They are also true nature lovers.

NUMBER 8

POSITIVE

Ambition, administration, authority, business,
command, competition, courage, discipline,
dynamism, energy, enterprise, enthusiasm, far-
sightedness, judgment, leadership, management,
optimism, organization, planning, practicality,
progress, resourcefulness, responsibility, system,
willpower

NEGATIVE

Aggression, bigotry, bluntness, crudeness, demanding, dictatorship, dishonesty, egotism, greed, ill-manneredness, opinionatedness, rebelliousness, rigidity, selfishness, stubbornness, tactlessness, uncaring, undignified, unreasonableness, unsociability

Whether positively or negatively inclined all Eight personalities aim for material success in life.

NUMBER 9

POSITIVE

Altruism, agreeability, benevolence, broadmindedness, compassion, cooperation, creativity, dedication, discrimination, emotion, enlightenment, forgiveness, friendship, generosity, honesty, humanitarianism, idealism, impressionability, loyalty, modesty, reliability, responsibility, tact, tolerance, understanding, wisdom.

NEGATIVE

Aloofness, bigotry, bitterness, defeatism, despondency, discourtesy, disagreement, dogmatism, egotism, evasiveness, humorlessness, indiscretion, intolerance, misanthropy, non-cooperativeness, over emotional, pessimism, unresponsiveness, unsympathetic, vindictiveness.

Whether positively or negatively inclined all Nine personalities possess a humanitarian outlook on life.

The Master Numbers: 11 and 22

Although a child may be born on the eleventh or twenty-second day of any month, as very young children they are rarely able to operate within the powerfully high frequencies of the Master vibrations of the 11 and 22 and so will likely be predominantly influenced by their base of 2 in the eleventh (1+1=<u>2</u>), and the 4 in the twenty-second (2+2=<u>4</u>). As these children grow into maturity, some may feel the powerful influences of these higher vibrations which will open them out to a vast range of opportunities. Otherwise, they will likely remain superior Twos and Fours.

First Day of the Month

All people with a first birth day are referred to as One personalities. They enter the world well equipped to face life with qualities of self-preservation, self-determination, independence, and self-consciousness. These attributes, among others, of the 1 vibration, form their fundamental personality structure. They do not need boosting of self-confidence since a strong sense of self-identity is a natural characteristic. Children with this birth day grow into leaders and decision makers, with the capacity to stand on their own feet early in life. Non-dependency, self-sufficiency, and self-promotion are some of their motivating forces.

As firm individualists, they will spend much time attending to their own affairs. They do not need, nor do they look for, frequent help or guidance from loved ones or others. Many would, in fact, resent excessive interest or interference in their decisions and actions. However, on the occasions One children feel the need to gain the attention of anyone, they do so without hesitation or consideration of the person, time, or place. Fluency of speech and an extensive vocabulary may not be among their best attributes, but they get their way by assertive and emphatic speech, and demanding body language. Being generally self-centered, the object of all their thoughts is their individuality. If they apply their attention to some other person, it will usually be in connection with that person's usefulness to themselves.

Most One personalities possess the willpower to do what they want or not to do what they do *not* want. They will not be led or misled by their peers. Although self-centered by nature, siblings, schoolmates, and friends can depend on their qualities of leadership, authority, and practicality whenever help or protection is required. A One child's first day at school will not be a traumatic experience. In the event of the break-up of a

1

family unit, a One child has the capacity to take over to a fair extent the responsibilities of a parent. However, cooperation and sharing are not natural qualities found in these children or adults. "Whatever is mine is mine, and whatever is yours is yours" is their natural attitude. These children should not be expected to willingly share their toys and other possessions. They may give but not share. The 1 vibration's strong sense of ownership is responsible for this attitude. This is also a vibration that prompts its subjects to go out and acquire and keep on acquiring. These attributes will eventually be reflected in the responsible use of money and material possessions.

Most One children are of an extroverted nature. In some rare instances, however, they can be loners. They are not easily amenable to restrictions, discipline, or censure. They can also be deeply resentful of criticism. They might react with defiance and rebelliousness. Strong egos and pride are basic attributes of the 1 vibration. They seldom admit that they have been in the wrong. Quite early in life they may develop expertise in justifying themselves in whatever they say or do, whether right or wrong. With a firm "I" and "my" mentality, they exhibit a strong, competitive spirit. They play to win in any form of competition and are not usually gallant losers. Emerging qualities of willpower, decisiveness, determination, leadership, courage, independence, self-reliance, guardianship, aggression, and obstinacy will be observed early in life, developing into fully fledged characteristics as they grow older.

As the 1 vibration operates within the physical plane, these children may not display or express much sentimentality. Sooner rather than later, they break loose from the affectionate and cuddly stage as they feel little need to be constantly kissed and hugged. A One child will cry—and cry loudly—in frustration or anger when deprived of something they want but not for sentimental reasons. Their emotions will be demonstrated in deeds, exceptional loyalty, and a protective manner toward all loved ones. One children are not likely to be bullied in school. However, some could turn into bullies if they have been nurtured in a quarrelsome home environment or exposed to the wrong role models.

One children possess a physically active temperament. For the most part, they learn through observation rather than direct instruction. They will need astute guidance if they are to reach a balance between study, play, and other responsibilities. Once set upon a course of action, a One child, or a One adult for that matter, is not likely to give up. They possess a high sense of achievement that they are loathe to surrender. One children have the capacity to resist demands or expectations not conducive to their natural abilities. A few who may suffer a temporary setback created by domineering parents soon come into their own as they grow older and begin acting under their own steam. Future employment prospects will always be good due to the 1 vibration's attributes of ambition, competition, self-promotion, enterprise, initiative, motivation, originality, and willpower. If these Ones do not end up as leaders in one form or other, they will be found striking out on their own as their own masters. On the rare occasions they enter into partnerships, they will hold the role of senior partner. The following is a summary of differences in One personalities when their birth months are taken into consideration.

Ones Born in January (first month)

A birth date containing different numbers or vibrations in the birth day and birth month provides two or more avenues for self-expression, those of the birth day being formative and the birth month contributory. The birth year, too, provides vibrations that contribute toward the formation of the integral personality. But these are minor forces that do not exercise an appreciable influence.

In the event of the birth day and birth month being the same as it is in One personalities born in the first month, the individual, on the one hand, does not possess a second significant opening for self-expression. On the other hand, attributes of the birth day vibration are intensified by repetition. Depending on the nature of the vibration of the birth day, such intensification may not always result in a strengthening of the integral personality. It may, in fact, give rise to certain negative aspects of the birth day vibration. This is a condition that can only be found with single-digit birth days.

In the case of a One personality, the repetition of the 1 vibration in the birth month could result in a strengthening of some 1 attributes and the hardening in negative ways of others. For instance, willpower, concentration, self-sufficiency, vital energy, memory, persistence, individuality, creativity, and single-mindedness are some attributes that are strengthened. At the same time, the personality tends to live in a black-and-white world with few shades of gray. Rigidity, inflexibility, a restricted imagination, dogmatism, obstinacy, fear, sensitivity, egotism, and above all, a real difficulty demonstrating emotion, are some problems. These children soon grow out of a need for close body contact. They can easily be misunderstood. The truth is that they are by no means insensitive toward loved ones as they do possess a soft center of love and loyalty. They display these attributes only on their own terms and in their own ways. Family ties are exceptionally strong. A first name reducing to 2, 3, 5, 6, or 9 will be best.

Ones Born in February (second month)

One personalities born in the second month possess an inlet for receiving and coping with emotion as well as an outlet for demonstrating emotion. However, as the 1 vibration is the controlling force, these One personalities are not subject to their emotions. The vibration symbolized by the number 2 is a genteel, sensitive, and receptive force. The 1 vibration is known for expenditure of energy, while the 2 is known for storage of energy. The 2 vibration's position in the birth month of a One personality has the effect of smoothing many rough edges of the personality. Inconsideration for the feelings of others, lack of cooperation, and demanding ways are some 1 qualities that are tempered by the 2. Some 2 qualities may emerge unconsciously from time to time, but their application for a balance within the personality is best done through conscious effort. Refer to the chapter on the second day of the month for a better understanding of these One personalities. These children will be more amenable to instruction and discipline than those born in the first, tenth, eleventh, fifth, or eighth months. It may be best to avoid a first name reducing to 1, 4, or 8. These vibrations may intensify the demanding and stubborn nature on the 1 aspect of the personality and stifle the helpful and cooperative nature of the 2 aspect.

Ones Born in March (third month)

Individuality, originality, leadership, and other self-sufficient qualities of the 1 vibration are reinforced in those born in the third month. At the same time, arbitrary, dogmatic, and controlling tendencies are reduced by open, youthful, friendly, and courteous attributes of the 3 vibration. The outlook of the personality is expanded, and flexibility is introduced. Self-consciousness and self-centeredness are characteristics shared by the 1, 2, and 3 vibrations, but they can be penetrated in the One personality born in the third month by gentle reminders to which a pure One may be immune. The chapter on the third birth day provides more details on this secondary aspect. Hardly any conflict will be experienced in the merger of the 1 and 3 forces. These children may not always conform to parental rules and regulations. Freedom of action and movement are their chief motivating forces. Do not expect much demonstration of emotion. They are loving and lovable children, but they pass the cuddly stage early in life. Discovery and adventure are much more attractive than intimacy and emotional contact. However, as they grow older, a strong romantic element will manifest itself. Emotion may be displayed in angry outbursts or tantrums when their demands are not immediately met. A first name reducing to 1, 3, 4, or 8 is best avoided as these will increase their demanding ways.

Ones Born in April (fourth month)

In addition to the 1, the number 4 is another vibration from the physical plane. Consequently, all the practical, pragmatic, and physical attributes of the 1 vibration will be considerably strengthened. Qualities of determination, perseverance, loyalty, vital energy, strength of purpose, obstinacy, and possessiveness are intensified. The 1 and 4 forces interact harmoniously. The personality should not experience conflicting elements. Parents can expect a good deal of stubbornness, but this is not necessarily a negative quality; it could have many positive applications in their teenage years and adulthood. With the capacity to give a firm and emphatic "No", they will stand on their own feet early in life. They cannot be influenced adversely by others. It will be most unlikely they would ever be bullied in school, but they may bully others.

Being almost entirely physically oriented, emotional expression will be at a minimum. They will express love and loyalty in deeds rather than sweet words and much body contact. A name with an emotional number 2, 5, or 9 will be best, while 1, 4, or 8 should be avoided. Consult the chapter on the fourth birth day for a better understanding of One personalities born in the fourth month.

Ones Born in May (fifth month)

A One personality will be enriched by a considerable variety of talents and personality traits introduced by the 5 vibration, which is a multi-faceted force. The ability to express emotion will be a special contribution. The controlling nature of the 1 vibration will also be enhanced and its adventuresome and pioneering qualities expanded. In short, the merger of 1 and 5 forces creates a totally resourceful personality. Restlessness will always be a problem with these children. They may not be too amenable to routine, punctuality, rules and regulations, and discipline. Freedom to do their own thing is most important. In general, they are quite able to look after themselves. They are physically courageous with a tendency to indulge in risky physical activities. Expect occasional injuries. Details shown in the chapter on the fifth birth day provide a good insight into this personality. Although the 5 vibration in the birth month is in a secondary position, its attributes are such that they take rank with those of the 1 vibration of the birth day. The combination of the 1 and 5 provide an adequate balance within the personality. It would be best to avoid a first name reducing to 1, 4, 5, or 8 as this would increase the individual's controlling tendencies.

Ones Born in June (sixth month)

Family and community orientation of the 6 vibration mitigates the individualistic and self-centered attributes of the 1 vibration in this birth day and birth month combination. Family pride and the protective and possessive nature of the 1 will readily accept family responsibility which is the chief attribute of the 6. Sociability and hospitality will also be expanded. These children will spend more time at home or in the company of family members than those Ones born in the first, third, or fifth months. Do not be surprised if they take an interest in cooking and other household duties. Their general habits will be orderly and methodical. Domestic disorder will harm a child's growth and wellbeing. Mental powers govern their thoughts and actions. Impulse will be exceptional. They can be quite argumentative as they will accept very little that is not factual or realistic. Although they possess a great capacity for love, they will hold displays of sentiment in check.

Many of these children can be quite unflappable toward events taking place around them. The chapter on the sixth birth day provides much more detail of the 6 aspect of this personality. However, bear in mind that 6 attributes are secondary features and some may be subdued by the power of the primary 1. By and large, however, both vibrations can interact in ways that create a strong positive personality. Disobedience and fits of temper will not arise if they are approached with reason and patience. As an outlet for emotional expression is lacking, a first name that reduces to 2, 5, or 9 will be helpful for rounding off the integral personality structure.

Ones Born in July (seventh month)

The vibration of the seventh month introduces a set of opposite traits which may confuse the fundamental personality formed by the 1 vibration. It is a strange combination of physical and spiritual elements. Compatibility with the 1 aspect will be found in practical and pragmatic aspects of life. But contrary features are introduced by the 7's spiritual side which contains non-competitive and non-acquisitive qualities. The chapter on the seventh Birth day shows that many such features of the 7 are different from those of the 1. However, despite some degree of uncertainty and confusion, these differences should not diminish the strength of the integral personality. These children will begin life with a strong positive mindset. They can be quiet and contemplative, showing a preference for their own company from time to time. Their sociability at all times cannot be taken for granted. They set their own conditions for interacting with people. They are loving and loyal children but will rarely show emotional demonstration. A first name with the numbers 2, 5, or 9 may provide a controlled release of emotion at proper times. They are happiest in natural surroundings. At an early age, they may not be conscious of a desire to look into the spiritual aspects of life but this will be displayed unconsciously in their love of nature in all its various forms. They may not be too talkative or communicative, but whenever they choose to speak out, whatever they say is thoughtful and purposeful. People pay attention to them.

Ones Born in August (eighth month)

The chapter on the eighth birth day reveals many similarities between the 1 and 8 vibrations. They merge effortlessly in this birth day and birth month to create a strong, positive, and controlling personality. An irresistible urge to take charge of people and circumstances will be their most prominent characteristic. This will be observed in children at a very early age. They may not be easy to teach and discipline. They learn more through observation and experience than by direct instruction. As natural leaders and organizers they succeed in anything they undertake, but will not necessarily always gain popularity. High ambition overrides any desire to compromise or please. These traits will be observed in their junior years when they participate in sport and invariably acquire leadership roles in school or college. They play to win as losing does not enter their mindset. They are extroverted and exceptionally active children who need to engage in many outdoor activities. It will not be easy to hold on to them with domestic interests or household hobbies. They will not be bullied or enticed into any activity contrary to their desires and beliefs. A first name reducing to 2, 3, 6, 7, or 9 will help them expand from a one-pointed desire for physical activity and their controlling nature, into community-conscious, artistic, and intellectual domains.

Ones Born in September (ninth month)

A comparison between the first birth day and the ninth birth day will reveal two different sets of personality traits as they are controlled by opposite forces; the major difference being, the ego-consciousness of the clear One personality and the expanded and inclusive characteristics of the 9 vibration. The direct impact of the 9 qualities upon those of the 1 will be a mitigation of self-centeredness and ego prominence. Although the 9 will be a secondary force, these individuals will acquire some degree of awareness and concern for the wellbeing and welfare of others and an extended outlook on life. Internationalism and humanitarianism are essential qualities of the 9 vibration. This is a fortunate combination of vibratory forces as it introduces physical, realistic, and practical abilities as well as ethical and moral values. In choosing a name for this child, it is best to avoid a name reducing to 1, 4, or 8. Such names may reduce the expansive nature of the 9 vibration. Another 9 name or any other will be quite suitable.

Ones Born in October (tenth month)

Please refer to the section on the first birth day. The repetition of the 1 vibration in the birth month indicates the absence of another outlet for self-expression which is now confined to a single sphere – the physical. The direst result is the strengthening of certain positive aspects of the 1 vibration and the hardening or stiffening of certain others. For instance, individuality, independence, self-determination, and concentration may be strengthened but some less desirable traits of obstinacy, rigidity, ego-centeredness, defiance and a restricted imagination will be emphasized. Many of these negative traits can easily be overcome or reduced in a caring and loving environment and a first name that reduces to 2, 3, 5, 6, or 9. Although the imaginative powers of these children may not be extensive, their creative powers in any form of work or activity will be enhanced. They will resent being disturbed when concentrating on anything. Emotional expression will also be restricted. Parents should not expect these children to need or give out much emotional contact. Acknowledgment and praise should be wisely given out and not withheld.

Ones Born in November (eleventh month)

With the 1 vibration spread over their birth day and birth month, these children are clearly confined within the powers of the 1 vibration and the physical plane. They move in narrow but deep channels of self-expression, usually in quite a rigid black-and-white world. The first observable traits will be absence of emotional demonstration, a restricted imagination and extraordinary powers of concentration. These children are in fact loving and exceptionally loyal and dutiful, but they soon outgrow sentimentality and the need to be fussed and cuddled. Not much variety will enter into their activities but whatever they undertake will be done with thoroughness and diligence. Certain positive traits of the 1 vibration may turn into less desirable forms of expression. For instance, strength of purpose may turn into rigidity and uncompromising ways. Decisiveness may turn into indecision and courage into excessive caution. A first name reducing to 2, 3, 5, 6, or 9 is essential.

Ones Born in December (twelfth month)

Characteristics of the 1 vibration shown on the first birth day are strengthened in those born on the twelfth day of the month. Active qualities of this vibration predominate but there may be moments when receptive qualities of the 2 vibration emerge. The chapter on the second birth day may be consulted. A given name reducing to 1, 4, 7, or 8 should be avoided as these will add to the authoritative and uncooperative nature of the clear One personality, and certainly stifle any genteel 2 qualities that may seek to enter their thoughts and actions. A name reducing to 2, 3, 5, 6, or 9 will be best.

Second Day of the Month

This day is governed by a receptive vibration as opposed to the 1 vibration, which is an active force. Once you have read this chapter, you will find the chapter on the first day of the month will be of considerable interest. The polarity of these forces is the outstanding feature. Basically, the 1 vibration symbolizes expenditure of energy and the 2 stands for storage of energy. So, the active nature of the One personality and the receptive nature of the Two personality can be manifested through their different personality traits.

Characteristics reflected in the receptive Two personality, among many other qualities are, adaptability, agreeability, companionship, consideration, cooperation, conciliation, courtesy, diplomacy, flexibility, gentleness, harmony, helpfulness, partnerships, peace, response, sociability, support, tact, and sensitivity to people and atmosphere. Two personalities are not free from self-centered qualities but they are certainly free from a prominent and assertive ego. They carry out self-promotion in unobtrusive and subtle ways. Some can resort to emotional manipulation in order to get what they want, but most Twos obtain their needs through obliging and winning ways. The law of attraction also works well for them. They often naturally attract things out of life that others have to work for.

A vital condition for the development of all Two children is a stable, peaceful, and quiet home life, free from discord, tension, vulgarity, and turmoil. Those who have been exposed to these negative conditions carry many emotional and mental scars into adulthood. They usually fail to reach their full potential and give of their best. Parents will observe that, from babyhood onwards, these children will become agitated by noise, especially when emitted from the human voice in anger, frustration, or argument. As they grow older they reveal themselves as warm-hearted children who give out, and in turn, expect a good deal of affection. They usually avoid being the center of attention and take up the role of observer. They enjoy being entertained rather than entertaining others. They are for the most part non-competitive individuals who enjoy participation. Although many can succeed as solo artists, their preference will be to enter into group performance. They could be tactfully taken out of this mindset as they have much to offer in entertainment and other activities. Gentle persuasion and encouragement from time to time by their elders, to overcome shyness and self-consciousness and uncover their multiple talents, is all they need. Many Twos have the habit of underrating themselves. This is unfortunate as all Twos possess more widespread talent than they give themselves credit for. They could do with more ego, strength, and ambition.

Most Two children are soft-spoken conversationalists who prefer person to person talk, enjoying exchange of intimacies rather than involvement in group conversation. They are more confident and talented with the written word than the spoken word. These children possess a natural tendency to fantasize and exercise a vivid imagination, which is usually channeled into writing and drawing. The practice of keeping up with pen pals is fairly common with all Two personalities. The receptive nature of the 2 vibration also makes them habitual collectors. Positive Twos collect useful, valuable, or marketable items while negatively inclined Twos are real bowerbirds who collect anything and everything. All Twos, however, resist dispensing with anything.

Twos prefer to play a supportive role in life rather than one of outright leadership and sole responsibility. They provide powerful support in conditions in which they feel supported. More often than not, a Two personality can be the "power behind the throne". An interesting contrast can be observed in the manner of One and Two children, or even in adults, when there is an occasion for them to sit for an unofficial group photograph. The One will obtain a prominent position in the front row while the Two will be content with an inconspicuous position. As mentioned earlier, Twos progress in life not through demand or assertiveness but through natural charm, winning and obliging ways, and dedication to whatever they undertake. Some characteristics that may delay advancement of certain Twos will be a fear of offending people, an over-keenness to please, fluctuation of mood, a tendency toward melancholy, indecision, fear of negative opinions, procrastination, and a tendency to imitate others rather than be themselves. Many negative Twos may suffer from imaginary illnesses. During their teens, especially, they may suffer from low self-esteem due to imaginary physical inadequacies. Two children need pleasant and quiet company. They do not enjoy prolonged periods of solitude.

Two children and adults are able to release their emotions by crying. They can instantly burst into tears which soon subside. School days can be a wonderful opportunity for opening their imaginative powers and need for friendships. But these personalities can also be traumatized if they encounter rough and aggressive characters. Such experiences will instantly inhibit their eagerness to progress. However, most Twos possess resilience as their strongest attribute. This comes in handy in a difficult domestic situation as well. They can be pushed or even pummeled only to a certain point, after which they can display firm resistance and stratagems to cope with most difficult situations. Once they acknowledge their powers, they can rise above imaginary limitations and find out one by one that they can actually do so. When all vibrations are considered, the 2 vibration is most likely to bring out the abilities within people who are sensitive to psychic phenomena. This non-physical aspect of life is manifested very early in Two children. Many outgrow their experiences while others carry them consciously or unconsciously into adulthood. Parents may observe these children talking and smiling to themselves. Often, this is because they are talking to fairies and other invisible playmates. The following is a summary of differences in Two personalities when their birth months are taken into consideration.

Twos Born in January (first month)

If you have read through the chapter on the 1 vibration, which is now manifesting as a secondary force, you can appreciate its impact on the Two personality. The strength of the 1 vibration is such that it could exercise a strong influence over a Two personality, ensuring the emergence of only the positive attributes of the 2 vibration. All negatives are automatically diminished in the process, especially uncontrolled emotion and sentimentality. Consequently, these Two children born in January take a positive stand when encountering people and conditions that are not conducive to their welfare and expectations. In short, they are able to say "No" when necessary. People seldom take advantage of these children as they may do with other Twos. Self-doubt, indecision, unaccountable fears, and reticence no longer hinder their progress in life. These Two children can assume positions of leadership and authority with confidence. A given name reducing to 1 or 2 is best avoided so that a fresh outlet for personality traits and talents is introduced. A name from the mental realm 3, 6, or 9 is ideal.

Twos Born in February (second month)

The repetition of the birth day vibration in the birth month invariably leads to a few personality problems. The overloading of a particular vibration in these two significant spheres of influence tends to activate its negative aspect and submerge the positive. A Two personality born in the second month will inevitably fall into the many negative features of the 2 vibration. These children will be gentle and sweet natured but they are most likely to be too gentle and too sweet for their own good. They could be ruled by their emotions and affected by worry, anxiety, fear, indecision, shyness, yielding ways, and emotional dependency. They will need constant boosting of self-confidence. They do not lose any of the multiple talents of the 2 vibration but their capabilities are delayed by a lack of faith in themselves. In other words they are much more talented than they think they are. "I can't do it" or "I am not sure" may be frequently expressed. Others may take advantage of them as they do not have the strength to say "No". They could be subject to negative psychic experiences, such as nightmares. These are truly beautiful children but they need a good deal of support and constant encouragement. They are much more comfortable expressing their thoughts and fantasies through drawings and writing rather than through oral expression. A name reducing to 1, 4, 6, or 7 should be chosen so that an excess of emotionalism can be controlled. All others, especially 2, 5, 8, and 9 should be avoided. These children need stability in the mental and physical realms.

Twos Born in March (third month)

Ego-centeredness is emphasized in this birth day and birth month combination. While the major 2 aspect of this personality gives and expects sentimentality and emotional expression, these characteristics are not prevalent in their secondary 3 nature. However, from an early age, people influenced to an appreciable degree by the 3 vibration are sure to demand attention. Such people simply refuse to remain unnoticed. They act and speak in ways that draw attention to themselves. Normal reserved attributes of the Two personality will be changed to a fair degree by these extroverted features of their birth month vibration. They will certainly assume a bolder stance in their interaction with others. They may no longer experience a real fear for occupying the spotlight.

Both chapters on the second and third days of the month indicate that the 2 and 3 vibrations provide several exceptional talents, especially in the performing arts. As especially intelligent children, they can progress through their studies during their student days without the additional aid of private tuition. However, these children do suffer a problem that may delay the emergence of their potential; a lack of inner self-confidence that may hold them back from going forward as fast as they should. Their self-confidence needs to be activated from time to time. Their lack of self-confidence may not always be obvious, as fluency of speech and well-mannered behavior, which are among their best qualities, may obscure feelings of inadequacy.

A powerful imagination, which is a special attribute of both the 2 and 3 vibrations, will be given free play in speech, writing, drawing, and all other forms of art, including dancing and gymnastics. Romanticism is also allowed free rein. Pragmatism may not be a strong element, especially in the future need for good financial management. A name reducing to 1, 4, or 7 is essential for these children. All others should be avoided if possible.

Twos Born in April (fourth month)

As a secondary force the 4 vibration will contribute some essentials needed by the primary 2. Emotional expression will be kept under control. The impulsive nature of the Two will be held in check. Manual dexterity will be introduced. With a sensitive touch, clear Two personalities are adept at handling anything that is delicate and fragile. With the aid of the 4 vibration they will acquire the ability to handle heavy loads as well. At a future date these children will be helped by their 4 aspect to stop and consider the value of an item before purchasing it.

While this is a helpful combination of vibrations it does not inject sufficient self-confidence and self-promotion. These children need to be reminded of their capabilities. They are not generally competitive individuals who favor prominent roles; neither do they like to be pushed or hurried into doing things. They may be slow but steady. They are obedient children, who are quite prepared to abide by domestic and school rules and regulations. Their school days are most likely to be free from trouble. A first name adding to 1, 3, 6, or 9 will be best. A 1 name will provide self-confidence while the 3, 6, or 9 will expand their mental horizons. The chapter on the fourth birth day provides more information on the 4 vibration. Its attributes should be treated as a secondary, yet effective force if found in the birth month.

Twos Born in May (fifth month)

If you refer to the chapter on the fifth day of the month, you will see that there is an over representation of attributes of the emotional plane in this birth day and birth month combination. The second birth day creates emotionalism of a passive nature while the 5 vibration or the fifth month introduces emotionalism of an active nature. We have here a curious mixture of emotional vibrations creating impulse, changeability, lack of direction, and uncertainty. It also introduces a certain dynamism into the Two personality by virtue of the extroverted nature of the 5 vibration.

Children born on this day and month are assuredly talented and lively personalities. However, an excess of flexibility, and fluid movement of body and mind, create restlessness and the need for frequent change of scene and activity. In due course, following a single career or system of study till completion is likely to be a perennial problem. Although the 5 vibration is in a secondary position it does not often play a secondary role. It is forceful enough to submerge many sedate and tranquil qualities of the 2 vibration. Quite often the child may act more as a Five personality than a Two. As the directness of the 5 vibration combines well with the subtlety of the 2, these children seek to organize their environment to suit their own needs. Tidiness, punctuality, and systematic habits cannot be expected. You will need considerable understanding and patience as these children may experience unaccountable mood changes and feelings of insecurity. A first name reducing to 1, 4, or 7 is essential. All other names should be avoided, especially one from the emotional plane, 2, 5, 8, or even 9, which contains a fair degree of emotion.

Twos Born in June (sixth month)

The chapter on the sixth day of the month will reveal the various influences that the 6 vibration could have on this Two personality, and the similarity between the 2 and 6 vibratory forces. They merge harmoniously despite the fact that one is on the emotional plane and the other on the mental plane. The immediate advantage in this combination is the moderation of the sentimental and emotional qualities of the 2 vibration by the rational and realistic thought processes of the 6. These children are not likely to readily burst into tears and tantrums. They are calm and restful children who do not suffer from conflicting elements within their personality structure. However, in their interaction with others and their activities they may experience disquiet and withdrawal due to a non-competitive nature. Ego-strength, assertiveness, and high ambition are not strong elements in this combination of vibrations. These children cannot be rushed or coerced into front-line activities or competitive pressures in order to satisfy the desire of ambitious parents. Their several talents are put to use at their own pace. Even the mildest form of harassment will inhibit their talent and potential.

These children really flourish in a peaceful home and family environment where togetherness is a fundamental factor. They will be closer to the parent who is accessible and has the time for communication. As their feelings are easily hurt, they will not open out unless they are certain of a sympathetic hearing. Adequate self-confidence and self-assurance are not strong qualities in their personality structure. A name reducing to 1, 4, or 7 will be most helpful. Other names are best avoided.

Twos Born in July (seventh month)

The various attributes of the emotionally oriented Two personality and those of the 7 vibration are not exclusive of each other. They blend harmoniously to create what will genuinely appear as a gentlemanly or ladylike personality. These children have no rough edges or uncouth features, except for those born on this day and month who are exposed to a harsh environment and negative role modeling. The chapter on the seventh day of the month provides much information on this 7 aspect. It is possible that the attributes of the 7 vibration function on equal terms with those of the 2 within this individual. It introduces into the Two personality many attributes of considerable strength. It releases the Two from excessive self-consciousness and outward emotional reactions. The Two becomes less dependent on others and more on their own initiatives. It is also sympathetic with the Two's psychic tendencies and introduces a love of nature.

Despite many wonderful and desirable characteristics in a 2/7 combination, these children are easily distressed and repelled by strident speech, coarse behavior, unfair treatment, and quarreling siblings and parents. They flourish only in harmonious surroundings. They imbibe knowledge and proper behavior from adults who take the trouble to explain in simple terms what they should or should not do in any situation. Discerning parents will know that their feelings are easily hurt and that they should never be shouted at. They could suffer from the mildest form of ill-treatment and not stand their ground and argue. They promptly retreat into silence when emotionally hurt. These children are often content with their own company and therefore take private time for themselves. Names reducing to a 3, 6, or 9 will be best, while 2, 5, and 8 should be avoided. 1, 4 and 7 will be fine also.

Twos Born in August (eighth month)

The Two personality operating on the emotional plane is heavily influenced by another from the same plane. However, there is a marked difference between the emotive powers of the 2 and 8 vibrations. The chapter on the eighth day of the month shows that they function in almost opposite ways. They are freely expressed in the Two personality due to the fluid and spontaneous nature of the 2 vibration. However, those influenced by the 8 vibration, do not tolerate an exhibition of emotion. Unrestrained sentimentality is regarded as transparent and undignified. Other contrasting features are the Two personality's attributes of cooperation, conformity, non-competition, partnership, and association, and the 8 vibration's attributes of competition, ambition, organization, administration, and control.

These contrasting elements are likely to create confusion in regard to decision-making and setting a clear direction in behavior and study. A certain degree of self-doubt will creep in. As these children grow older they can be directed to combine these mutually desirable forces within their personality. Parents will observe that these children are emotionally vulnerable. They do possess an urgent need for understanding. A given name reducing to 1, 4, or 7 will be best, while emotional numbers 2, 5, 8, and 9 should be avoided. 3 and 6 will be acceptable but best avoided if possible. Stability on the physical plane is what they need.

Twos Born in September (ninth month)

If Two personalities are taken out of the confined world of their own concerns into the world at large, they cannot do better than absorbing the attributes of the 9 vibration. This is, therefore, a fortunate condition for those born in the ninth month. An expansion of their personality will take place whether or not they are conscious of it. The chapter on the ninth day of the month indicates the extent to which a Two can extend their integral personality.

Two personalities can merge harmoniously with this 9 aspect of their personality as the 9 vibration is, above all, an understanding and sympathetic force in which a forceful ego does not operate. Another strong attribute contributed by the 9 vibration is a compassionate nature. This aspect does not help the emotionally oriented Two. Consequently, Twos born in the ninth month are easily subjected to emotional demonstration. These Two children cry often as they are easily touched by sorrow, sadness, or by any sort of misfortune suffered by others, especially their loved ones. Their sensitive nature suffers greatly in despotic and discordant conditions at home or at school. They refuse to stand up for themselves as arguments and quarrels are repellent to their genteel constitution. What these children need is a first name reducing to the 1 vibration. This will provide the strength and willpower they need to bring out the best qualities of the 2 and 9 aspects of their personality. A 4 or 7 will be next best. All other names are best avoided, especially 2, 5, 8, or 9. These children need stability on the physical plane.

Twos Born in October (tenth month)

Please refer to the section on Twos born in January, the first month. There will be no difference in the personality of a child born in the first or tenth month. The zero does not count as it has no attributes of its own.

Twos Born in November (eleventh month)

Please refer to the section on Twos born in January, the first month. In this birth day and birth month combination, the help provided by the 1 vibration is doubled. These Two personalities therefore reap a double measure of the attributes of the 1 vibration. It is possible that these children may at times act more as qualified Ones than Two personalities. One way or the other this is a good combination as the best qualities of the Two can be manifested and the rough edges of the plain 1 vibration smoothened over.

These are strong, self-confident children who do not depend on a name to provide them with initiative and willpower. However, it will be best to avoid another 2 or 1 name. A number from the mental plane, 3, 6, or 9 will provide a fine balance between physical, emotional, and mental planes. A 4 or 7 name will increase practicality but not expand their vision as a mental plane number would do.

Twos Born in December (twelfth month)

Attributes of the 2 vibration are widespread in this birth day and birth month combination. Unlike Twos born in the second month, the repetition of the 2 vibration does not create a negative condition. It does in fact create a strong positive Two as the 2 vibration from the birth month is buttressed by the 1. These children have a genteel temperament aided by inner strength. It would be best to avoid a name reducing to a 2, 5, or 8. Any other name will be fine.

Third Day of the Month

Ego and egocentricity are inherent characteristics in all people born on the first, second and third days of the month, as well as those born on the twentieth and thirtieth. They have inherited a personal outlook that estimates the nature of events and people primarily by the way in which they affect their own existence and only secondarily by the way in which they affect others. This condition is not to be taken as a negative trait but as just the nature of these vibratory forces. Concentration on self is not done in the same way by One, Two, and Three personalities. In the One, egocentric traits are prominent and affirmative. The Two's ego is disguised and persuasive. The Three's ego may be conspicuous but, with a few exceptions, it is not always resistant or defensive. It can be open and accommodating.

Three children need to be drawn out of themselves from time to time. When this is done they readily follow any reminders of their obligations toward others, as selfishness is not part of their personality. Most children do not take offense when their self-absorbed habits or instances are pointed out to them. But no one should be surprised when they soon retire into their self-involved world. Sins of omission are more common than sins of commission. A genuine zest for living and concentration on what they may be doing at any given time makes them forgetful. Adults who objectively observe their behavior invariably cannot fail to enjoy their enthusiasm, enterprise and their sparkling personalities.

All Three children respond better to reason and understanding than overbearing treatment. They are certain to relate better to a kindly parent, be it the mother or father, than to the one who dictates to them. This attitude is not the result of any weakness on their part but resentment against the sterner parent's manner, which will be regarded as an assault

21

upon their individuality. Most Three children avoid challenging a parent due to a natural sense of courtesy and respect inherent in all those influenced by the 3 vibration. Found in such a situation, they are most likely to fall back on their own sense of values and assume responsibility for their lives. These children possess a vivid, creative imagination that they put to use on their own initiative. Keen observers of their behavior will find that in one sense they are non-dependent, and in the other, they need frequent praise and acknowledgment. However, demonstration of emotion will be exceptional in these children. The 3 vibration is a mental force. Consequently they do not always express their emotions in their interaction with loved ones. Their love is of a mental quality. In addition, they are much too active, individualistic, and adventuresome to spend time seeking or giving affection. Emotion is usually released in their artistic creations, and in their love of music and all beautiful things.

Self-expression is the strongest urge in all Three children. They are extroverted personalities who need and demand to be the center of attention in almost every situation in which they find themselves. They feel frustrated if compelled to take a back seat rather than the spotlight, and they need constant company. Aloneness is a state that they cannot cope with. The truth is that they do possess all the attributes needed to occupy the spotlight. They are natural entertainers. Unlike Two children, they are seldom found as part of a group. Solo performance is their natural role. Uncontrolled activity could be a problem with many Three children. They are easily carried away by enthusiastic activity that does not last. The grass is always greener on the other side of the fence. At the same time, they possess the rare ability to enjoy the present moment. They are easily bored if not constantly kept occupied. A physical vibration 1, 4, or 7 in their birth month or given name will provide a better sense of permanence.

Their school days will be an adventure enriched by an admiring following. Their enthusiasm in whatever they do as leaders will be infectious. They maintain friendships without being led or adversely influenced. They are naturally intelligent children who pick up knowledge quicker than average. They are innovators and trendsetters. Early in life they display a love for fashionable and colorful clothing. Artistic talents are exceptional in all Three children. It will be difficult to foresee what form of artistic activity they may engage in as their versatility is such that they could develop expertise in more than one. They could excel in a variety of sports but heavy body contact sports may be avoided. They are good-natured competitors as sportsmanship is another good attribute of the 3 vibration.

All Three children possess a natural expertise with the spoken word. With a voice of fine tonal quality, which is carried into adulthood, they begin to speak earlier than average. Accuracy in what they say and an expanding vocabulary are additional features. They do not hesitate to initiate conversation or respond immediately to questions put to them. Often, they may not allow others to finish their sentences. They will instantly point out flaws or inaccuracies in the speech of others. The pronoun "I" is most frequently used in their speech. Sooner or later all Three children develop a fine sense of humor which is enriched by their extensive vocabulary and their joyful temperament. A good way to entertain Three children is to listen to them.

Some other attributes of the 3 vibration not mentioned earlier are, sociability, friendliness, inspiration, energy, and romance. This vibration is not without its negative aspects. Certain birth months produce some of these negatives, such as, conceit, boastfulness, self-promotion, condescension, extravagance, verbosity, criticism, indecision, and fear. The following sections explain how Three personalities may change when their birth month is taken into consideration.

Threes Born in January (first month)

Egocentricity and firm individuality are emphasized in people with this birth day and birth month combination. You will see the extent to which these traits exist in the chapter on the first day of the month. These are exceptionally intelligent, creative, and self-confident children who will eventually take responsibility for their speech and actions. But they are much more demanding and difficult to discipline than other Three children. Their extroverted and independent temperaments cannot be restrained or restricted by routine, timetables, or an excess of discipline. Quite early in life they display a tendency to take charge of their lives. They cannot be made to sit down even for brief periods. Motivated by an abundance of physical and mental energy they need to be constantly on the move.

This combination does not contain an open display of sentimentality and emotion. However, their "love nature" is deep and abiding, and displayed in the care and devotion they give their loved ones. Their protective nature is exceptionally strong.

A first name reducing to an emotional number 2, 5, or 9 will suit them well. Although the 8 is on the emotional plane, it should be avoided due to the controlling nature of the 8 vibration. Additional controlling qualities are not needed. A first name reducing to 1 or 3 is also best avoided. What these children need is a vibration that takes them out of excessive concentration on their own affairs. Reduction to a 4, 6, 7, or 9 will be best.

Threes Born in February (second month)

An outlet for emotional expression is a beneficial contribution by the 2 vibration of this birth month. These children need not suffer from pent up emotions as they are able to release their feelings in the occasional outburst of tears and in other sentimental ways. Another advantage with this birth month is the combination of the 3 vibration's potential with the spoken word and the 2 vibration's potential with the written word. All other artistic talents of the 3 vibration are also enriched, as attributes of the 2 and 3 vibrations generally merge harmoniously. The chapter on the second day of the month will confirm this condition.

This birth day and birth month, while creating a multi-talented personality, do not form an assertive ego or a competitive nature. These children may not possess as much self-confidence as they need for maximum use of their abilities. Consequently, they can do with gentle encouragement from time to time. They are neither stubborn nor self-willed. They are flexible, adaptable, and open to instruction and advice. A first name reducing to 1 will be an excellent choice as it will provide the extra self-confidence they need. Another 2 or 3 is not advisable; nor is a 5, 6, or 8 or 9. If a name reducing to a 1 cannot be decided upon the next best will be a 4 or 7.

Threes Born in March (third month)

Three personalities born in the third month are faced with a twofold problem. Firstly, with an overloading of the attributes of the 3 vibration and secondly, with the absence of another strong outlet for self-expression provided by the birth month. Invariably, this condition permits negative attributes of the 3 vibration taking control of the personality. These children do not lose the multiple talents and versatility of the 3 vibration but the condition that emerges is an excessive, or even an obsessive, desire to be the center of attention created by a loss of self-assurance. They can be resentful of anyone or anything that deflects from their constant demand for attention. If they are overlooked they are likely to resort to speech and action, mostly of a negative nature, that compels the attention of others.

In order to help these intelligent children use their multiple talents effectively, a name reducing to 1, 4, or 7 is needed. They need to be grounded with a vibration from the physical plane. Reduction to all other numbers should be avoided.

Threes Born in April (fourth month)

Interplay of mental and physical forces motivate Three personalities born in the fourth month. The creative imagination of the 3 vibration and the practicality and manual dexterity of the 4 vibration provide an outstanding combination of talent. The amazing capabilities of these children resulting from the reciprocal relationship of the 3 and 4 forces can be also be seen in the chapter on the fourth day and third month. The 4 vibration, in particular, helps them conceive of a project, do it and see it through to the end before moving to something else. It helps check the tendency of those influenced by the 3 vibration to keep changing course.

Attributes of the emotional plane do not play a role in this birth day and birth month combination. Consequently, these children may not respond to emotions displayed by others or give vent to their own feelings. They are not touchers, nor do they like to be touched. They excel in all forms of sport. They are not highly competitive by nature but the combination of mental and physical skills overcomes any need for strong opposition. Their natural skills can be enhanced by an injection of self-confidence from time to time as they can be inclined to underrate themselves. A first name reducing to 3 or 4 should be avoided. Any other name will be OK

Threes Born in May (fifth month)

The chapter on the fifth day of the month reveals how the 3 and 5 vibration have many shared attributes. This condition emphasizes characteristics such as enthusiasm, self-expression, sociability, variety, motivation, alertness, flexibility, adaptability, changeability, and restlessness. These children are great talkers but poor listeners. Their natural aptitude in many directions, especially in the performing arts, needs to be encouraged and harnessed. This will not be an easy task as they are not amenable to strict discipline, routine, timetables, and punctuality. They cannot be confined to a small living area. Unit-dwelling families will have a hard time quietening these noisy and energetic children. They are happiest when they are most active. They require physical outlets for their feelings. School children are likely to be restless and talkative in their classrooms.

A first name reducing to a 3 or 5 should be avoided. The best choice will be one that reduces to 4, 6, 7, or 9. Names with the numbers reducing to 1, 2, or 8 are best avoided as these will increase their demanding nature.

Threes Born in June (sixth month)

With both primary and secondary spheres of influence operating on the mental plane these children are clearly mentally oriented. Emotional expression will be minimal while reasoning powers are maximized. The 6 vibration in its positive aspect represents balance in all things. Consequently, this vibration in the Three personality's birth month restricts any extravagant, over-imaginative, and impulsive tendencies. Changeability and other fluctuations in behavior are kept to a minimum.

The 6 vibration also intensifies the artistic talent and social graces of the Three personality. To a fair extent, it removes the Three personality from self-absorption as this is also a community-oriented force. But it does not provide qualities of self-confidence and self-assurance to a degree that allows the Three to act without hesitation and without encouragement. These children may underestimate their talents. But it will not be difficult to instruct them. They are more peaceful and family-oriented than other Three personalities. The chapter on the sixth day of the month indicates the additional assets provided by this vibration. The best name these children can be given is one with a number from the physical plane, i.e. 1, 4, or 7. All others are best avoided.

Threes Born in July (seventh month)

The mentally oriented and imaginative Three personality is brought down-to-earth by the physical 7 vibration. As this is a mature and realistic force, these children will not have too many illusions about themselves. The influence of the 7 vibration creates a quietly confident manner with measured and accurate speech. These are the least talkative of all Three personalities. If you refer to the chapter on the seventh day of the month you will see, among other things, that the 7 vibration is not an extroverted force. There is a reserve in those influenced by this vibration that makes them selective of the company they keep.

The artistic talents of the Three will be greatly enriched by the manual dexterity of the 7. This vibration also introduces a love of nature and brings to the surface their spiritual aspect. Their emotions will be directed into their artistic creations, their love of natural surroundings and a love of animals. A given name reducing to 1, 2, 5, 8, or 9 will be best. A 3 or 7 are best avoided. A 4 or 6 will do no harm but these too are best avoided.

Threes Born in August (eighth month)

Leadership talents of the 3 vibration will be combined with the organizational and administrative powers of the 8. The chapter on the eighth day of the month will indicate the extent to which these forces work together in these personalities. These children are likely to be quite demanding of attention and their needs. Although outward expression may indicate a strong, positive, and confident personality, this will not be quite the case. There is very likely to be an inner insecurity that emerges in a self-promoting and loud-spoken manner. They are clever children but their relationship with others may be harmed by critical, intolerant, and boastful behavior. They are also susceptible to flattery. If they fail to receive the adulation they expect, they resort to self-praise and exaggerated notions of their capabilities. A 7, 6, or 9 name will be best as these will reduce certain inflated ideas they may have of themselves. Other numbers are best avoided.

Threes Born in September (ninth month)

The best attributes of the 3 and 9 vibrations combine to function effectively in these children. Their natural disposition displays politeness, and a kindly and friendly manner. Please consult the chapter on the ninth day of the month to ascertain the contribution that will be made by the 9 vibration.

The 3 vibration operating as the primary force always needs a secondary feature that provides self-confidence, self-belief, and firm decisions, to effortlessly bring out their best attributes. The 9 vibration in the birth month, while contributing so many superior attributes, does not provide the ego-strength, self-assertiveness, and firm decisions that may be needed at times. This condition cannot be considered an inadequacy in the 9 vibration. The fact is that the 9 has moved beyond ego-consciousness and self-centeredness into a humanitarian, compassionate, and global outlook on life. These are qualities that will be introduced into the Three personality.

Three children born in the ninth month can benefit from an injection of self-confidence from time to time so that their multiple talents are used to their maximum. A first name reducing to the number 1 will be the best. A 7 name will be helpful. All others are best avoided.

Threes Born in October (tenth month)

Please refer to the section Threes born in January (first month) above. The zero does not make a difference in the personality structure. 2, 6, and 9 names are best for these children.1, 4, 7, and 8 are best avoided. 3 and 5 are controlling forces and are also best avoided.

Threes Born in November (eleventh month)

The section Threes born in January (first month) will apply here. It may be noted to this day, however, the double 1 will emphasize the influence of the 1 vibration on this Three personality. The best names are a 2, 6, or 9. Others should be avoided as they could be too assertive and controlling.

Threes Born in December (twelfth month)

Although the 1 and 2 vibrations operate as a secondary feature, the section Threes born in January (first month) will apply here, as the 1 vibration is a stronger and more assertive force than the 2. However, these children can be slightly more amenable to discipline than those born in the first, tenth, and eleventh months. The best names for these children will be those reducing to 2, 6, and 9. All others are best avoided as they would be too controlling.

Fourth Day of the Month

The 1, 4, and 7 vibrations operate on the physical plane – each with its own span of attributes, many of which have very little in common. However, a realistic approach to life is one that is contained in all three. Occupying the central position in the spectrum of physical forces, the 4 vibration is one that provides features that manifest within strictly confined areas of operation. It is a stable and solid force with attributes such as balance, caution, deliberation, dependability, discipline, duty, economy, endurance, loyalty, method, moderation, obedience, steadfastness, and above all, practicality. As with other vibratory forces it is not without negative features. Four children who have not been nurtured in a favorable environment could easily slip into negative traits such as, bluntness in speech and manner, discourtesy, insensitivity, obstinacy, argument, rudeness, laziness, indecision, and lack of motivation.

In general, all Four children possess an inherent respect for discipline and law and order. For the most part, they accept things as they are and fit into routine and regularity. They could react to unfamiliar conditions with real anxiety as they possess methodical and orderly minds that cannot easily be hurried, changed, or misled. An ancient maxim "make haste slowly" can be applied to them. There is nothing they dislike more than being forced into completing a task, or making instant decisions or sudden changes in their daily activities. Although these children are placid and easy-going by nature, they could react aggressively or obstinately if they are coerced into doing something that is contrary to their temperament, such as being pushed into highly competitive situations or being made to be in the spotlight. Although not fiercely competitive, they are usually physically strong children who would be successful in any form of sport. Body contact sports do not worry them. In a football game, for instance, their natural position is one of defense rather than one of attack. In a social event, and subsequently in a work scene, their natural area of choice will be activity in the background.

Their imaginative powers may not be wide but common sense is an outstanding quality. They may not be outright leaders such as those controlled by the 1 or 3 vibrations, but they are not defenseless followers either. Their ample measure of common sense and level-headedness safeguards them from being swayed by undesirable associates. If they make a mistake it will be of their own doing and not the result of someone else's prompting. For the most part, they are quite able to make up their minds as to whom and when their support is extended. However, there may be occasions when they allow others to take advantage of their helpful ways. As they mature, Four personalities are fairly certain to be tight with their money but they are generous with their time and skills. Using their manual dexterity, Four children are happiest when taking things apart and putting them back together. The 4 vibration produces the natural builder and engineer. Building blocks and other mechanical gadgets are ideal gifts for Four children, whether they are boys or girls. They will also display an early attraction toward military music and the drums. Four children are home and community-oriented personalities. They do not wander far from familiar surroundings but remain close to home and their friends and acquaintances. Domestic harmony is essential in order to foster their full potential. They could easily under-perform in dysfunctional family life.

The number 4 is not a strong speech vibration. Four children may take a little longer to begin speaking than those with a speech vibration. But when they do develop this faculty their speech is precise and meaningful. Action rather than words will invariably be their best form of self-expression; in other words, a steady hand but not necessarily a ready tongue. To their disadvantage, many Four children and adults may in certain circumstances fail to explain themselves adequately or promote themselves and suffer some adverse consequences. They are most likely to pursue and acquire specialized practical skills and remain in a chosen field of work rather than change trades or professions. An effort has to be made by parents to get them into a reading habit as most Fours are not attracted to books dealing with general knowledge or even fiction. If these Four children are not helped by a flexible vibration in another strong sphere of influence they can confine themselves to restricted thought processes and consequently restricted ambition. It will not be easy to get them to change their minds or venture into new and experimental fields, even if it is to their advantage. A name with any number, except another 4, will help these children expand their vision.

Fours Born in January (first month)

The physical attributes of people born on the fourth day are substantially increased by the 1 vibration of the first month. See the chapter on the first day of the month to confirm this condition. In addition, these attributes are directed into positive channels by qualities of self-confidence, self-esteem, non-dependence, self-sufficiency, and competitiveness. These are natural attributes of the 1 vibration. Birth months without the 1 vibration do not provide these qualities to the same degree. In such months, certain negative features may appear side by side with those that are positive. This should not be the case with One children born in the first month.

Stubbornness and the absence of emotional demonstration will be obvious features of these personalities. But they need not be regarded as negative qualities. They will be valuable assets in the pursuit of studies, sport, and eventually, in the work scene. These children will also develop the ability to deal with challenges and conflicts without losing emotional balance. They will hold very firm opinions. They are not likely to give up an argument until they have had the last word. At the same time, it will not be easy to draw them into argument. They will also not be moved or misled by people who attempt to influence them against their wishes. They are quite able to give an emphatic "No" as an answer.

A name reducing to numbers 2, 3, 5, 6, or 9 will broaden their horizons and provide more flexibility and adaptability, whereas 4, 7, and 8 should be avoided as these vibrations add intolerance to an already self-assertive personality.

Fours Born in February (second month)

The 2 vibration of the second month introduces, among other things, an emotional outlet into a physically oriented Four personality. However, the 2 is a gentle and unobtrusive force which, as a secondary feature, does not favor the Four personality with desirable qualities of self-confidence, self-appreciation, and self-promotion. The chapter on the second day of the month shows the receptive qualities of this vibration as opposed to those that are active, and which are needed for a clear positive approach to life. Four personalities born in January or the first month are noticeably different from those born in February. Basically, the former are self-sufficient while the latter need boosting of self-confidence from time to time with a constant reminder of their multiple talents. Elders should not make negative remarks to these children that may instill ideas of limitation in them, either in private or in the presence of others. Unless these children are frequently and gently encouraged they may suffer from insufficient faith in their capabilities and consequently lack high ambition, drive, and self-assertiveness.

While the 2 vibration does not inject sufficient self-belief, it does introduce a good measure of flexibility, adaptability, imagination, and sociability. It also enhances the manual dexterity of the Four personality. All people influenced by the 2 and 4 vibration possess strong and sensitive hands and fingers, providing them with delicacy of touch. Both vibrations are non-competitive forces. Those influenced by the 2 and 4 will willingly participate in most activities but they are not fierce competitors or outright leaders. The best first name that can help bring out their potential will be one reducing to 1 or 7. The numbers 2 and 4 should not be repeated. Other numbers will be helpful but they may not provide the self-confidence innate in the 1 and 7.

Fours Born in March (third month)

Thought processes generated by the 4 vibration are generally directed into the physical realm while those of the 3 function within the mental realm. Their interaction within the birth day and birth month creates an imaginative and productive combination of talent. The manual dexterity of the 4 is merged with the creative imagination of the 3. A high sense of accuracy and exactitude is a special feature with both forces. These are clever, practical, and multi-talented children. They are mentally and physically active but emotionally undemonstrative. The chapter on the third day of the month explains that the 3 vibration introduces a degree of elegance, extroversion, friendliness, and clear oral expression.

Despite their wide range of talents, these children may not realize how smart they are. They may suffer from a measure of insecurity or inadequate self-confidence. These can be inner conditions not noticeable in their general behavior. A first name reducing to 1 or 7 will be ideal for a necessary injection of self-confidence. Avoid a repetition of 3 and 4. Other numbers will expand their potential but not provide the self-confidence they need.

Fours Born in April (fourth month)

When the number of a single-digit birth day is repeated in the birth month an intensification of the attributes of that number takes place. In most instances this may not be an advantageous condition. It deprives the personality of an opening into a fresh avenue for self-expression from the important sphere of the birth month. It consequently confines the individual to a particular set of personality traits and talents. (Minor openings may certainly be available in the numbers of the birth year and first name. But these are not as influential as those of the birth month).

A Four personality born in the fourth month will experience little departure from the circumscribed condition formed by the 4 vibration. This is not necessarily a negative situation but it does emphasize attributes of the 4 vibration while being deprived of strong elements of other forces. Imaginative powers and fluent oral communication, which are not strong in this vibration, may be further reduced. However, its qualities of stubbornness, concentration, determination, and manual dexterity are enhanced.

These are quiet children who, despite many physical and practical attributes, may be inclined to be lazy, and they may need help to motivate themselves toward high achievement. Otherwise, they may be content to be low achievers although they do possess the potential for high achievement. A first name reducing to 4 should be strictly avoided. Any other name will open out their personality, each in its own way, and add versatility and flexibility.

Fours Born in May (fifth month)

An additional outlet for creativity is provided by the 5 vibration of this birth month. While manual talents and practicality are strong points of the 4 vibration, flexibility, adaptability, and sociability are some of their weaker qualities. These and many others are supplemented by the 5 vibration of this birth month. The personality is expanded with an interest and capacity to experience life to a much greater extent than that offered by the attributes of the 4 vibration.

These are energetic, active, and multi-talented children who constantly look for some physical activity to entertain themselves. As they grow older they are certain to excel in all physical contact sports. However, they may experience a degree of confusion when the staid nature of their primary 4 nature is invaded by the changeable and dynamic attributes of the 5. Although the latter is a secondary feature, its qualities will not hesitate to interfere with the fundamental nature of the Four personality. This may account for occasional erratic behavior. Avoid a first name reducing to 4 or 5. Any other name will be beneficial.

Fours Born in June (sixth month)

The down-to-earth nature of the 4 vibration and the logic and rationality of the 6 vibration combine harmoniously to provide ample physical and mental energy to these children. Both vibrations contribute balance and stability in all aspects of life. These children are unlikely to fall into extreme forms of behavior. They will hold firm opinions and argue against anything they find irrational or inconclusive. They will be attached to home and family.

Some of these children may need an occasional nudge directed toward strengthening their self-confidence. They may be inclined to take life easily and not hasten toward reaching their high potential in both the mental and physical realms. A first name reducing to an odd number will be best while those reducing to an even number should be avoided. These children need an adventurous spirit.

Fours Born in July (seventh month)

These children possess some of the best attributes of the physical plane. Their primary 4 vibration directs them into physical channels such as farming, geology, mining, gemology, and anything else that has a connection with Mother Earth. Their secondary 7 aspect, along with many practical skills, complements these features with poetic, aesthetic, and spiritual qualities directed into the wide world of nature. Refer to the chapter on the seventh day of the month to see this complementary condition.

These are quiet, contemplative, soft-spoken and self-sufficient children who avoid argument and strong competition. They are not dependent too much on company and are quite content doing things on their own. Any name other than a 4, 7, or 8 will suit them.

Fours Born in August (eighth month)

The practical, businesslike, methodical, and money management skills of the primary nature of these children will be carried to higher levels by the 8 vibration of their birth month. This is confirmed in the chapter on the eighth day of the month. High ambition, which is not strong in the 4, is very strong in the 8. Similarly, competitiveness, which is not powerful in the 4, is a powerful attribute in the 8.

These children are most likely to end up in the world of business, finance, executive authority, and building construction. However, they will need to develop self-confidence, certain social graces, fluency of speech, flexibility, and open-mindedness. A 1 name will provide ample self-confidence but it may also increase self-assertiveness and dogmatism. Any other name will open out the personality into wider horizons and a more genteel manner. Avoid 4 and 8 names.

Fours Born in September (ninth month)

This is a most advantageous month for a Four personality to be born in. The 9 vibration will introduce the staid Four personality into the wide world of sociability with fluency of speech, imagination, flexibility, and above all, a humanitarian outlook on life. Reference to the chapter on the ninth day of the month will provide a good understanding of these children. It will be seen that most of the attributes of the 4 and 9 vibrations are poles apart.

Although the 9 vibration provides many outstanding features, it does not provide sufficient self-confidence. These children may depend on caring parents to wisely inject qualities of self-belief, strength of purpose, and self-assurance. A 1, 7, or 9 name will be ideal. Other names will provide fresh avenues for self-expression but they may not provide sufficient self-confidence. It is best to avoid 4 and 9 names.

Fours Born in October (tenth month)

October children will be the same as Fours born in January. The zero does not provide any new attributes.

Fours Born in November (eleventh month)

These children will be the same as Fours born in January (first month). However, as there are two 1 vibrations here, their influence upon the personality will be stronger.

Fours Born in December (twelfth month)

Qualities of the 1 and 2 vibrations combine to influence the Four personality. As the 1 is an assertive force and the 2 a passive and receptive force, attributes of the 1 may have a stronger impact on the Four personality. This will benefit the Four. These children will not lack self-confidence. Their 2 qualities will remain in the background but will modify some of the rough edges of the 4 and 1. A wide range of names is available for these children. However, it will be best to avoid another 4.

Fifth Day of the Month

The number 5 or the 5 vibration is known as the most multi-sided force within the single-digit spectrum—1 to 9. Its holistic nature functions effectively within the physical, emotional, and mental realms. The following random selection of 5 attributes reveals its widespread and mercurial nature: Activity, adaptability, adventure, alertness, animation, changeability, curiosity, demonstration, dynamism, energy, enterprise, enthusiasm, excitability, impulsiveness, restlessness, impatience, extravagance, flexibility, independence, spontaneity, individuality, opportunism, and sociability.

Needless to say, many of these vibrant and extroverted characteristics will be exhibited, even at a very early age, by children born on the fifth day. For instance, oral frustration will not be a problem. These children begin to speak with conviction and often without fear of disapproval. Early in life they develop the capacity to influence others through the spoken word and certain distinctive mannerisms. The written word may not be one of their best talents. Their emotions, which are easily released, are usually accompanied by expressive body language and animated facial expression. They do not hesitate to use their powers of persuasion and manipulation to get what they want; nor will they hesitate, if the occasion demands, to tamper with the truth.

Much patience will be needed to understand and nurture a Five child. Guidance offered to them should be based on a study of their complex personality and not always on what adults expect them to be. Due to their restless nature, their greatest source of pleasure is in a diversity of interests and activity. Their constant search for novelty could be quite irksome to parents and guardians. Enthusiasm in one area of interest is usually short-lived. They may begin projects zealously but never finish them. Curiosity is one of their stimulating features. With an urgent desire to know the whys and wherefores of things they could be constantly questioning elders. Expect many awkward questions. Basically, they are highly intelligent and alert children who set out to experience life in its rich diversity. They seldom retreat into a comfort zone as most other children do. Change is an inherent component of their nature—change initiated by them or change brought about by circumstances. They possess a better than average talent to sense the feelings and thoughts of people. Consequently, they rarely miss out on anything that is said in their presence, even in whispers. A flair for showmanship is another attractive aspect of their personality.

When these children feel like doing something you will find they do not look for approval or permission, but unconsciously proceed to act according to their natural urges. They are well equipped to be in the accelerated lifestyle of the present century. They may promptly show genuine impatience toward anyone unable to keep up with their speed, energy, enterprise, and adaptability. Their energy is expended in activity rather than in interaction with people. They are excellent communicators and good mixers, but their association with others is usually a by-product of their need to indulge in various activities. They do acquire many admirers due to their vitality, optimism, and flair for organizing people and circumstances, although their various schemes are often related to self-interest. There is invariably an element of unpredictability in their behavior. They are attracted to everything but held down by nothing and are hopeless in keeping in touch with family, friends, and acquaintances. Many could also be accident-prone due to their impulsive nature. More often than the average child, they fall into some sort of strife. But, more often than not, they talk themselves out of any trouble they create for themselves or others. The older they grow, the better they will be at providing plausible explanations for their conduct. Love of personal freedom is one of their strongest qualities. They are easily bored, seldom able to keep still, and always seeking the limelight. They usually resent the need to abide by routine, rules and regulations, and domestic duties. They are not rebels but their tendency to make their own decisions often comes into conflict with authority. Their inherent desire is to experience rather than follow. A worry here is that they do not fear strangers.

A name reducing to 1 will be best. What they need is a clear sense of direction and resistance to change for change sake. The 1 will help them with a degree of willpower to do so. The next best choice will be a 4 or 7 name. A 6 name may be considered. All other names are best avoided as they may not control impulse and changeability. A 5 name should be strictly avoided. It is important to note that vibrations or numbers of the birth month exercise a significant influence in the fundamental traits of the 5 vibration within the birth day. The following sections are therefore of considerable interest.

Fives Born in January (first month)

This is one of the best months for a Five personality to be born in. The others are the tenth, eleventh, and twelfth. The number 1 or the 1 vibration is responsible for this fortunate condition. In the chapter on the first day of the month, you will see how many of the attributes of the 1 vibration complement and strengthen those of the 5. The most beneficial are those that help to provide self-discipline in order to maintain clear direction in life and, as a consequence, curtail impulsive actions and the desire for frequent change. The extent a Five child benefits from this secondary sphere of influence will also depend on upbringing.

At an early age, these children will certainly display characteristics of individuality, self-confidence, authority, leadership, and adventure. They will not indulge in complaints that they have been harassed or bullied in school or anywhere else. Wherever they function they are bound to gather around them a following of faithful friends. They do not need a name which reduces to a 1 or 5. Any other name will better suit them.

Fives Born in February (second month)

This is not the most ideal month into which Five children are born. They will need careful nurturing as the 2 vibration does not provide the essential support a Five personality needs. In the first instance, it increases emotionalism. Secondly, it fails to provide the willpower and firm decisiveness needed for a steady course of action. Changeability is also increased. The 2 vibration certainly adds multiple talents to the Five personality but these children will need help to harness these talents and guide them into definite areas of self-expression. To further your understanding, refer to the chapter on the second day of the month.

These children are, in fact, much smarter than they think they are. Their problem is inadequate self-confidence. They should be given a number 1 name. A 4 or 7 would also be fine. Avoid 2 and 5 names. Names with other numbers will do no harm but they will not provide the self-confidence and proper direction these children need.

Fives Born in March (third month)

The chapter on the third day of the month will reveal that the 3 and 5 vibrations possess several shared attributes; the most common being, extroversion, independence, authority, enthusiasm, flexibility, adaptability, popularity, charm, and verbal effectiveness. In regard to the last attribute, the Five's voice does not contain the fine tonal quality and accuracy of speech of the Three. The quality of speech of 5 children born in March will be improved by their 3 aspect although the quantity of words may not be reduced. The Five's tendency toward imprecise speech will also be checked.

These children will habitually draw attention to themselves. There is a perennial need for company and entertainment. Solitude and quietude are states they cannot abide by. They could get into all sorts of mischief if left alone or without sufficient mental or physical stimulation. They are exceptionally alert and intelligent children who pick up knowledge with amazing speed. At the same time, they experience difficulty channeling their knowledge into definite directions. They also feel that the "grass is always greener on the other side of the fence". A 1, 4, or 7 name will suit them best as these will establish a measure of stability in their lives and readiness to take responsibility for their actions. All other names are best avoided.

Fives Born in April (fourth month)

The 4 vibration of the fourth month will provide these Five children with essential attributes not found in their birth force. Refer to the chapter on the fourth birth day to see how the 4 contributes many balancing features such as constancy and stability. Emotionalism and changeability will also be held in check. Almost all 4 attributes are the opposite of those of the 5. Although the 4 vibration of the birth month is a secondary feature it resolutely encroaches upon 5 attributes. It also greatly increases the Five personality's practical talents. These children will be much easier to manage than other Fives. Any name other than another 5 or 4 will suit them.

Fives Born in May (fifth month)

The repetition of the birth day number in the birth month does not augur well for a well-directed application of the attributes of the birth force; namely, the 5 in this instance. On the one hand, it creates an overloading of the attributes of the 5 vibration, and on the other hand, this condition deprives the personality of an outlet for manifestation of a secondary feature. The inevitable result is a tendency for the personality to be drawn into certain negative aspects of the 5 vibration. This can take place in greater or lesser degrees depending on the upbringing of the child. Some of these negatives could be: excess of restlessness, changeability, impulse, and sensationalism. Some other negative tendencies that may be observed in these children are: instability, waywardness, hyperactivity, abuse of personal freedom, and lack of taking responsibility.

Many such children, and subsequently adults, use persuasive and evasive speech and methods to obtain their needs and offer excuses for their actions. It will not be easy to hold them down to a factual explanation of their conduct. Although these negative traits may appear extreme, do not think that a particular child will not be subject to some of these traits, because they will be, at least to some extent. At the same time, a child whose personality has been shaped by the combined efforts of concerned parents can overcome many of these negative traits. What these children need is a clear direction in life. A first name with the 1, 4, or 7 vibration will be most helpful. All other names should be avoided.

Fives Born in June (sixth month)

The Five personality reaps many benefits from the 6 vibration of the sixth month. The chapter on the sixth day of the month shows how this mentally oriented force can exercise a good deal of control over the mercurial temperament of a pure Five personality. Although operating as a secondary force, the 6 vibration reduces 5 qualities of impulse, the need for constant activity and constant change, and excess of emotional expression. Deliberation, being one of the 6 vibration's prominent attributes, will have a salutary influence on these Five personalities. They are likely to feel the urge to "look before they leap".

These are versatile and multi-talented children who would, nevertheless, need help and guidance toward balanced development and, from time to time, a boosting of their self-confidence. It will not be difficult to gain their attention when you give them instructions, as long as you approach them subtly and rationally. These children need a first name that gives them access to the physical plane. A 1, 4, or 7 name will be ideal. Any of these will help them persevere during rough patches in their lives. Other numbers are also best avoided, in particular a 5 or 6.

Fives Born in July (seventh month)

The 7 vibration of the seventh month introduces many qualities that are unrelated to those of the 5. These children may experience a degree of inner conflict as a result of the pull of opposite forces. The chapter on the seventh day of the month will reveal the likelihood of this condition arising. This can, in fact, be turned into a positive state as the 7 attributes will slow down the unnecessary speed, desire for frequent change, and impulsiveness of the natural Five personality. They also lead to a child displaying an attraction to books and to the love of natural surroundings. Most importantly, the 7 vibration may introduce a good measure of non-dependence on too much activity and interaction with friends and acquaintances. A quiet self-confidence which will eventually help them define their goals in life will also be the result of the influence of 7 attributes. Any name, except those reducing to a 5 or 7, will suit these children.

Fives Born in August (eighth month)

Reference to the chapter on the eighth day of the month will reveal some fundamental attributes that the 5 and 8 vibrations have in common and some that are of an opposite quality. Those that are similar are the controlling nature of both forces and the emotionalism they contain. These are the most prominent characteristics of Five personalities born in the eighth month. From an early age, Five children will adopt various means to control their elders, their contemporaries, and circumstances in which they find themselves. If their attempts are frustrated, their natural reactions will be emotional outbursts and possibly some destructive behavior. Both 5 and 8 vibrations operate on the emotional plane. Emotionalism of the 5 is expressed outwardly in speech and action while that of the 8 is usually suppressed and released in outbursts of anger or frustration. A name reducing to 3, 6, 7, or 9 will relieve to some extent their controlling nature. A name with the vibration 6 or 7 will restrain emotional outbursts. Names with 1 and 4 vibrations should be avoided as these will increase their controlling nature. Avoid 5 and 8 names.

Fives Born in September (ninth month)

The expansive horizons of the natural Five personality is extended even further in people born in the ninth month. At the same time, attributes of the 9 vibration will be responsible for diminishing self-interest, which is a natural trait with Fives, and increase their consideration for the needs of others. These 9 qualities of wisdom, compassion, and generosity will increasingly seek entry into their thought processes. This process will be facilitated and expedited in a favorable home environment. Please refer to the chapter on the ninth birth day for a good understanding of Five children born in September.

You will only reach these children by using a mental approach. You will not succeed with an emotional approach or physical threats. As these children are emotionally and mentally oriented at birth, a physical vibration 1, 4, or 7 will provide a source of practicality and down-to-earth values. Other numbers are best avoided.

Fives Born in October (tenth month)

These Five children will be the same as Fives born in January (the first month). The zero does not add any new attributes. This is a desirable month for Five children to be born in. The 1 vibration of their birth month provides self-confidence, decision, and above, all a clear direction in life. Repetition of a 1 or 5 in their first name is not needed. All other numbers will enrich their personality. However, an 8 name may introduce too much authority and controlling habits. So, this number is best avoided.

Fives Born in November (eleventh month)

With the 1 vibration in double strength these children enjoy the best attributes of the 1 vibration and the best of the 5 in almost equal strength. However, the authoritative and leadership qualities of the 1 and the controlling and organizational attributes of the 5 could be taken too far. These children could be eventually successful in whatever they undertake but this may be done at the expense of popularity and close friendships. They will display individuality, self-reliance, self-confidence, and decisiveness very early in life. Their strong egos can be diminished with a first name reducing to 2, 6, 7, or 9. Other numbers are best avoided.

Fives Born in December (twelfth month)

Five personalities are enriched by the combined influence of the 1 and 2 vibrations from the birth month. These children can achieve anything they set out to do at an early age. All they need is chance and opportunity. If deprived of these, success may be delayed but they will sooner or later create opportunities for high achievement. First names reducing to 2, 3, 6, 7, and 9 will increase their perspectives and talents. 1, 4, 5, and 8 names are best avoided as these will increase authority and controlling habits which they already possess in sufficient strength.

Sixth Day of the Month

The vibration operating within this day contains, among other things, all matters relating to family, home, and community. It is known as the vibration of love, harmony, peace, and balance. Functioning on the mental plane, these wonderful attributes are manifested through reason, logic, analysis, and deliberation. All other personality traits and habits are an elaboration of these essential aspects. The natural Six is a candid and unsophisticated individual. There is nothing fake about a Six personality, especially a Six child.

As the 6 vibration is clearly a mental force, those under its influence depend on a vibration from the emotional plane, especially a 2 or 5, for easy release of emotion. If one of these is not present, emotional expression is limited. Such children pass the cuddlesome stage early in life. But qualities of love, loyalty companionship and bonding are in no way diminished. Purposeful speech and action take precedence over emotional demonstration.

As peace and quiet are fundamental aspects of their constitution, these Six children are exceptionally sensitive to atmosphere. As babies they are instantly disturbed by inharmonious music or other harsh noises, and calmed by silence, or pleasant and harmonious sounds. These responses are carried into childhood and adulthood. Consequently, these children blossom in peaceful surroundings. Placed occasionally in discordant conditions, they can easily absorb negative vibrations and at a later stage suffer from a state of anxiety without knowing its cause.

These children constantly seek genteel company and togetherness. Left to their own devices they can become quite unsettled and slow in development. They are cautiously extroverted and sociable, and carefully selective of the company they keep. They relate with ease to all age groups.

Given a reasonable upbringing they acquire and display social graces at an early age. Being home-oriented by nature they are not likely to become drifters, wanderers, or even bona fide travelers. Travel may be undertaken for educational purposes at any age but the homing call will always pull them back.

These children will grow into adults who lead organized and well-adjusted lives. They do not entertain revolutionary ideas but will always remain prepared to fight for their principles, especially those of justice and fair play. They are generally non-competitive children—more so if their birth month also contains a non-competitive vibration, such as a 2, another 6, 7, or 9. A Six child's first day at kindergarten or school could be a fearful experience. Leaving the closeness of home and family, especially the mother, could be quite traumatic. However, once they have overcome the initial mixing with non-family members, the natural sociability of the 6 vibration will help them make friends and enjoy school life. Rarely, if ever, will they enter into fierce rivalries or enmity with schoolmates. Their best expression is given in group activity rather than in solo performance. They are studious children who take their studies earnestly. However, some may display a tendency to worry about their performance, not only in their studies, but also in extracurricular activities. They may need a boost of self-confidence by an occasional reminder that they are invariably better than they think they are. All Six personalities possess a keen appreciation for the fine arts. As adults they could emerge as art critics, connoisseurs, and collectors.

A most endearing and valuable asset in Six children is their capacity to take upon themselves the responsibilities of domesticity in the event of a breakdown of the family unit. The motherly/fatherly instinct within the 6 vibration will emerge unselfishly in support of a single parent and care of siblings. Expertise in the culinary arts is another special attribute of their birth force. The kitchen will be the jealous preserve of a Six homemaker. Listening to stories and telling stories is another special quality with all Six children. Almost all turn into avid readers.

Most Six personalities are a balance between left brain (mind) and right brain (heart). With a few exceptions, children and adults stand out for their evenness of disposition. A desire for peace and restoration of peace when peace has been lost are urgent needs. They do not rely on others to restore peaceful conditions, but will rather take up the task themselves. Consequently, they acquire a reputation as arbitrators and peacemakers. A Six child should not be given a name with a mental vibration, 3, 6, or 9. A name converting to any other number will suit them well. Attributes of the 6 vibration do not manifest in the same ways in all Six personalities. There are other spheres of influence, particularly the birth month and the given name, that are responsible for certain changes. The following is a list of possible changes made by each birth month.

Sixes Born in January (first month)

January is one of the best birth months for a Six personality to be born in. The others are, October, November, and December. The 1 vibration operating within these months is responsible for positive manifestation of all 6 attributes. Although the 1 is found in a secondary position, it works as a strong operative force. Consequently, all negative qualities of the 6 are usually restricted and positive ones activated. The primal or essential Six personalities have the potential to achieve anything they set out to do. However, due to the inevitable exposure to outside influences the attributes of their blueprint could be either enriched or damaged. Fortunately, with the 1 of the birth month having an influence, the fundamental positive nature of these children will help them resist much negative conditioning and absorb positive influences as soon as they begin thinking and acting as individuals in their own right. And this will begin early in life. The chapter on the first day of the month should be read in conjunction with this birth day and birth month.

Contributions made by the 1 vibration, among other things, are self-confidence and self-esteem. At the same time, as the 6 is the primary force, it softens the 1 vibration's tendency toward egocentricity and certain abrasive qualities. These children possess all the mental and physical attributes to stand on their own feet early in life. They should be handled with care as they will not hesitate to challenge anything or anyone that does not measure up to rational analysis of things. A first name with an emotional vibration 2, 5, or 9 will round out the personality. Another 6 or 1 will not be necessary.

Sixes Born in February (second month)

The chapter on the second day of the month should be read in order to gain a good understanding of the Six personality born in February. There are many similarities between the Six and the Two, despite the former operating on the mental plane and the latter on the emotional plane. This condition serves to emphasize these attributes, especially their peaceful disposition. Such emphasis could be advantageous as well as disadvantageous, depending on circumstances and the company these children interact with. They blossom in a harmonious family atmosphere and in close friendships but the rough and tumble days of schooling and the hurly burly of public life could take a toll on their sensitivity and non-competitive nature. Their endearing qualities of peace, tranquillity, kindness, generosity, helpfulness, and congenial ways will be treasured by those close to them. Unfortunately, some negative traits of both the 6 and 2 vibrations are also likely to manifest themselves, such as, mood changes, unaccountable fears, anxiety, fear of crowds, aversion to strong competitive demands, and noisy living or working conditions.

These children need careful nurturing. They should be encouraged to hold a good opinion of themselves and their capabilities. Left to their own devices they could fall into the trap of underestimating themselves. They are much more capable than they think. A name with the 1 vibration will help change a generally fearful outlook on life into a bolder one. A 4, 5, or 7 name could also be helpful. Naturally, another 6 or 2 should be avoided. It is best to avoid a 3, 8, or 9 as these may not help with the practicalities of life.

Sixes Born in March (third month)

Vibrations from the mental plane operate within both birth day and birth month. A mental orientation of children and adults with this combination can be expected. At the same time, a direct consequence is a restriction of emotional expression, and an inadequacy of skills at a practical level. However, demonstration of one or the other can be generated to some degree by a given name from the emotional or physical plane. A physical number 1, 4, or 7 will be better. Any of these numbers will provide stability which an emotional plane number may not.

Some personality traits that will be expanded in this combination will be articulate speech, artistic appreciation and creativity, extroversion, sociability, and social graces. These are highly intelligent children, but their degree of self-confidence and self-sufficiency may not match their degree of intelligence. When a need arises to face and overcome inevitable difficulties and problems in practical living, they may look to others for support. This will not be withheld at any stage of their lives. Nurturing and associating with these children will be a perennial source of pleasure due to their natural courtesy, sense of humor, entertaining speech, and a natural capacity to pick up new knowledge and skills.

Sixes Born in April (fourth month)

Children born into this combination of birth day and birth month are favored with a blueprint formed by mental and physical vibrations. Emotional expression may be restricted but its limitation is amply compensated by unswerving loyalty and devotion to home and loved ones. Their helpful nature will be extended to community and country in adulthood. These children are certain to be great little helpers in household duties, especially in the kitchen; in general, girls with their mothers and boys with their fathers.

These are good children within the simple meaning of the word good. Any attributes harmful to themselves or to others will be introduced from outside sources. The chapter on the fourth day of the month should be read for a better understanding of this birth day and birth month combination. The Six personality's tendency to think and rationalize will be enhanced by their birth month. A special fondness will be shown for good food and physical comforts, but they are not likely to fall into extremes of indulgence. They will not be easily influenced by others. As teenagers and adults they will not be slaves to fashion or fall victim to sales gimmicks. They will look for value and utility in all their acquisitions. They do not need an additional vibration from the mental or physical plane. One from the emotional plane, 2, 5, or 8 will be helpful.

Sixes Born in May (fifth month)

Six personalities born in the fifth month find themselves in a condition of contrasts. Refer to the chapter on the fifth day of the month to see the many differences between the 6 and 5 vibratory forces. A major difference will be the Six personality's love of domesticity and a peaceful, settled, and unexciting way of life, and the 5 vibration's attributes of changeability, unpredictability, adventure, movement, restlessness, and impulse. These children are bound to receive mixed messages or conflicting desires which could result in some degree of uncertainty and an unsettled state of mind. Reconciliation of these two aspects in their nature may take time and effort but it will certainly work to their advantage. Their lives will be opened out into extended dimensions of living. Though the 5 is in a secondary position, it is powerful enough to lead the Six out of a comfort zone of home, family, and community. At the same time the 6 vibration's sense of balance will always deter them from falling into extremes of behavior.

Parents of these children should note the dichotomy in their personality and expect occasional changes and surprises in their conduct. The best given name will be one from the physical plane, 1, 4, or 7. Repetition of the 6 and 5 is inadvisable. Other numbers too should also be avoided.

Sixes Born in June (sixth month)

All single-digit birth days are exposed to repetition. This is the repetition of the same number or vibration in their birth month. This condition, on the one hand, tends to overload the personality with attributes of the birth force, and on the other hand, deprives the individual of an opening into other significant spheres of expression. The inevitable result is the entry of certain negative aspects of the birth force.

Six personalities born in the sixth month seldom escape them. Some problems they could face are anxiety, dependability, fear, possessiveness, selfishness, pessimism, suspicion, and a martyr or victim complex. All these are possibilities but not necessarily certainties. Careful nurturing could help them overcome one or more that may appear. A good boost of self-confidence and counseling from parents or guardians should help them get a better understanding of themselves. Do not leave it to them to gain an understanding of their own nature or human nature in general. They are likely to show distaste toward touching others or being touched by others. A name with a physical number 1, 4, or 7 is essential. All other numbers should be avoided. These children need stability on the physical plane.

Sixes Born in July (seventh month)

The sixth birth day and the seventh birth month are a rich composition of very desirable personality traits and multiplicity of talent. The chapter on the seventh day of the month will indicate that these children are usually deep thinkers and keen students. At an early age, they are certain to display a widening interest in books and communication with interesting and knowledgeable people.

As they do not possess an effective vibration from the emotional plane their sentiments are not freely expressed either verbally or physically. They are not touchers, nor do they enjoy being touched by others who use this as a means of communication. This condition certainly does not diminish their love and devotion to loved ones and loyalty to friends. Their love nature is displayed in actions rather than words and physical demonstrations. The most endearing aspects in the personality of these children are the absence of a prominent ego and self-centeredness, and non-demanding and non-competitive ways. These attributes contribute toward an elegant individuality. Left to their own devices or in company of their choice, their overall strength and resourcefulness emerges. However, their Achilles heel becomes evident in discordant conditions and in company of rude, noisy, and uncouth individuals. A name with numbers reduced to a 1 or 5 will help them cope to some extent in unpleasant company. A 2 name should be avoided as this vibration is not strong enough to help in this respect. A 6 or 7 name should also be avoided. Names with other numbers should be fine.

Sixes Born in August (eighth month)

A merger of the 6 and 8 vibrations create quite a few contradictory personality traits and talents. With a little effort these can be acknowledged and used as advantages rather than disturbances and disadvantages. The Six personality is strengthened by the ambitious and competitive qualities of the 8 vibration while these same 8 qualities are held in control or balance by the many sensible 6 attributes. Please consult the chapter on the eighth day of the month for further understanding.

Though these children may receive mixed messages from this personality structure, concerned parents can help them understand the differences that motivate them. On the one hand, they could be advised to use the 8 aspect of their nature to engage in substantial contact with competitive living, thus preparing for the challenges of teen years and adulthood. On the other hand, by using their 6 aspect they could use their clear reasoning powers to maintain a balance between a harmonious private life and an active public life. This is a rare feature that is certain to help them in their need and talent for organization and method in all aspects of life. A name with a number from the physical plane, 1, 4, or 7 will suit them best. A repetition of a 6 or 8 will be undesirable. Other numbers are also best avoided.

Sixes Born in September (ninth month)

The numbers 6 and 9 symbolize compatible forces operating on the mental plane. Please refer to the chapter of the ninth day of the month. These children will not be pulled in opposite directions or receive mixed messages from within themselves. They will face life with a strong set of values generated by the blending of these vibratory forces. As a vibration from the emotional plane is conspicuous by its absence, these children will be mentally oriented with limited emotional expression and limited manual skills. The abundant love and loyalty, and sense of duty they possess will be displayed in caring, sympathy, devotion, and service. In adulthood they invariably turn into professional counselors or private confidants.

They will rarely, if ever, be taken as egotistic, self-centered, and selfish personalities. Early in life they are certain to exhibit consciousness and concern for the wellbeing of loved ones and others they come into contact with. They need people and eventually people will need them. They do not suffer from the illusion of an isolated self, self-sufficiency, or non-dependence. Wisdom and understanding are attributes they display early in life. As many of their personality traits are of a delicate nature they will not escape from suffering from many of the harsh realities of life. They will need to develop a sense of detachment without losing their helpfulness and concern for others. Parents and guardians can help by giving these children a strong injection of self-confidence. A first name reduced to a physical number, 1, 4, or 7 is most essential. One of these will help them assert themselves when necessary. All other numbers are best avoided.

Sixes Born in October (tenth month)

Please refer to the section on Sixes born in January, (first month). The influence of this birth month on the Six personality will be the same. The zero does not add any new features.

Sixes Born in November (eleventh month)

Please refer to the section on Sixes born in January (first month). The influence of the 1 vibration will be strong as it is present in double strength. Attributes of this vibration may often override those of the 6 without altogether overmastering them.

Sixes Born in December (twelfth month)

This is a good month for the mentally oriented Six personality to be born in. Their 6 birth force is reinforced by the 1 vibration providing access to the physical plane and by the 2 providing access to the emotional plane. Please consult the sections on Sixes born in January and Sixes born in February.

Seventh Day of the Month

The 7 vibration is the third member of the physical plane; the previous ones being the 1 and 4. While these earlier numbers, for the most part, contain attributes that are allied to the physical plane, the number 7 also contains elements that impel its subjects to reach beyond the purely physical and material. Consequently, people born on the seventh day display certain propensities not found in other numbers or birth days. Commencing at childhood these qualities may manifest in different ways according to the child's upbringing but a common undertone will be present in all.

Special personality traits that distinguish a Seven child from others and which are emphasized in adulthood are: an introspective and reserved disposition, a need for, and ability to enjoy silence, a need for private time and solitary activities for the pleasure of their own company, and an enduring love for everything contained within natural surroundings. They may be alone but they are never lonely. They are easily disturbed in noisy, unfriendly, and rough company, and they are strictly selective of the company they keep. Even in chosen company they can be reserved yet still enjoy themselves. Their friendliness cannot always be taken for granted. Wherever they may be, they choose to observe, draw conclusions, and keep the results to themselves. It is not easy to extract information or opinions out of a Seven personality. They respect the privacy of others and, in turn, expect their privacy to be respected.

They are self-sufficient children who use their imagination and manual dexterity to find and enjoy hobbies in an extended range of activities. It would be most unusual to hear a Seven child complaining of boredom. They are certain to engage in indoor as well as outdoor hobbies. They show lasting interest in music; literature, especially poetry; nature studies; and pets, especially birds.

These children do not realize that they possess considerable depth of personality although this is usually observed by others. They may be found often lost in thought. Rare qualities of poise and grace are expressed in their demeanor. They are neither loud-spoken nor demanding, and express their thoughts and needs in a quiet, soft-spoken manner which captures the attention of listeners. They are skilled at using a minimum of words when they speak and using skilful body language to convey non-verbal messages. They do not expect to be fussed over as they are not emotionally dependent or emotionally expressive. Their love nature is deep and abiding, and shown in deeds rather than in demonstrations. Sevens resent being touched too often, especially by non-family members, and communication by touch is not a means they use. They are likely to avoid body contact sports. They are not talkative children, although they observe and know much more than they give out. They usually speak when they have a question to ask or a worthy subject to discuss. These are unusually perceptive children who are not susceptible to flattery, nor do they submit themselves readily to hero-worship, unless they know someone of real substance.

Some other general characteristics these children possess are: accuracy, a strict individuality, calm, dependability, intuition, idealism, intellectualism, and initiative. Any name will suit these children. But 3, 5, and 9 names will take them out of their reserved disposition and provide greater fluency of speech. The birth month contributes a strong secondary influence upon the fundamental personality structure formed by the birth day. The following sections indicate how each month affects certain changes in the Seven personality.

Sevens Born in January (first month)

Two powerful energies intermingle in this birth day and birth month. The result is a combination of self-assurance, self-sufficiency, and self-defense. The chapter on the first day of the month should be read in order to appreciate the independent nature of these children. The fundamental 7 vibration forming the birth day has the strength to use attributes of the 1 vibration that are relatively the same and remain impervious to those that are not. For instance, characteristics of the 1 vibration that are not uncommon, such as, egotism, pride, self-centeredness, and demanding and arbitrary ways, will not find entry into the integral Seven personality. But a positive outlook on life, a spirit of adventure, initiative, leadership, decisiveness, courage, and energy will be readily absorbed—thus greatly strengthening the Seven personality.

These children should be allowed to blossom without too much interference. Actually, they will insist on a minimum of interference. A first name reducing to 1, 4, 7, or 8 is best avoided. These may add too much authority and assertiveness. Any other name will be most suitable.

Sevens Born in February (second month)

Unlike Seven children born in the first month who may absorb certain 1 attributes and reject others, those born in the second month take in all the qualities of the 2 vibration. Strong attributes of the 2 vibration will expand their Seven personality while weaker aspects may find sympathy with weaker aspects of the Seven. Please read the chapter on the second day of the month for a better understanding of these children.

Endearing qualities that will be strengthened are: a soft-spoken and courteous manner, love of quietude, peace and harmony, gentility and sensitivity. Attributes of the 2 that may not always help the integral personality are: shyness, dislike of strong competition, imaginary fears, reserve, and self-consciousness. Although these are clever and versatile children they would need a harmonious atmosphere to open out to their full potential. They could easily close in when placed in inharmonious conditions. The courage and incentive to overcome their sensitivity can be gained with a name that reduces to 1, 3, 5, or 8. Another 2 or 7 should be avoided. Other numbers will open out the personality into more avenues for self-expression but they may not provide the self-confidence these children need.

Sevens Born in March (third month)

This birth day and birth month combination results in an enrichment of the personality. The 3 vibration will introduce many opposite attributes which may incur a degree of confusion and uncertainty in the minds of these children. But these very opposites, once they have been reconciled, will be responsible for innumerable attractive personality traits and multiple talents. Refer to the chapter on the third day of the month for a good insight into the many positive features the 3 vibration will contribute.

Although the 3 is a secondary force, it will certainly take these children out of the accustomed reserve of their Seven nature. In addition, a melodious tone will be added to an already fine speaking voice, and perhaps singing voice. Artistic talents will also be expanded by the manual dexterity of the 7 and the powerful creative imagination of the 3. The Seven child's reluctance to take a prominent role in social activity will be reduced. The 3 vibration does not introduce any features that could adversely influence the Seven personality. This is an advantageous month in which a Seven child is born. These children will be known for their artistic and creative talents as well as many charming personality traits. Another 3 or 7 in the first name will not be of much use. Any other name will expand further an already expanded personality.

Sevens Born in April (fourth month)

People born with this birth day and birth month combination inevitably acquire the best attributes of the physical plane. Mental faculties are directed toward creativity, activity, and the pleasures of this plane. Please refer to the chapter on the fourth day of the month. Although a strong affinity exists between these vibratory forces on physical aspects of life, the 7 vibration's awareness of non-physical aspects of life is not lost.

These are down-to-earth and practical children who are not swayed by impulse or other forms of emotional demonstration. For the most part, they control their emotions rather than let their emotions control them. This attribute will be increasingly manifested as they grow into maturity. With feet firmly placed on the ground they are not likely to be influenced against their better judgment. Both 7 and 4 vibrations create doers rather than talkers. These children will invariably prefer to go about their business without excessive communication. They generally prefer to be left to their own devices but every opportunity should be provided for these children to use their creative imagination and manual dexterity. They are attentive children whose minds do not wander during instruction.

A name with an emotional vibration 2 or 5 will provide an opening into the emotional realm. The emotional content in the 9 vibration will also help them. An 8 should be avoided as this will increase stubbornness and intolerance which are negative features in the 7 and 4. Other numbers will do no harm.

Sevens Born in May (fifth month)

The chapter on the fifth day of the month shows the presence of many conflicting features in the 7 and 5 vibratory forces. Acknowledging and using these differences in equal proportion, without an inner conflict, is a challenge these children will undertake, both knowingly and unknowingly.

Although the 5 vibration plays a secondary role, it contributes a layer of strength which the Seven personalities can rely upon. It will certainly draw them out of their customary reluctance to participate in group activity and also introduce a greater variety of social interests. At the same time it will not alter the Seven's quiet, soft-spoken disposition. These children will often surprise their parents and elders with many moments of fearlessness, ingenuity, and initiative—qualities that are not usually suspected in their quiet temperament. From an early age the 5's influence will help a shy Seven child shine in areas in which they have a keen interest.

These children possess such a considerable variety of personality traits and talents that they do not need a supporting name to booster their integral personality. Any name other than one reducing to 7 or 5 will suit them very well. A repetition of a 7 or 5 will be unnecessary.

Sevens Born in June (sixth month)

The chapter on the sixth day of the month reveals many congenial sets of vibrations that intermingle in the personality with this birth day and birth month combination. It will not be easy to pin-point any significant elements in either vibration that could create conflict or undesirable traits in these children. All the superior attributes of both forces are manifested without hindrance. These children will be largely free from affectation and attention-seeking behavior. Their non-assertive egos, non-competitive ways, and refined manners may not meet with the approval of people involved in the rough world of fierce competition and self-assertive habits. This should be of no concern to them as they are certain to be held in high esteem for these same characteristics by more discerning individuals.

Two factors that do not control these children are emphatic egos and uncontrolled emotions. If a special "fault" can be attributed to them, it would be modesty and self-effacement. They are infinitely more capable than they think they are. They do not need 7 or 6 names. 2, 5, or 9 names will help them with emotional expression. 1, 3, and 8 names will help overcome their modesty to a fair extent. A 4 name will greatly increase their practicality.

Sevens Born in July (seventh month)

The repetition of the 7 vibration in the birth month accentuates all 7 attributes. This may not necessarily mean a beneficial condition for Seven children born in July. Their generally reserved nature may fall deeper into varying degrees of introversion and distance. Sociability becomes limited. Negative qualities of doubt, mistrust, suspicion, secrecy, and insensitivity may take hold of the personality in various forms. At the same time positive attributes of the 7 vibration, such as accuracy, erudition, contemplation, and an attraction to philosophical, as well as, scientific studies are emphasized.

These children may feel quite frustrated by their inability to open out and freely express their thoughts and feelings. A given name reducing to 2, 3, 5, 6, or 9 will help them overcome the restrictions placed on them by the repetition of 7 traits. A 7 name should certainly be avoided. 1, 4, or 8 names are not ideal and best avoided.

Sevens Born in August (eighth month)

Contradictory as well as complementary attributes appear in this birth day and birth month combination. Many of these await progress into adulthood before being manifested. As children, these personalities will be strong-willed and determined to organize their lives, and even others, to suit themselves. They will not be led or influenced by their peers. Compatible features of the 7 and 8 forces that merge and provide greater strength to the personality are: deliberation, organization, responsibility, judgment, justice, practicality, skilful money management, and emotional control. Contrary features that could create a degree of conflict within the personality are the 8 vibration's strong competitiveness, high ambition for acquisition of power and material wealth, and the possibility that this aspect will not share a love of nature, and peace and tranquility. In other words the Seven's need for mental and spiritual freedom may be frustrated by the 8 vibration's promptings. However, these are not opposites that cannot be unified. A fine balance can be achieved over time with success in both aspects of life. Please refer to the chapter on the eighth day of the month for a better understanding of the influence of the 8 vibration upon a Seven child.

These children cannot be placated by empty promises, excuses, or false praise. One needs to be completely truthful with them. When parents cease to demand a certain code of conduct they may often find these children behaving in ways they want them to. All they need is wise guidance. A name with any number will suit these children.

Sevens Born in September (ninth month)

The numbers 7 and 9 are exceptionally harmonious vibratory forces. Please refer to the chapter on the ninth day of the month. Many desirable human attributes manifest in this combination. There is, in fact, nothing in either set of vibrations that could interfere with the formation of a much admired and successful personality. Among other things, the 9 vibration's sociability will exercise a gentle yet effective influence on the Seven personality's reticent nature. At the same time the 7 vibration's practicality and emotional control will not permit the 9 vibration's impulsive nature to enter the Seven personality's thoughts and actions.

Egotistic and self-centered traits are hardly present in these children. Limited thoughts of "me" and "mine" are not natural features. Very early in life these children will distinguish right from wrong. With a non-demanding nature they gain pleasure more in giving than in receiving. Names that reduce to 7 and 9 are not needed. Any other name will suit these wise and intelligent children.

Sevens Born in October (tenth month)

Seven children born in October are the same as Sevens born in January. The zero in the tenth month does not contribute any additional features. Please refer to the section on Sevens born in January (first month).

Sevens Born in November (eleventh month)

This is very much the same as Sevens born in January, the first month. But as the 1 vibration is present in a dual capacity its influence upon the Seven personality is stronger.

Sevens Born in December (twelfth month)

The best attributes of the 1 and 2 vibrations combine to exercise a very positive influence upon this Seven personality. An examination of the chapters on the first and second days of the month will indicate the overall strength of all children born in this month. This is the best month in which a Seven child can be born. The combined strength of the 7, 1, and 2 vibrations does not permit any of their negative aspects from entering the integral personality. They do not need a name adding to 7, 1, or 2. Any other name will suit them.

Eighth Day of the Month

Some of the strongest personality traits and talents related to the material aspects of life are contained in this birth day. Their potential is such that most children born on the eighth day do not have to wait until maturity before many of these traits are fully manifested. They will be observed in emergent ways—strengthening with each year of growth.

Instinctive traits that surface both consciously and unconsciously are willpower, determination, stubbornness, assertiveness, practicality, methodical habits, and early leanings toward authoritative behavior. Bold attempts to organize living conditions and the lives of others to suit their needs will be seen as a frequent practice. They can become quickly irritated when others do not fit in with their desires and plans. This is a habit that will be carried from early life into adulthood. Many Eight children could suffer from an unrealistic sense of entitlement before they are qualified by maturity for any such privileges. A premature claim would be the right to exercise authority over others. They would need to slow down such expectations lest they earn unpopularity and hinder an acceptable rate of growth.

These children are not rebels or revolutionaries. They are, in fact, happy to live within the established rules of living and discipline. It is their claim, or at least their desire, to have a say in most matters that have to be contended with. It will also be their chief motivational factor in adulthood. They are not types who uncomplainingly accept decisions of others. Authoritative body language will be displayed at an early age. In speech they will be direct and to the point. Physical activity is needed to focus their emotions, which are normally held in check. While these children may present a stern and often demanding façade, there are warmer, caring, protective and sensitive feelings behind outer appearances.

While nurturing them, avoid direct commands and orders, as these will be instantly resisted. A quiet, reasonable approach will easily capture their attention. In addition, take care to avoid excessively questioning their behavior. Their nature is such that they resent giving explanations or accounting for their conduct. They are not secretive types, but, relieved of interference, they voluntarily relate their experiences.

These children are seldom comfortable with body contact. They may avoid being kissed and hugged too much. But body contact in sport will be an exception. Their highly competitive spirit takes over during play and overrides their dislike of body contact. In sport and other activities they do not remain long as team mates, but sooner or later assume a controlling or leadership role.

Attributes that reach maturity in adulthood are high ambition, authority, competitiveness, organization and administration, a keen business sense, skill in money management, discipline, planning, pragmatism, enthusiasm, responsibility, and leadership. Names with emotional vibrations such as 2, 5, or 9 should be avoided, as well as another 8. A name with any other number will be suitable.

Not all personalities born on the eighth day are the same in character and talents. They are not uniform as the birth month extends a strong secondary influence, creating certain specific changes in each. The following sections indicate the nature of these changes.

Eights Born in January (first month)

The 1 vibration in this month is a tremendous advantage. All positive attributes of the Eight personality are strengthened and given a clear sense of direction. This beneficial condition is due to the many similarities between the 8 and 1 forces. Please refer to the chapter on the first day of the month for a greater understanding. Their combination creates a "power-plus" personality. The predominant disposition of these Eights is the exercise of authority. They are equipped to do so with contributory attributes of leadership, decisiveness, assertiveness, organization, willpower, self-control, high ambition, and a strong sense of individuality. Potential for success in these children in education and subsequently in public life is unlimited. They are not types who willingly settle for secondary roles, or who will work successfully in equal partnerships or as team members. They need to be in charge.

In almost all situations, Eight children are capable of defending themselves. Success in family and other close relationships will depend on the degree to which they are able to check their controlling habits. They will respect authority administered with fairness and moderation, but are certain to rebel against arbitrary and despotic measures. Names that reduce to 2, 3, 6, 7, or 9 will soften to some degree their controlling habits. Avoid names with numbers, 1, 4, 5, or 8.

Eights Born in February (second month)

Vibrations from the emotional plane control both the birth day and birth month. The inevitable result in this condition is an excess of emotion as well as emotional disorder. Disorder is due to the fact that the 8 and 2 vibrations are in different modes of expression. The tendency of those controlled by the 8 is to exercise restraint as demonstration of emotion is regarded as undignified; the result being occasional outbursts. People influenced by the 2 are able to release their emotions easily. Reconciling these opposite modes of emotional expression is a problem faced by all those born with this birth day and birth month combination. Readers may refer to the chapter on the second day of the month for more information on the 2 vibration.

As a secondary influence the 2 vibration can mitigate many arbitrary traits in the Eight with desirable qualities of cooperation, adaptability, good fellowship, and the ability to consider the other person's point of view. There is no doubt that these children are multi-talented but due to their emotional nature, they struggle to maintain a clear sense of direction and self-assurance. They may need frequent reminders that they are capable of completing anything they set out to do. A name with a 1, 4, or 7 will help them acquire a good measure of self-confidence. Avoid 2, 5, and 8 names. Also avoid 3, 6, and 9 names as these do not provide a strong footing on the physical plane which is what these children need.

Eights Born in March (third month)

The 3 vibration in the month of March opens out many enlivening facets in a relatively conservative Eight personality. Maturity and youthfulness meet in this combination of birth day and birth month. Refer to the chapter on the third day of the month for more information about the 3 vibration's influence.

These children possess prominent egos and an enhanced sense of individuality. The organizing nature of their Eight personality and self-centered qualities of the 3 vibration demand attention and frequent praise for their actions. They are certainly versatile and multi-talented children, proud of their achievements. They can easily be won over by flattery. A fair amount of noise and activity can be expected in their daily lives. They may not be too easy to discipline. A firm hand may be needed to keep them under control. They will respect a firm hand but take full advantage of a soft approach.

Some of these children can entertain inner feelings of insecurity and seek to cover them up by an inflated opinion of themselves, as well as a good measure of self-promotion. At the same time, they can be generous and active in all forms of social life. They possess a high sense of accuracy and organization. A name with a 1 vibration will help overcome a lack of adequate self-confidence and the need to self-promote. Names with a 2 or 5 may upset emotional stability. Names with mental vibrations 6 and 9 are not necessary as the 3 in their birth month is more than adequate. They will benefit most from physical vibrations 1, 4, and 7.

Eights Born in April (fourth month)

Attributes of the vibrations of this birth month blend with those of the birth day. The chapter on the fourth day of the month shows that the 4 vibration has many qualities similar to those of the 8. On a closer examination, you will see that they are in an escalated form in the 8. The blending of these forces is not an entirely advantageous condition. Many attributes of the 4 contribute to the strengthening of the Eight personality. But some tend toward hardening the individual into negative ways.

Positive characteristics found in these children and subsequently in adults are: accuracy, attentiveness, ready response to discipline, caution in all their dealings, conformity, vitality, endurance, practicality, manual dexterity, careful money management, and a keen business sense. Some attributes that could be strengthened to their disadvantage are: excessive emotional restriction followed by outbursts of anger, tendency toward selfishness and possessiveness, laziness, stubbornness, and clumsiness.

These children need an outlet for frivolity, openness, humor, and fluency of speech. Names with 2, 3, 5, 6, and 9 vibrations will provide these needs to some degree. These children may suffer from a lack of self-confidence. A name with a 1 or 7 will help. Names with a 4 or 8 should be strictly avoided.

Eights Born in May (fifth month)

Children with this birth day and birth month contend with opposite and often conflicting forces. The chapter on the fifth day of the month reveals that there is an appreciable difference between the 8 and 5 vibrations. The 5 may be a secondary force, yet it has a persistent and intrusive influence upon the basic personality formed by the birth day vibration. Fundamental 8 characteristics of conservatism, responsibility, steadfastness, deliberation, planning, and organization will be contested by the contrary needs of the 5, such as, the desire for frequent change, movement, speed, and freedom of thought and speech. The freedom to challenge prevailing conditions and engage in a variety of activity are other aspects of the 5 that will challenge the fundamental Eight personality.

These opposites may unknowingly create disturbance in the minds of these children. They will spend their whole lives recognizing and reconciling these characteristics. This may take time but real success in life is assured when they do. These children are certainly versatile multi-taskers. They need a given name that provides a clear sense of direction, self-discipline, and self-confidence. A name with a 1 or 7 will fill in these needs. Avoid 8 and 5 names. All other names may add more facets to their integral personality but they may not provide the stability these children need on practical aspects of life. They also need emotional stability. This can be provided by 1, 4, and 7 names.

Eights Born in June (sixth month)

Similarities and contrasts exist in this birth day and birth month combination. Organization in all aspects of life is a shared attribute. However, there is a clear difference in the method of organization. People influenced by the 8 vibration govern their own lives and at the same time actively endeavor to govern or take charge of the lives of others. Those influenced by the 6 vibration also govern their own lives efficiently but do not seek to exercise authority over others. Their expertise in organization tends toward helpfulness, protection, support, instruction, and many compassionate ways.

These Eight children may be a changeable mixture of these opposite qualities. The 6 vibration is, for the most part, a non-competitive, cooperative, team-playing vibration. It may, in a small way, mitigate the competitive, individualistic, dynamic, and authoritative attributes of their 8 aspect. Their basic Eight nature does not contain too many domestic interests but their secondary 6 aspect is a strong domestic force. When their cooperative 6 aspect is accessed these children can be made to sit down, listen, and follow instructions and counseling. The chapter on the sixth day of the month provides more information on this secondary sphere of influence.

Self-confidence is a quality that can be increased in these children. A first name reducing to 1 or 7 will suit them well. While 6 and 8 names should be avoided, names with other numbers will be OK

Eights Born in July (seventh month)

The chapter on the seventh day of the month indicates that 8 and 7 vibrations possess certain attributes in common. However, these are not strictly complementary forces. Some conflicting elements may prevent the Eight personality from maintaining an even mode of life using all attributes of the 8 vibration. On the one hand, the reserved, non-competitive, non-demanding, studious, and idealistic attributes of the 7 vibration interfere with the competitive, ambitious, and assertive nature of the 8. On the other hand, the 7 provides exceptional qualities of diligence, competence, accuracy, practicality, and creativity that will help Eight personalities in all their ventures. But any ventures that include ruthless ambition, aggressiveness, excess of materialism, and unfair competition will be prevented by the influence of their secondary 7 aspect.

The 7 vibration, despite its many noble attributes includes a streak of intolerance which combines easily with the 8 vibration's authoritative qualities. These children are certainly intelligent and resourceful. They can also display recalcitrance and pig-headedness when they do not get their own way. First names reducing to 8 or 7 should be strictly avoided. A 4 name is also best avoided as stubbornness could be increased. A 1 name will provide more self-confidence and is advisable. Other numbers will add fresh openings to the integral personality but they may not increase self-confidence.

Eights Born in August (eighth month)

Repetition of the same number or vibration in a single-digit birth day results in a restricted personality structure. In these cases, the individual is burdened by an overloading, and consequently, an over-emphasis of the attributes of the birth force. The personality is deprived of an opening into fresh avenues of self-expression the birth month provides. This condition invariably invites negative aspects of the birth day vibration.

Some personality difficulties that may arise in this present combination are: an inferiority complex that is covered up by aggression, dictatorship, vulnerable emotions, irrational fears, lack of consideration for others, unpopularity, and an unsettled temperament. Bluntness, greed, and possessiveness could be some other negative qualities. Many of these negative traits could be mitigated by a first name reducing to 1, 2, 3, 5, 6, 7, or 9. An 8 name should be strictly avoided. A 4 name is also undesirable. The 4 is too close in nature to the 8.

Eights Born in September (ninth month)

An examination of the attributes of the 9 vibration in the chapter on the ninth day of the month will reveal that many are of a different nature to those of the 8. The merger of these forces does not create disharmony or confusion. On the contrary, it hugely enriches the Eight personality with

69

many superior qualities of the 9, such as understanding and wisdom which curtails many controlling and authoritative qualities of the 8. Although serving as a secondary force, this 9 aspect will moderate the strictly businesslike disposition of the average Eight personality. Humanitarian sentiments and a global outlook on life will be introduced.

Parents and guardians should note the wisdom and understanding of the second nature of these children and approach this aspect in the event of disobedient or obstinate conduct. Any name except a repetition of and 8 or 9 will suit these children.

Eights Born in October (tenth month)

This will be the same as Eights born in January (first month month). The zero does not have any bearing on the personality.

Eights Born in November (eleventh month)

This will be almost the same as Eights born in January (first month). The only difference will be a strengthening of the powers of the 1 vibration.

Eights Born in December (twelfth month)

The presence of the 2 vibration in the birth month will help with emotional expression, flexibility, and adaptability. These children are blessed with a positive outlook on life. All the best attributes of their birth day vibration will manifest in their lives. A name with any number except an 8 will suit them.

Ninth Day of the Month

As the last vibration in the single-digit spectrum, the 9 manifests as an all-inclusive force, containing elements of the preceding vibrations, in various degrees. A touch of the outgoing nature of the 1, the receptivity of the 2, the imagination of the 3, the form and order of the 4, the progress of the 5, the responsibility of the 6, the spirituality of the 7, the judgment of the 8, culminating in the wisdom and compassion of the 9, all merge in the personality of the Nine child and adult.

An endearing quality in all Nine children is the absence of intensive ego activity. In other words, they are not bound within a narrow circle of ego-consciousness. The pronouns "I" and "My" are seldom used in a possessive and self-promoting sense. Their outlook on life can be said to be an even balance between concern for personal welfare and an awareness of the needs and wellbeing of others, with the latter aspects increasing in early adulthood. This condition is the direct result of the 9 vibration's breadth of vision and global outlook on life. Some typical attributes of this vibration that will be seen developing in all Nine children and maturing in adulthood are: agreeability, altruism, benevolence, broadmindedness, sociability, charity, compassion, cooperation, personal magnetism, emotion, enthusiasm, friendliness, honesty, generosity, hospitality, idealism, intuition, kindliness, grace, and unselfishness.

There are also certain negative 9 attributes, as in all other vibrations, that detract from the many superior traits listed above. These are confusion, changing or swinging moods, despondency, fear, indecision, impressionability, impulsiveness, restlessness, impracticality, and disunity. Nines who choose a negative path, and these are very few, can be warm and affectionate at times and cold and unapproachable at others. The birth month is usually responsible for the manner and degree in which positive or negative traits will be manifested. This will be shown briefly in the sections that follow.

Nine children cannot be confined to a small circle of friends and acquaintances. They interact with people on an even level. They are not compulsive leaders, controllers, or even manipulators. Nor are they willing followers or loners. For the most part they are their own person. Their disposition is such that they gather around them a circle of admiring and faithful friends. They do not need to put in much effort to gain the respect and esteem of friends and acquaintances. These tributes are earned largely by their habit of taking a sincere interest in the affairs of others rather than needing others taking an interest in their own. With very few exceptions they are extroverted and socially-oriented children who adopt goodwill and a trusting approach to all people. They are pleasant and easy conversationalists. But they will avoid argument and controversial topics. Parents and adults are often taken aback by statements and comments made by them. As wisdom is an innate quality, many things about life need not be explained in detail to them. They seem to understand instinctively. They need not be told twice to make them understand the need for proper behavior. Early in life they will be capable of distinguishing between right and wrong.

These children will not hesitate to converse with strangers. Being trustful and open-minded by nature they could be vulnerable to deceit. Freed to a large extent from a possessive mentality of "me" and "mine" they are usually unselfish children prepared to share their possessions or part with them for those in need, especially when their sympathetic emotions are aroused. Adults should be careful to treat them truthfully, lest they fall into confusion and disillusionment. These children are easily adaptable to changing circumstances and situations. They also enjoy speedy recovery from illness, or any sad or hurtful experience. They can forget and forgive without bearing grudges. They are blessed with the power of rejuvenation, which is a special attribute of the 9 vibration. Anything to do with humanity at large elicits their interest. Some may not be adept with their hands and may avoid manual tasks. The energies of most Nines are directed toward music, art, literature, and abstract subjects such as religion and philosophy.

Many superior 9 attributes lie dormant, awaiting various stages of growth before emerging in full strength. Nine children often experience confusion when they become weighed down by a flood of thoughts that enter their minds from time to time. There is often a clash between the physical and material versus the moral and conscience-driven values. They may take some time to sort things out. In the process of doing so they may appear as slow starters. But when they do get matters reasonably clarified they find themselves streets ahead of their contemporaries in almost all aspects of life.

The best names for these children will be those adding up to 1, 4, or 7. These will provided great strength of purpose into their personality. 2, 5, 8, and 9 names are best avoided as they would introduce too much emotionalism at the expense of rational thought. 3 and 6 names may be given but they may not provide great strength of purpose and adequate self-confidence.

Nines Born in January (first month)

All people born on the ninth day of the first month are favored with a well-integrated personality structure. Children with this combination who have been blessed with a loving home environment and reasonable socio-economic conditions develop all the noble attributes and potential of the 9 vibration. Those who have not been so favored still do so under their own steam a little later in life. All Nine children are energized by the secondary powers of the 1 vibration of their birth month. They imbibe the self-confidence and self-assurance for effective application of the best 9 attributes. The chapter on the first day of the month, which provides many details of the 1 vibration, will help in understanding these Nine children.

There is a dual advantage in this combination. Certain weaker attributes of the 9 vibration are strengthened by the 1 and certain disadvantageous traits of the 1 are overcome by many noble attributes of the 9. For instance, qualities of impressionability, blind/open trust, indecision in some circumstances, and impracticability are overcome and strengthened by the 1. A prominent ego with an "I" and "My" mentality is replaced by a "We" and "Us" mentality by the ninth birth day.

In short, the 9 and 1 combination creates a fine balance between unmercenary thought processes and worldly wisdom. The lives of these children will open out into broader than average pathways with many useful contributions made to society at large. The vast range of potential open to all Nine personalities is unlikely to be wasted by these children. A given name adding to 9 or 1 will not be necessary. Any other name will open out their broad-minded personality even further.

Nines Born in February (second month)

Sensitivity and emotionalism are major components of the personality of children with this birth day and birth month combination. They possess beautiful, loving, and genteel temperaments that seldom create trouble at home, school, college, and subsequently in public life. At the same time, they may often unknowingly and unintentionally create problems when their emotions are aroused. They often burst into tears much too easily. They are easily swept away by their own real or imagined painful experiences and by the problems and suffering of loved ones. See the chapter on the second day of the month for information about why these children are of such a refined and sensitive nature.

More often than not they speak the language of the heart and less the language of the mind or of practicality. Communication by touch is reinforced by oral communication. But they will always avoid close physical contact, especially with strangers and in sport. Their self-esteem and self-confidence could be demolished by crude, critical, and overbearing people. Many may not possess a strong defensive armor and consequently be at a loss to defend themselves. These children do not like to be left alone. Company is essential to their wellbeing. They are popular team players. In order to fulfill the wonderful potential of their birth day they need to view life's events objectively. A name with a 1, 4, or 7 will be ideal in this respect. All other names are best avoided.

Nines Born in March (third month)

The mental orientation of children born on the ninth day will be amplified when they are born in the third month. This may take place at the expense of practicality. Read the chapter on the third day of the month for a fuller understanding of these Nine children.

While imaginative powers, artistic expression and creativity, quality of speech, natural courtesy, friendliness, social graces, and a keen sense of humor are enhanced, these children may depend on support to make firm decisions and to boost their self-confidence. It is not easy to see their lack of self-confidence. It usually manifests when they are faced with real practical problems. They are often unaware of their multi-talented nature.

The world is a friendly place to these children as openness is their predominant attitude. Negative displays of anger, resentment, discourtesy, and silence will be exceptional. A first name adding to 1, 4, or 7 will be ideal. They need to be more grounded on the physical realm. Emotional names with the numbers 2, 5, and 8 will not help. Names with numbers 3, 6, and 9 are not needed.

Nines Born in April (fourth month)

Nine children born in the month of April are a fine combination of mentality and practicality. They are not as easily carried away by the compassionate nature of many other Nine personalities. The stable and down-to-earth 4 vibration acts as a sensor when impulsive feelings of the 9 vibration are aroused. It enables them to stop and think before acting or reacting, especially reacting. It also provides manual dexterity and a keen grasp of practical values. Refer to the chapter on the fourth day of the month for more helpful advice.

These are genuinely resourceful and creative children who are not motivated by self-serving ambition but by a sincere desire to help out of benevolence, in physical and other helpful ways. They are sensitive children whose feelings can be deeply hurt by indifference or ill-treatment. Strong self-esteem and self-confidence are not among their dominant attributes. They need to be given honest and well informed answers to any questions they put to elders. They will be mildly competitive in sport or other activities. Participation and camaraderie are more important to them than winning.

A number 1 or number 7 name will be ideal. While other numbers will provide wider dimensions for self-expression, they may not provide the strong self-confidence that is needed by these children. 9 and 4 names are best avoided.

Nines Born in May (fifth month)

A prominent feature in this birth day and birth month combination will be emotionalism. It will be felt and displayed in a somewhat confused condition as the emotional nature and content of the 9 vibration are different from those of the 5. They could be non-personal, reactive, and compassionate in the 9 but personal, active, changeable, and uncertain in the 5. Please refer to the chapter on fifth day of the month for more information.

These children are, without doubt, multi-talented and multi-faceted personalities. They are exceptionally active, energetic, and not too easy to control or discipline, as they need mental and physical freedom for full self-expression. They are quite outspoken in their demands. It is possible that they may expose themselves to a scattering of their talents which may end in disappointment. The 5 vibration introduces restlessness in a personality that is already infused with a wide range of thought. They need to be carefully handled so that clarity of purpose and steadfastness is introduced into their lives. They do possess an inner knowledge of these needs. All they need is a firm act of will to choose and complete a particular course of action that will be beneficial. A name with a 1, 4, or 7 vibration is essential. All other numbers should be avoided, especially another 9 or 5.

Nines Born in June (sixth month)

People influenced by the 9 and 6 vibrations are givers rather than takers. There may, however, be a small minority that are of the opposite temperament. The generosity of these Nines born in the sixth month involves parting, within reason, not merely with their material possessions but especially with their services. Anyone influenced heavily by either of these vibrations is a natural helper, confidant, counselor, peace maker, and teacher. These altruistic traits are reinforced when both the 6 and 9 vibrations operate within a single personality. See more on this subject in the chapter on the sixth day of the month.

By nature, these are loving, lovable, and home and family-oriented children. Their love nature is displayed in actions, loyalty, and dependability rather than outward demonstration of emotion. As both vibrations operating within their personality belong to the mental plane they are blessed with rational thought processes and inspiration. You will not see self-promotion as one of their characteristics. Despite the fact that they succeed in anything they undertake, there may be a need to overcome an underestimation of their capabilities. These children will be a delight to guide, teach, and instruct, as they are potential future teachers, guides, counselors, and peacemakers themselves. They will voluntarily take to reading at a very early age. They are generally non-competitive children who revel in togetherness rather than separation.

A given name with a 1, 4, or 7 will be best as these will contribute many earthly values to their naturally altruistic nature. A 1 name, especially, will boost their self-confidence and self-worth which may not be as strong as they should be. Names with emotional numbers 2, 5, or 8 will help with emotional expression but they may not add to self-confidence.

Nines Born in July (seventh month)

Given a proper environment, the key note that will manifest in Nine personalities born in the seventh month, is studiousness with interests in humanity, nature, music, poetry, history, and philosophy. The chapter on the seventh day of the month reveals many similarities between the 9 and / vibrations. At the same time, a significant difference will be seen in the 9 vibration's extroverted qualities and the 7's reserved nature. Children with either vibration require periods of silence and time for themselves but those with a combination of both need an increased amount of contemplation and self-examination.

As the 7 operates on the physical plane it adds many pragmatic and manual talents to this Nine personality. These children will grow into self-motivated teenagers and adults. Ego-projection will be at a minimum or not at all. Even at an early age concern for themselves will not exceed thoughtfulness for others and the wellbeing of animals in their care. Whenever possible they should be exposed to nature in all its aspects. They are sensitive and truthful children whose feelings are easily harmed in inharmonious conditions and by falsehood and deceit. They may also suffer from a poor self-image despite the fact that they may be superior in many ways to their contemporaries. Adults who use their position to put them down are often inferior to them as human beings. A name with any number will suit them but 9 and 7 should be avoided.

Nines Born in August (eighth month)

The 9 and 8 may be consecutive numbers but the vibrations they symbolize are of an opposite quality. There is no carry-over from one to the other. Consequently, people born with this birth day and birth month combination are faced with contrary sets of personality traits and talents. The chapter on the eighth day of the month exposes these differences.

As the 8 vibration is a secondary force when in the birth month, it will not overpower basic 9 attributes. It will certainly influence Nine personalities, more often than not to their advantage. This vibration's customary traits of fierce competitiveness, assertiveness, control, ambition for power, practicality, financial acumen, organization, and a businesslike approach to life will be watered down and used to strengthen the integral personality.

These children may take some time to establish a reasonable balance between these major aspects. They may undergo periods of confusion and uncertainty but an eventual outcome as successful adults is certain. A tertiary education will ensure steady progress into extended fields of knowledge and activity. From childhood to adulthood they will be involved with people. Solitary activities will not suit them. A first name with a 9 or 8 should be avoided. Any other name will suit these children.

Nines Born in September (ninth month)

This birth day and birth month combination is likely to introduce certain negative aspects of the 9 vibration. It is not an unusual occurrence when a single vibration has control over a major portion of a personality. The absence of another avenue or outlet for self-expression which results in an enclosure of personality traits and talents within a confined range deprives the individual from reaching into a comprehensive view of life.

These children do not lose many superior attributes of the 9 vibration.

They remain in potential until negative qualities are overcome in a caring and loving environment. They cannot be let loose to figure out life's problems by themselves. Some personality problems they may face are confusion, lack of self-confidence (which often results in a scornful and cynical attitude toward life), hypersensitivity leading to misinterpretation of the motives of others, and irrational fear of emotional hurt. They may resort to unnecessary and often unpleasant measures to defend themselves. A name with a physical number 1, 4, or 7 is most essential. Avoid all other numbers.

Nines Born in October (tenth month)

Please refer to the section on the Nines born in January (first month). All the best attributes of the 9 vibration are manifested in these children. Any name will suit these children.

Nines Born in November (eleventh month)

Please refer to the section on Nines born in January (first month). In this combination, the powers of the 1 vibration function in double strength. Attributes of the 9 and 1 vibrations operate in almost equal force. Nine children born in this month are bound to succeed in all their endeavors. They do not need a name with a 1 vibration. Any other name will suit them.

Nines Born in December (twelfth month)

This is a most favorable combination of birth day and birth month. These Nine children are reinforced by the positive attributes of the 1 and 2 vibrations. Any name will suit these children.

Tenth Day of the Month

Please refer to the chapter on the first day of the month. The zero in the 10 does not add any fresh attributes. The most it may do is emphasize some of the attributes of the 1 vibration.

Eleventh Day of the Month

11 reduces to (1+1=2)

All people born on this day are influenced by an exceptionally powerful vibration, commonly known as one of the two Master vibrations (11 and 22). It places a vast range of potential at their disposal. All they need are reasonable opportunities to spread their wings over physical, emotional, mental, and spiritual realms. Not all people will be so privileged. But these children retain the potential to emerge into their natural powers when the right conditions are presented.

Eleven children will most likely operate within the influence of the 2 vibration with the powerful Master vibration 11 boosting them along as they mature. They can be equally at home in any of the arts, sciences, humanitarian, and spiritual activities. They may possess in varying degrees a strong inventive spark, visionary trends, willpower, concentration, intuition, clairvoyance, and clairaudience faculties. Their life path indicates a desire to seek a balance between external and internal aspects of life. Their natural condition is to think ahead of the times in which they live.

They begin to stand on their own feet early in life and possess the strength to resist external pressures that may expect them to be what they are not meant to be or to do what they decide not to do. As they enter their teens they will seldom expect or desire much parental involvement in their affairs and ambitions. During their school days, or even in adulthood, they will not be a target for bullying or other measures to undermine their self-image. They may, on the contrary, use a wise and courageous approach to convert a bully or someone who is a disruptive element. They are sensitive to people and atmosphere but emotional demonstration is limited. They could be emotionally reactive but not reveal their reactions. They are not touchers and could be uncomfortable with too much body contact.

All Eleven children are good communicators who enjoy hearing themselves talk. Early in life they develop a trend to tell others what they should or should not be doing. While they enjoy giving free advice they may not always follow or practice what they preach. They could be intolerant of others who do not subscribe to their views on things. They are, in fact, genuine "ideas people", especially regarding ideas for improvements and advancement. However, not all Elevens come out with ideas acceptable to others as practical or profitable. There could be at times a degree of impracticability and insubstantiality in their ideas. This occurs when they do not balance practicality with higher reaches of thought.

All Eleven children who have been allowed natural development without parental pressures or over indulgence display a positive application of their personality traits. Talents emerge early in life. A first name with a 1, 4, 7, or 8 is best avoided. The nature of many Elevens is to take life too seriously. These numbers may not help enliven the personality. Any other number will open them out into livelier realms.

Eleven personalities do not fall into one division of personality traits and talents. There are sub-divisions formed by the vibration of their birth month. The following sections will provide the differences that exist.

Elevens Born in January (first month)

All attributes of the Master vibration will be reinforced by the repetition of the 1 vibration in the birth month. However, this strengthening may lead to contraction of the Eleven personality's range of thought and activity. In other words, there will be concentration on smaller and specialized fields. Sensitivity will be increased but emotional demonstration will be further reduced. These children are able to give their full attention to whatever task they undertake. They do not welcome any sort of distraction or disturbance while concentrating on study or any sort of work. Pride of achievement is very strong. They could be inclined to take life seriously, and although they appreciate humor expressed by others they seldom initiate humor themselves. A little more imagination, conviviality, and relaxation will be gained with a first name reducing to 2, 3, 5, 6, or 9. The numbers 4, 7, and 8 are best avoided as these may add to the customary earnestness of their nature.

Elevens Born in February (second month)

Eleven children born in the month of February potentially possess all the powerful attributes of the Master vibration of their birth day. In addition, their personality is expanded in positive ways with all the genteel and serving qualities of the 2 vibration. See the chapter on the second day of the month.

Active and receptive human characteristics operate in harmony within the personality of these children. This gives them the opportunity to develop as outstanding citizens in all aspects of life. Every dollar spent on their education will bear rich fruit. There will be no loss or wastage of what they have learned. There is really no need for another vibration to boost their self-image and confidence because these are innate traits. Choosing a first name will be quite easy, as a name with any number will suit them, although a name with a 1 or 2 should be avoided.

Elevens Born in March (third month)

The best attributes of the 3 vibration will be absorbed and displayed by Eleven children born in the month of March. Please refer to the chapter on the third day of the month. These children will be altogether positive on their outlook on life. Their optimism and enthusiasm is infectious. Some other outstanding characteristics are excellence of speech, humor, sociability, romance, accuracy in speech and action, and creativity in areas such as music, art, and literature. Love and loyalty will be deep and abiding but these tender qualities may not be displayed in frequent emotional contact. While the numbers 1 and 3 should be avoided, a name with any other number will benefit these clever children.

Elevens Born in April (fourth month)

The most down-to-earth Eleven personalities will be found with this birth day and birth month combination. Their secondary 4 attributes will draw these children into practical and physical application of all the humanitarian attributes of the master vibration of their birth day. They are able to stand firmly on their own feet. They are genuine survivors who will not be intimidated or allow their self-assurance to be demolished by adverse circumstances. Nor will they panic in emergencies. They are also conscientious and dependable. Emotional expression in these children will be limited. Please refer to the chapter on the fourth day of the month. A first name reducing to 1, 4, 7, or 8 should be avoided. What they need is an expansion of imagination and a sense of humor. These qualities will be found in the remaining numbers.

Elevens Born in May (fifth month)

The most active and energetic Eleven children are found with this birth day and birth month combination. Please refer to the chapter on the fifth day of the month for a fuller understanding of these children. Although the 5 vibration is a secondary force it will exercise considerable influence in shaping their personality.

Their activities will not be disconnected, but well planned. A strong pull toward internationalism will eventually involve much travel and interaction with a great variety of people. They are inquisitive and questioning personalities, demanding freedom of speech and movement. Early in life they display an absence of fear. They are exceptionally alert children who miss nothing that is going on around them. They can learn more than one foreign language. While the 1 and 5 numbers may be avoided, a name with any other number will suit them.

Elevens Born in June (sixth month)

As a secondary force the 6 vibration, operating on the mental plane, reinforces the mind of the Eleven personality with logical and rationalistic thought processes. The predominant disposition of these children will be one of reasonableness and fair play. They are also clear-headed and trusting personalities who view the world as a friendly place and are open-minded and willing to listen and learn. They do possess a strong argumentative streak which helps them resist or challenge anything they consider irrational, unreasonable, or inconsistent.

Their intelligent and kindly nature does not resort to uncouth speech or conduct. They will eventually establish a good balance between domestic responsibilities and public duties. Their love of nature cannot be questioned but emotional expression will be limited. Love is displayed by service and good deeds.

These children are gifted with a well-balanced personality. Consequently they are not dependent on a name that could supply a lack of some essential feature. A name with any number can be chosen.

Elevens Born in July (seventh month)

The 11 Master vibration is a surprising combination of earthliness and spirituality. The 7 vibration is the same. When both forces operate within a single personality, the potential for success in both spheres is amplified. For obvious reasons the earthly and practical side of these children will take precedence. But during their years of growth they are certain to receive promptings from sub-conscious levels.

These children are naturally studious, observant, open-minded, perceptive, and curious. Research will be their forte in adulthood. Their investigations will embrace scientific and metaphysical realms. At quite an early age they are looked up to by their contemporaries for their knowledge and eagerness to seek knowledge. They will always know much more than they are prepared to give out unless they are in special company. They are self-assured children who take responsibility for their actions and do not demand preferential treatment in a family scene. Their emotions are contained. Touching and other emotional demonstrations are kept at a minimum and they may be inclined to take life rather seriously. A first name adding to 2, 3, 5, 6, or 9 will be most helpful. Any of these will bring more laughter into their lives. Avoid numbers 1, 4, 7, or 8.

Elevens Born in August (eighth month)

This is a "power-plus" combination of authoritative forces. Children and adults will display a natural tendency to take control of circumstances in which they find themselves. It is natural for them to walk and talk with self-confident body language. The physical, practical, and commercial aspects of life will take precedence over the 11 vibration's humanitarian features. At an early stage these children will expect to be given freedom to make their own decisions. They are quite capable of doing so, and possess more than sufficient self-confidence to remain independent of the opinions of others. They are able to express their emotions without being controlled by them.

They could often be at odds with their schoolmates and teachers if they are prevented from having their own way or if their actions are challenged or questioned. They quickly learn when they are shown and instructed, but not when they are told or ordered. The spiritual element of their birth day vibration will come to light with maturity and after success has been achieved in public life. They will be welcome benefactors in society. A first name adding to 2, 3, 6, or 9 will add friendliness and a more relaxed attitude. Numbers 1, 4, 7, and 8 should be avoided.

Elevens Born in September (ninth month)

An outstanding feature in all people with this birth day and birth month combination is a collective rather than an individual mentality. The interdependence of all living things is an inner knowledge that will emerge from time to time and increase in duration as these children grow older. In addition, these children are of an independent nature, with an inner knowledge that interdependence is not equated with dependency.

Apart from gentle guidance and support in the physical and material aspects of life, these children should be allowed to blossom on their own initiative. There could be instances when some are wiser, more compassionate, more understanding, and open-minded than their parents and other adults in the family circle. Any really troublesome personality traits they display may be an acquisition from external forces and may not be carried into adulthood.

These are highly perceptive and intelligent children who should be encouraged to express their opinions without fear or embarrassment. The chapter on the ninth day of the month will reveal that the combination of the 11 and 9 vibrations generate in these children a global outlook on life. Any name will suit these outstanding children.

Elevens Born in October (tenth month)

Please refer to the section on the Elevens born in January (first month). The zero in the tenth day does not exercise any difference.

Elevens Born in November (eleventh month)

The presence of the 1 vibration in quadruple strength has the effect of narrowing but deepening the perspectives and performance of these children. Their expectations too are limited. Chances are they will live in a black-and-white world with few shades of gray. They possess strong-willed and unyielding minds that could operate in positive as well as negative ways, depending on the situations they are in. They need flexibility and imagination. A name with a 2, 3, 5, 6, or 9 will be most suitable. 1, 4, 7, or 8 should be avoided.

Elevens Born in December (twelfth month)

All the attributes of the Master vibration of their birth day will be reinforced in most positive ways in Eleven personalities born in December. Welcome elements of flexibility and adaptability will be provided by the 2 vibration, as well as a certain freedom with emotional expression. These are truly gifted children who will be a pleasure to nurture, educate, and befriend. Any name will suit them, although another 1 is best avoided.

Twelfth Day of the Month

12 reduces to (1+2=3)

Children born on the twelfth day have the influence of the 1 and 2 vibrations in the outer personality and the 3 vibration functioning in the background. They emerge with a keen sense of individuality. They will function in any situation with self-confidence and a positive attitude toward life. They possess a multiform personality structure resulting in an equal distribution of vibratory powers over physical (1), emotional (2) and mental (3) planes.

Some prominent characteristics and talents that appear at an early age and mature in adulthood are: leadership, self-esteem, decisiveness, imagination, humor, creativity, extroversion, sociability, flexibility, loyalty, ambition, optimism, and constructive thought processes. Parents and others will notice that they are not followers who can be influenced or misled. The Twelve is not a clinging type of child. They need to strike out on their own. But they will always do so within company. They are not loners.

All three vibrations operating and motivating them contain egocentric qualities. These are essentially "I" and "My" vibrations. Consequently, Twelve children and adults concentrate on personal wellbeing before they give thought to others. However, the anomaly here is that they are not uncaring or selfish by nature. They are, in fact, quite generous with their help and possessions. These children need gentle but frequent reminders of their obligations toward others. When this is done they do not fail to cooperate. But they may soon fall back into a 'getting' mode.

Being naturally multi-talented they are sure to involve themselves in several activities, usually outside home. They may find it difficult to stick to one task or activity until a task has been completed or expertise has been developed in a chosen activity. This is often a problem faced by multi-talented children. The grass is always greener on the other side of the fence. Unless suppressed by arbitrary authority within the home, these children are active, energetic, restless, noisy, light-hearted, and entertaining.

Self-expression is their most urgent need with a natural urge to hold the spotlight wherever they are. And the fact is that they are capable of holding the center of attention. If they find themselves ignored they resort to all sorts of strategies to make their presence known. They are popular social mixers and remain so as long as they do not focus attention too long upon their own affairs and ignore or pay scant attention to what others have to say. They are easily bored when made to listen for a length of time to a subject that does not interest them. They are not likely to pay attention as a matter of courtesy. Impatience takes precedence over natural good manners. This is a tendency with all people influenced by the 1, 2, or 3 vibrations, individually or collectively. These children will not hesitate to strike up a conversation with people of all ages. A most marketable talent enjoyed by these children and adults is excellence of speech with a good quality of voice and above average vocabulary. This talent should always be positively exploited. Certain changes in their personality and talents will take place through the influence of the vibration of the birth month. The following sections deal with these changes.

Twelves Born in January (first month)

All aspects of the birth force, i.e. the combined strength of the 1, 2, and 3 vibrations, are strengthened in many positive ways by the repetition of the 1 vibration in the birth month. Individualism and independence will be increased. The capacity of these children to get things done under their own steam, and also get things done by others, will be extended.

Augmentation of these attributes may expose them to certain disadvantages if careful self-education is not constantly practiced. Ego-strength and self-centeredness will be enlarged. The direct result will be an unconscious tendency to take charge of people and situations, and resentment of any challenge to their authority. Their immediate reaction to correction, instruction, and advice is likely to be resentful; hence, the need to engage in the difficult task of self-education. The natural bent of these children is to learn through observation and experience rather than direct instruction. A first name with the numbers 2, 5, 6, 7, or 9 will moderate their egos and their tendency to take control of their environment.

Twelves Born in February (second month)

In the case of single-digit birth days the repetition of the birth day number in the birth month overloads the personality with a single set of creative forces, leading to certain negative tendencies entering the integral personality. This does not take place with a multiple digit birth day such as the twelfth.

With Twelve children born in the second month, attributes of the 2 vibration exercise a positive influence upon their personality. It provides, among other things, a capacity to temporarily overlook their own needs and show appreciation for the needs of others. The chapter on the second day of the month will provide some information on the 2 vibration's contribution to these Twelve children.

These children approach life with a confident but sensitive touch. Their temperament includes sympathy, understanding, cooperation without loss of individuality, and the absence of an overly assertive ego. Although their power of speech is not reduced, the written word is stronger than the spoken word. There is a good deal of rhythm in these children which provides skills in any form of dance or rhythmic activity. They are also real water babies. Their love of water is carried well into adulthood. A first name with another 1 or especially another 2 should not be chosen. Any other name will suit these talented children.

Twelves Born in March (third month)

An escalation of artistic talent will take place with the repetition of the 3 vibration in the birth month. These children will display a compelling need for social interaction. They should not be left alone to enjoy their own company. Self-expression in speech and action is their chief motivating power. They function principally on the mental plane with a powerful creative imagination. With a first name adding to the number 4 they can effortlessly transfer their mental creations into physical forms.

They demand to be the center of attention more than other Twelve children. When this is not provided they create situations to compel others to pay attention to them. These children possess an extraordinary sense of accuracy and exactitude which could be taken to extremes. They do not hesitate to point out a fault or omission in someone's speech or straighten a hanging picture that is slightly askew. Possessing extraordinary word power they can excel in debate or any form of argument. They can also be critical and cynical when they choose to do so. During their school days they are sure to shine in mathematics due to their high sense of accuracy.

Apart from a first name with a number 4, other numbers that suit them are, 1, 7, and 8. These will also combine their creative imagination with manual dexterity. Other numbers will be suitable but they may not help too much with practical aspects of life.

Twelves Born in April (fourth month)

This is an excellent birth day and birth month combination. These children possess a creative mentality and manual dexterity. There is nothing they cannot do. It is not possible to suggest a line of study and subsequently a line of work. They could do anything they choose, and do it well. White collar, blue collar, or any other collar work will suit them. They will not fail to reach excellence in any type of work or profession they choose. Once set upon a course of study, they are not likely to change or give it up. Determination and the capacity to work hard are inherent traits.

These children should have clear and well-formed hand writing due to the combination of the 3 vibration's artistic talents and the 4 vibration's desire for form and design. However, these children may turn out to be talkers and doers rather than writers. They need to be kept constantly occupied. Any name will suit these multi-faceted and multi-talented children.

Twelves Born in May (fifth month)

All the extroverted attributes of the Twelve personality will be magnified by the influence of the 5 vibration of their birth month. Characteristics that will be prominent are: curiosity, movement, travel, adventure, alertness, flexibility and adaptability, ego-centeredness, fluency of speech, romance, and activity.

These children need outlets for expenditure of energy to accommodate their desire for frequent change. They find it hard to keep still or retain interest in a particular activity for long. Concentration is difficult as very little escapes their attention. They are tempted to get involved in many things at the same time. They are multi-talented children but their urgent need is to harness their talents.

From an early age these children may be noisy and demanding, with only a slight reduction as they grow older. A name with a 4, 6, or 7 may slow them down to some extent. Other names are not advisable as they may increase unnecessary activity and manipulating habits.

Twelves Born in June (sixth month)

A salutary condition resulting from the influence of the 6 vibration in the birth month is a reduction of egocentricity, natural to the Twelve personality. The 6 vibration is a family and community-oriented force. The chapter on the sixth day of the month will reveal this. The best attributes of this vibration can be used by the positive nature of the Twelve personality.

Twelve children will be a delight to nurture and educate. A good deal of reciprocity can be expected of them, provided they are approached with reason and fair play. If not, their argumentative and reasoning powers are considerable. These children possess well-balanced personalities. They do not need an additional vibration from a first name to round off their personality. Any name will suit them.

Twelves Born in July (seventh month)

The lessening of a controlling ego or a perennial "I" and "My" mentality is a pleasing feature in Twelve personalities influenced by the7 vibration. Their temperament will be one of sensitivity, discrimination, and selectivity, and not one of assertiveness and demand. Although the 7 vibration is a secondary force in this combination of birth day and birth month it is certain to mitigate many self-centered attributes of the Twelve. The chapter on the seventh day of the month which reveals many other attributes of the 7 vibration will be interesting reading. You will find that many other personality traits developed by the influence of the 7 are almost opposite to those of the 1, 2, and 3 vibrations within the Twelve personality.

The 7 is also a spiritual force operating on the physical plane. It contributes many practical talents which are often used for non-personal reasons. These children are not as restless as other Twelves. Their sociability also cannot be taken for granted at all times. Self-sufficiency, non-dependence, and an occasional need for their own company are among their prominent characteristics. Emotional demonstration will be limited, although their love and loyalty cannot be questioned. Any name will suit these well-balanced children.

Twelves Born in August (eighth month)

Children with this birth day and birth month combination are able to take charge of their own lives at an early stage and they also possess a natural urge to take charge or control the lives of others. Family members, friends, and acquaintances will not fail to observe a progressive development of both modes of conduct. Leadership, organization, and ego-strength combine forcefully within their integral personality. The designation "Boss" will be applied to them sooner or later. They will carry this "title" with aplomb.

These children, and subsequently adults, will be involved with people of all sorts of temperament, needs, and skills. Such interaction will help them break out of ego-centered thought processes as they observe the diversity of personality types. The best names for them will be those that reduce to 2, 5, 6, or 9. These will help them relate to others on a mutual basis.

Twelves Born in September (ninth month)

Twelve personalities need a strong vibration in the influential sphere of their birth month in order to diminish ego-centered thought processes. The best month to do so is September, the ninth month. Twelve children born in this month need not be constantly prompted to be conscious of the needs and sensibilities of others. With the compassionate and wide perspectives of the 9 vibration they are able to do so spontaneously. But the degree in which they do so will depend on careful nurturing. They are not children who will resent advice and instruction, as long as they are given due respect to their individuality. Any name will suit these wise children.

Twelves Born in October (tenth month)

These children will not be any different to Twelves born in January (first month). The zero in the month has no real influence upon the personality.

Twelves Born in November (eleventh month)

Attributes of the 1 vibration are emphasized in these children. Please refer to the chapter on the first day of the month. These children are most likely to insist on having their own way and not share their possessions. They are not ungenerous, but sharing is not in their nature. Their policy is "What's mine is mine."

A strong will and stubbornness in many ways could be advantageous, but also disadvantageous in many ways. A first name adding to 2, 6, or 9 will be most helpful. Other numbers may not help ease many self-centered ways.

Twelves Born in December (twelfth month)

These are strong-willed and positive children whose first reactions will be to put self before others. However they do possess the capacity, when reminded, to see the other person's point of view. Reference to the chapters on the first and second days of the month will be helpful. These children are influenced by attributes of the 1 and 2 vibrations. These are reasonably well-balanced children. Any name except another 1 or 2 will be suitable.

Thirteenth Day of the Month

13 reduces to (1+3=4)

Children born on the thirteenth day have the influence of the 1 and 3 vibrations in the outer personality, and the 4 vibration functioning in the background. Parents with a boy or girl born on the thirteenth day may rest assured that they have been gifted with a multi-talented child. A person born on this day possesses a rich multiplicity of all the positive attributes of the 1, 3, and 4 vibratory forces that operate within the thirteenth day. The chapters on the first, third and fourth day of the month provide a comprehensive idea of how the personality of these children will unfold. Although they possess the attributes of these forces in relatively the same degree in a harmonious interaction, there may be times when one is likely to be more operative that the others.

These children have sufficient self-confidence to step out of a protective pattern of life and stand on their own feet at an early age. Preferential treatment or dependency are not aspects of their temperament. They are moved by an inner stimulus to take charge of their lives. Reason and pragmatic thought processes govern their actions. They are seldom, if ever, swept away by their emotions in their interaction with people. Instead, emotions are channeled into their creative activities. They are among the easiest children to teach as they earnestly pick up fresh knowledge. The potential for rapid development in many departments of life is one of their best assets. They are not children who complain of boredom as they possess the imagination and energy to involve themselves in one activity or another. In disciplinary matters they need not be told twice in order to understand such directions, but they may not always abide by them. They are too independent-minded to show much sensitivity to reprimand or react to the opinions of others. They are obliging, helpful, and courteous children but you cannot gain their attention on demand. They need to be treated as intelligent individuals who cannot be manipulated.

These children are multi-faceted and versatile, as well as responsible. As their needs will be many, expect involvement in a variety of projects. Nurturing and education could be costly but the cost will be worthwhile.

The numbers of their birth month add further features to their many-sided nature. The following sections on the twelve birth months are interesting reading. The repetition of the 1, 2, or 3 vibrations adds strength to that aspect of their personality but does not introduce any negative qualities. This is a problem only with single-digit birth days. Any name will suit these well-balanced and talented children.

Thirteens Born in January (first month)

As mentioned above, children born on the thirteenth day are strong-willed, self-confident, multi-skilled, and many-sided personalities. The effectiveness of these positive attributes is enhanced in those born in January. By virtue of the affirmative qualities of the 1 vibration, some special characteristics that will be reinforced are: a stronger sense of individuality, inventiveness, exploration, creativity, imagination, manual dexterity, willpower, and leadership.

These children can be quite recalcitrant if they do not get their way. They are also types who cannot be led or influenced by direct or arbitrary means. They can only be reached by those who share their same interests or with the same affinity to their own nature. Physical chastizement for wrongdoing will have little effect. In any case there will be few occasions for correction if they are kept occupied in a variety of mental and physical outlets. They can be demanding but not complaining.

They tolerate physical contact in sport but in all other interactions with people they are uncomfortable with body contact. Emotional expression, which is not effusive in the Twelve personality, is further restrained by the 1 vibration in the birth month. But loyalty and the incentive to protect loved ones will be strengthened. Younger siblings will be taken under their wings. Names with a 1, 3, 4, or 8 are best avoided. Any other number will add fresh openings to an already enriched personality.

Thirteens Born in February (second month)

The 2 vibration of the second month introduces many gentle, adaptable, and cooperative attributes into an otherwise strong-willed and independent-minded personality. However, these receptive qualities do not exercise an immediate influence or change. They may be delayed until early maturity and act in the background. The chapter on the second day of the month provides more information on this vibration.

An advantageous role played by the 2 is that it acts in cooperation with the fundamental 4 vibration in the Thirteen. Both are receptive forces while the 1 and 3 are active forces. The 2, among other things, joins the 4 in contributing service and supportive qualities usually seen in the caring professions—nurses, doctors, counselors, caretakers, personal secretaries etc. The 4 also cooperates with the 2 providing physical protection in services such as the police force, fire brigade, the army, ambulance service etc. At the same time, the combined strength of their 1 and 3 forces provides the incentive and power to reach the peak of their chosen professions.

The combined 2 and 4 vibrations also reduce self-centeredness and increase community consciousness. The 2 is also a sensitive and emotionally demonstrative vibration. Thirteen children will be able to release their emotions occasionally. These children possess well-rounded personalities. A name with any number will suit them. Names reducing to 1, 2, 3, or 4 will do no harm but those with other numbers will add further openings to their integral personality.

Thirteens Born in March (third month)

Due to the repetition of the number 3 in the birth month, attributes of the 3 vibration will be much more prominent in these children than the 1 and 4 vibrations. A careful study of the chapter on the third day of the month is recommended. Self-consciousness will certainly be increased, along with sociability, self-expression, and the need to excite activity around them. These children ensure that they are not overlooked in any company and will use the power of speech as a means to achieve this. They may speak their minds without much awareness of the conditions they are in or of the sensibilities of others. In most discussions they put forward their opinions before others finish their sentences. Yet, they are natural entertainers and a joy to have around. An emerging sense of humor should be encouraged.

A very early introduction into instrumental music, song, and dance will reap a fruitful harvest. In music and literature these children will be drawn naturally to the romantic side of life. Their love and sentiments will be expressed through fine speech, poetry, and song, rather than in demonstrations of emotion. They may not be comfortable with too much physical contact as they are essentially mentally oriented. It will not be easy to convince these mentally active children that every moment of their time need not be filled with some form of activity or interaction with people. They can never be at ease in a quiet place. A name with any number except the repetition of the number 3 will suit these children.

Thirteens Born in April (fourth month)

All Thirteen children are qualified Four personalities by virtue of the underlying 4 vibration (1+3 = 4). Children born in the month of April are invariably oriented toward physical plane characteristics and talents. The chapter on the fourth day of the month provides much information on the 4 vibration.

The number 1 in their birth day is also a very strong physical force. This adds to their outlook and expertise in all physical activities and creations. From an early age, these children can be found deconstructing then reassembling any toy or article they can get their hands on. There is a natural urge to know how things are put together and how things work. Sooner or later they will be making things themselves. They are never happier than when the means to do so are provided.

These are strong-willed and self-confident children who can never be pushed around. They need to make their own mistakes and learn by them. With considerable staying power they can excel in any form of sport that demands stamina—both mental and physical. As an emotional vibration is conspicuous by its absence, demonstration of their sensitive feelings will be at a minimum. But expect occasional outbursts of ill-temper. Names with the numbers 1, 4, 7, and 8 are best avoided. These could increase stubbornness. Other numbers will loosen up the personality.

Thirteens Born in May (fifth month)

Thirteen children born in the fifth month are indisputably, all-rounders. Their birth day alone makes them multi-talented and versatile. With the addition of the 5 vibration in their birth month they experience a tremendous upsurge of their 1, 3, and 4 attributes plus fresh attributes of the 5 vibration itself. Refer to the chapter on the fifth day of the month to learn about the extensive influence of this additional force. These four vibrations comprising the major portion of their personality do not conflict with one another. Yet, this intensified condition may not always remain conducive to their wellbeing and to that of others.

In a normal domestic scene, opportunities may not be available for expenditure of the tremendous mental and physical energy that activates these children. To get them to quieten down could be a perennial problem until opportunities widen as they grow older. The advantage here is that they have the capacity to create opportunities. They are difficult children to keep indoors, as the outdoors is their element. They need to have something happening around them. If not, they create something. With a thirst for experiences, practical skills exceed book-learned skills. Without much effort or nurturing they are able to take charge of their lives. They look after themselves by using physical courage, a natural perceptiveness, quick reflexes, and fluency and flexibility of speech. They do not find it difficult to extricate themselves from adverse situations or tight corners they may fall into. The best names for them are with the numbers 2, 7, or 6. These may slow them down somewhat without loss of capacity. Other numbers may not do so.

Thirteens Born in June (sixth month)

The chapter on the sixth day of the month shows that self-centered traits common to the 1 and 3 vibrations are considerably reduced in the 6. This is a family and community-oriented force. A further examination of the 4 vibration in the chapter on the fourth day of the month indicates that this vibration, which operates at a fundamental level in the Thirteen personality, has many features in common with the 6. The desire to serve and safeguard are among their chief shared features.

There is a reasonable balance in the personality of these children between self-interest and self-assertive qualities on the one hand, and the desire to help and serve, on the other. Usually, they need not be reminded to attend to personal care or to fulfill their obligations toward others. They will be happy to spend an equal amount of their time in indoor activities and outdoor activities. Helping in the kitchen may be one of their favorite interests. They are popular children who earn the admiration of their peers and are much sought after for advice and support.

The need for any form of chastizement will be exceptional. At the same time, they will not hesitate to argue or challenge incorrect views or revolt against irrational and unfair treatment. They are self-assured personalities who expect to be treated with the same respect they give others. Any name will suit these well-balanced children.

Thirteens Born in July (seventh month)

Practical talents and down-to-earth values of Thirteen children are extended and strengthened by the 7 vibration in their birth month. At the same time, a fresh and often contrary set of qualities are introduced. The chapter on the seventh day of the month will disclose the reserved and non-egotistic attributes of the 7 vibration. These children are likely to be selective in their choice of company and less vocal at home and among their friends. They may speak in shorter sentences, but those sentences will be full of meaning. Their opinions on matters may often be withheld. Their greatest strength lies in their self-sufficiency. They do not experience boredom or difficulty entertaining themselves.

With a studious and generally non-demanding nature they get what they need through their own efforts, especially as they grow older. They do not suffer from any difficult personality traits or necessary talents that would eventually shut them out of a particular trade or profession.

These are children who quickly pass the cuddly stage. Emotional display will be at a minimum. Any name will suit these well-balanced children. But a name with an emotional vibration 2, 5, or 9 will help them more easily release emotion when there is an inner need to do so.

Thirteens Born in August (eighth month)

The authoritative, leadership, and disciplinary aspects of the 1, 3, and 4 vibrations comprising the Thirteen personality are emphasized by the 8 vibration. Provided they have not been deprived of natural growth by despotic parents, at an early age, these children should feel an inward sense of power followed by an outward display of leadership and authority. This will be their natural disposition. Even if they have been subdued during their upbringing, they are certain to come into their own as soon as they are free to take charge of their lives and open themselves to the vast range of potential at their disposal. These are children who can succeed in any line of work, sport, or occupation they choose.

With confident body language and commanding speech, they will be early leaders who may not hesitate to push others out of their way while on their own road to success. They will not hesitate to challenge orders or instructions given at home or any other place. Their emotions are well contained but occasional displays of affection or displeasure can be expected. They cannot be emotionally manipulated. Names with the numbers 2, 6, 7, or 9 are best as any of these may reduce their dictatorial ways. Numbers 1, 3, 4, 5, and 8 should be avoided.

Thirteens Born in September (ninth month)

The personality of Thirteen children born in September is best understood by referring to the chapter on the ninth day of the month. You will see that these children benefit for the most part from a different and fresh set of attributes. Most importantly, the influence of the 9 vibration has the potential to ease them out of personal and localized thought and activities, and lead them into the international arena and out of a narrow field of "me" and "mine". The considerable variety of talent provided by their birth day vibrations can be employed much further afield than town, state, or country.

The 9 vibration also introduces high-minded attributes of wisdom, understanding, and compassion which create greater sensitivity to pain in themselves and in others. It also takes them closer to the cultural aspects of life such as music, drama, poetry, and spiritual studies, and further from purely physical pleasures.

These positive children regard the world as a friendly place. They may show no hesitation in taking the initiative in getting to know people and interacting with them. They acquire popularity early in life as the controlling nature of the Thirteen personality has been changed to a more friendly approach. Every dollar spent on the education of these multi-talented children will reap a rich harvest. There is no trade, business, or profession that will not profit by their personality and talents. Any name will suit these children.

Thirteens Born in October (tenth month)

Please refer to the sub-chapter on Thirteens born in January (first month). The zero in the month of October has no attributes of its own that could influence the Thirteen personality.

Thirteens Born in November (eleventh month)

Please refer to the sub-chapter on the Thirteens born in January (first month). As the 1 vibration is present in double strength, its attributes are emphasized in children born in the eleventh month.

Thirteens Born in December (twelfth month)

Attributes of the 1 vibration are strengthened in children born in December. At the same time, certain gentle qualities of the 2 may emerge from time to time. Please refer to the chapter on the second day of the month.

Fourteenth Day of the Month

14 reduces to (1+4=5)

Children born on the fourteenth day have the influence of the 1 and 4 vibrations in the outer personality and the 5 vibration functioning in the background. The three vibratory forces (1, 4, and 5) operating within this birth day, combine to form an exceptionally powerful physically oriented personality. The potential to use the best attributes of the forces within the physical plane and none of their negative aspects exists in these children. The chapters on the first, fourth and fifth days of the month contain these attributes. While the 1 and 4 vibrations relate exclusively to the physical plane the underlying 5 radiates over the physical, emotional, and mental planes, with an emphasis on the physical.

These are undoubtedly self-sufficient and confident children who eventually make the transition into adulthood without undue self-depreciation or self-reproach. In cases where natural growth has been hindered by adverse circumstances in family life they are certain to shed many fears and other negative beliefs soon after they become independent. These are essentially non-dependent children who choose to make their own decisions rather than relying on others to make them. They could be rebellious and resentful of parents and elders who are too meticulous or severe in guiding or disciplining them. Any form of physical punishment will not change their self-willed nature. They do not hesitate to stand up for themselves when they feel that chastizement may be unwarranted. They do not have to be told twice to understand the need for certain rules and regulations. The best approach for promoting their growth and maintaining domestic harmony will be to observe and appreciate their multiple talents and provide opportunities for their expression. Parental ambitions should not be imposed on them, unless they are of the same temperament.

These are competitive children who excel in any form of sport. Body contact sports will not be excluded. They are not children who need to be constantly entertained. They usually find their own sources of entertainment and activity. They choose to involve themselves in any form of activity rather than watch others performing. They develop naturally as all-rounders and handypersons. They do not seek the limelight although they do invariably move in and out of the limelight with ease. Although they undoubtedly possess leadership talents, they may not actively seek leading roles. At the same time, they can never comfortably remain long as followers. Parents may be assured that such children cannot be led, misled, or bullied by their contemporaries. Their school days will be spent with an adventurous spirit and a keen interest in learning. They will always display a good deal of physical courage. These children may learn to walk and run well before the average child. But fluency of speech may not appear too early. As they grow older their emotions will be held in control by their realistic minds. Fantasy and imagination are not aspects of their personality. They are generally healthy children who recover quickly after any form of illness or emotional hurt.

Any name will suit these self-confident and multi-talented children. This birth month will be responsible for certain variations in the personality of these Fourteen children. The following sections reveal these variations.

Fourteens Born in January (first month)

The physical orientation, practicality, individuality, and willpower of a Fourteen child will be reinforced by the addition of the 1 vibration from their birth month. Beginning from early childhood, into their teens, and then into young adulthood, these children will be independent. Dependability on their parents will be at a minimum. While providing the means for self-reliant growth, parents will need to resist a natural urge to control or have close participation in these children's choice of activities, unless participation is of mutual acceptance and benefit. The independent nature of these children will resist emotional attachment and interference with their decisions. Their temperament will cause them to shy away from accepting other people's convictions and beliefs unless they fit into their own scheme of things.

These children may not be emotionally close or demonstrative but they do possess a great deal of unexpressed emotion, often shown in outbursts of temper. They may be self-sufficient, usually following their own interests but are exceptionally loyal and dependable in times of need. They can be called upon for help and support in family matters at any stage of their lives.

While any name will suit these self-confident and practical children, a name adding to 1 or 4 should be avoided as they do not need further attributes from the physical plane. Any other name will suit them.

Fourteens Born in February (second month)

Two physical and two emotional vibratory forces operate within Fourteen children born in February. The physical attributes function for the most part as outer forces and emotional attributes as restrained inner forces. The latter are usually held in check in the presence of general company, but released as the occasion demands within the family and in intimate relationships. The personalities of these children are therefore formed by two modes of expression that interact to form a confident and well-intentioned child.

There is another aspect in the formation of their personality to be considered. Two active forces (1 and 5) intermingle with two receptive forces (4 and 2). The former provide the energy, determination, and initiative to obtain for themselves all the good things physical and material life has to offer, and the latter instills in them the additional need and desire to help, share, and serve others. These children therefore possess the potential to develop into very useful members of their families and communities. They are exceptionally adept with their hands, both in heavy and delicate tasks. They need to be kept occupied with indoor as well as outdoor activities. Children who receive encouragement and support excel in all forms of sport. Operating under their own steam, they are backed up by willpower, quick reflexes, and physical strength. While any name will suit these talented children, those reducing to 3, 6, 7, or 9 will be best. Any one of these will provide a fresh outlet to their overall personality.

Fourteens Born in March (third month)

A creative imagination, originality, manual dexterity, and practicality are among many advantageous attributes acquired by children with this birth day and birth month combination. In addition, there are several other special characteristics and talents that are backed up with self-confidence and good self-esteem, which enable them to make maximum use of their multi-faceted personality structure. Attributes of the physical, emotional, and mental planes interact harmoniously to provide them with the potential for quick study and early growth. These children may study any subject and eventually undertake any line of work. They are genuine all-rounders.

These children are both mentally and physically active. Parents will need to provide several outlets for expenditure of their energies. If not, they become restless, fidgety, and demanding. They view the world as a friendly and adventuresome place. They are not likely to remain home-oriented children. Social and outdoor activities will be their usual fields of operation. They pass the cuddly stage early in life and enter the world of adventure. They are quite capable of standing up for themselves and resisting unreasonable demands upon their time, and arbitrary rules and regulations. Their independence and individuality are well preserved. They are natural leaders and poor followers. Any name will suit these well-balanced children.

Fourteens Born in April (fourth month)

Children born with this birth day and birth month combination are influenced almost entirely by attributes of physical vibrations. The 1 and 4 are predominantly physical forces, and the presence of the 4 in double strength enhances all physical and down-to-earth characteristics. Please consult the chapter on the fourth day of the month for a better understanding of these children. The underlying 5 in their birth day also contains many physical features that interact with the 1 and 4.

These are physically strong and self-assured children who develop firm ideas and unshakable opinions. They may listen to advice and instructions attentively but they are likely to take in what they agree with and effectively block out the rest. They cannot be adversely influenced or lead astray by members of their age group, or even by older friends and acquaintances. With independent reasoning they are capable of making their own decisions and standing their ground in most circumstances. It is most unlikely that they will ever be a target for bullies.

They are not emotionally demonstrative or talkative children. They would rather be doing something than engaging in unproductive conversation. They do not usually seek to entertain others. By nature they are exceptionally loyal and protective of loved ones. They can be depended upon to do their part in normal domestic duties as well as in emergencies. They are usually found fixing things around the home and garden. They excel in all forms of sport. Offensive or defensive roles can be taken up with equal success. A given name reducing to the number 4 should be avoided. Any other name will suit these children.

Fourteens Born in May (fifth month)

It is important to read the chapter on the fifth day of the month for a better understanding of children with this birth day and birth month combination. People born on the fourteenth day are qualified Five personalities. As this vibration operates as an underlying force in the birth day and is also seen in the birth month, the attributes of the 5 vibration are predominant in the integral personality of these children.

The 1 and 4 vibrations are also strong formative forces and these coalesce advantageously with the 5. They strengthen its physical aspects but they also control qualities of emotional demonstration, impulse, and changeability. Usually, these children are healthy physically oriented individuals. With strong constitutions they possess a tremendous quantity of energy awaiting release. They are fearless and adventuresome in all physical aspects of life. They are also highly competitive, non-dependent, and self-motivated.

To a large extent they foster their own interests before extending their concern for others. But they do not hesitate to willingly help anyone at any place or time when called upon to do so. They are most valuable in emergencies due to their courage, quick reflexes, and practical talents. The repetition of the 1, 4, and 5 in a first name should be avoided. Any other name will be beneficial.

Fourteens Born in June (sixth month)

The physical, emotional, and mental planes are well represented in this birth day and birth month combination. This indicates a multiform personality structure. The 6 vibration introduces an awareness of family and community responsibilities. These children will consequently use all the practical talents inherited from their birth day vibrations in service of family and community. Not only will they be found doing odd jobs around the house and garden but they will also show a keen interest in the kitchen. The 6 vibration is responsible for the love of quality food and good cooking. A pleasant demeanor seen in these children has its source in the combined positive aspects of the 1, 4, 5, and 6 vibratory forces.

These are loyal and loving children but they do not always show these qualities by emotional demonstration. They are shown in action rather than in words. Emotional outbursts are exceptional. They are self-assured individuals motivated by logical and realistic thought processes. Impulse and changeability, which are usual attributes of their underlying 5 vibration, are subdued by the rationality of the 6 and the down-to-earth qualities of the 1 and 4. It is these combined forces that ensure qualities of dependability, responsibility, and practicality. These children are capable of expressing themselves in speech but action will always be more evident than words. Parents should allow the fine characteristics contained in their personality to emerge naturally, in an upbringing that does not contain suppression, deprivation, or good nurturing. Although these children are well able to progressively stand on their own feet they need reasonable care to prevent inhibition of many of their fine qualities. These children are not rebellious, but they will not hesitate to question authority in the event of unfair or unreasonable treatment.

Fourteens Born in July (seventh month)

All three vibrations from the physical plane operate within this birth day and birth month combination. In addition, the underlying 5 in the birth day (people born on the fourteenth day are qualified Five personalities) has many physically oriented qualities, despite being an effective force on the emotional plane. The intermingling of these forces therefore results in the formation of a personality structure with a variety of attributes relative to the physical plane. The interesting condition here is that each number or vibration provides a relatively different set of talents and personality traits. The 1 in the birth day offers originality, self-assurance, decisiveness, and a host of other positive qualities. The 4 provides manual dexterity, stability, and down-to-earth values among many other things. The 5 introduces physical courage, a spirit of adventure and movement, and once again several other characteristics. Lastly the 7 introduces a love of nature and a consciousness of a spiritual element in all living things. As this is a complex personality structure, the chapters on the first, fourth, fifth and seventh days of the month should be examined for a better understanding of these children. The attributes of a particular vibration will not be predominant. Each will contribute its share toward the integral personality.

As a consequence of the above, these children will emerge as competent, well-adjusted, and multi-talented personalities. They are emotionally stable with very early indications of individuality. By nature, they are neither followers nor conformists. They are not likely to be constant talkers, but when they do speak out others listen to them. They are certain to turn out as conscientious and self-motivated students. Any name will suit these talented children, but a name with the numbers 3, 6, or 9 will serve to open out even wider perspectives.

Fourteens Born in August (eighth month)

Fourteen children born in the eighth month possess the potential to develop and exercise considerable power in the public service and the business world. They will be strongly competitive in all forms of activity. An authoritative demeanor will be accompanied by a keen desire for power and material wealth. A natural sense of entitlement will be backed up by the capacity to achieve their ambitions. Nurturing these children may not be too easy as they could be demanding and many of their demands will need to be met. Their demands will not be frivolous or subject to change.

These children are likely to be spic and span in their personal lives and resentful of poor organization in the lives of those close to them. Provided ideas of limitation have not been instilled into them, they will become independent early in life and take great pride in their achievements. They can make clear-cut decisions and not mince words when they give out their opinions. They resent contradiction. They may not hesitate to push others out of their way if they interfere with their plans. They are not children who could be easily intimidated. In early adulthood their ambitions will be self-serving, but once success has been gained, a fine sense of generosity will emerge. Any name will suit these competent children.

Fourteens Born in September (ninth month)

Fourteen children born in the ninth month are gifted with an expanded outlook on life. Please refer to the chapter on the ninth day of the month. The 9 vibration activates attributes of the discoverer and pioneer in the 1 vibration of their birth day and drives them into global and international perspectives. It does the same with the underlying 5 vibration's desire for activity, movement, and travel. The powerful 4 in their birth day provides practical application to all their ventures and acts as a safeguard against excessive movement and change. These are consequently well-balanced children who are likely to look upon life as an extensive adventure in which they will make many positive contributions. You will not need to explain to them too many details about life. They seem to instinctively understand and easily adapt to changing circumstances.

These children are also blessed with an openness of manner and a willingness to listen to what others have to say. They are not likely to demand preferential treatment in a family with many siblings but will happily contribute their share of domestic responsibilities. The 9 vibration has released them to a fair extent from ego-consciousness and replaced it with a willingness to help others. Self-correction has also become easier. They are easily reactive to atmosphere, especially when something has been said or done that touches a chord in their sensitive nature. They can only be influenced by people with the same affinity with their own nature. They may avoid close interaction with others. Any name will suit these intelligent children.

Fourteens Born in October (tenth month)

Please refer to the sub-chapter on Fourteens born in January (first month). There will be no difference between these children. The zero in this position has no influence on the personality of children born in October. A first name reducing to 2, 3, 5, 6, or 9 will be advisable. A name reducing to 1 or 4 should be avoided.

Fourteens Born in November (eleventh month)

Please refer to the section on Fourteens born in January (first month). Children born in November will not be too different to those born in January. However, they will show a greater degree of determination and down-to-earth values. Emotional expression will be restricted. A first name reducing to 2, 3, 5, 6, or 9 will be very helpful. Avoid names with 1 and 4.

Fourteens Born in December (twelfth month)

Children born in December are strong positive personalities who have some of the best attributes of the 1, 4, and 5 vibrations. Please refer to the chapters on the first, fourth and fifth days of the month. The 2 vibration in their birth month is overpowered to a large degree by these forces. However, it does provide these children with a small outlet for expression of their emotions. A good first name for them will be one that reduces to a 2, 3, 5, 6, or 9.

Fifteenth Day of the Month

15 reduces to (1+5=6)

Children born on the fifteenth day have the influence of the 1 and 5 vibrations in the outer personality and the 6 vibration in the inner personality. The fifteenth day is one of the few near complete birth days. People born on this day have the potential to function successfully in a unified condition in which attributes from the physical, emotional, and mental planes operate in equal strength. They also manifest their positive aspects, leaving all negative features in abeyance, unless the latter are introduced in a dysfunctional upbringing.

Decisiveness, rationality, and enterprise are some of their outstanding attributes. Early in life these children will display characteristics of physical courage, non-dependence, ample kinetic energy, and a keen desire to be involved in the world of experience. Attributes of loyalty to home and family are also strong although these may not be evident in their younger days. They become active and operative in early maturity. These qualities are in the nature of their underlying 6 vibration. They take a back seat, so to speak, in the Fifteen child's development. You may rest assured that these children, within reason, are able to look after themselves. They may influence others but are not likely to be influenced by them, unless a suggestion meets with their approval. They are seldom affected by boredom, melancholy, or depression. They have no time. Self-confidence and self-assurance arise from within them, not from outside influences. They do not rely on the opinions that others may have of them.

Despite an inner peaceful nature, by virtue of their 6 vibration, these children could rebel against arbitrary restrictions and unfair disciplinary measures, speaking their minds without hesitation. They are naturally drawn to physical activity rather than a need for close interaction with people. Social intercourse may be connected with their activities but not their first priority. Oral expression will also be subordinate to physical activity. They will usually speak in short sentences. Book learning will also take second place to practical and physical experiences. While their need for various activities should be catered to they should also be taught that every moment of their time need not be filled with some form of change or movement. They will accept this advice as they grow older and the quiet nature of their 6 vibration emerges more fully. Although their 5 aspect has no problem with touching and hugging, these tendencies are restricted by their 1 and 6 aspects. Fifteen children therefore are not comfortable with excessive hugging and kissing.

These are multi-faceted and multi-talented children who can choose any line of study and future employment. There will often be a preference for movement and outdoor work. Any name will suit them.

Fifteens Born in January (first month)

The overall strength and positive nature of the Fifteen personality are lifted into higher levels of manifestation by the 1 vibration in their birth month. This elevation takes place in the outer 1 and 5 aspects of their personality at the expense of some attributes of their inner 6 nature. Self-confidence, assertiveness, competition, authority, decisiveness, determination, strength of purpose, and the desire to explore all aspects of the physical world are some areas that are enhanced. At the same time, the peaceful, non-competitive, and home-oriented features are overtaken in Fifteen children by their need for constant physical activity and fearlessness. The 1 vibration, among other things, is known chiefly as the activator. When it appears in the birth day and birth month, and in combination with the 5, it is easy to understand why these children need several outlets for expenditure of physical energy. The chapters on the first, fifth and sixth days of the month provide more details on this birth day and birth month combination.

One of the best outlets for release of energy and the competitive and adventuresome nature of these children will be a variety of sport. They may eventually specialize in one or two and distinguish themselves. Similarly, their education is open to a variety of directions. These are multi-talented, energetic, and multi-faceted personalities whose assets are not confined to specialized or limited areas. While any name will suit these positive children it will be best to choose one that does not add up to 1 or 5. They are amply endowed with the qualities of these forces already.

Fifteens Born in February (second month)

The fundamental personality formed by the fifteenth day is expanded and enriched by the presence of the 2 vibration in the birth month. Its attributes are quite opposite to those of the 1 and 5 in the outer personality of the Fifteen. At the same time it has a good deal in common with their inner nature symbolized by the number 6. The combined receptive nature of the 2 and 6 and the active and controlling nature of the combined 1 and 5 operate within these children. Parents will discover that their 1 and 5 aspects are more prominent that their 2 and 6. However, the latter have a calming effect upon the personality. These children are prevented from falling into extremes of behavior by moving into physical activity at the expense of study and family togetherness. They will be more amenable to discipline and a balanced approach to life. They will not be as restless within the home as some other Fifteen children. As competitors they will be fair, sportsmanlike, and sensitive to other peoples' feelings. They will also be helpful around the home. They lose nothing of the positive and self-confident aspects of their 1 and 5 nature and these will also be manifested with a mixture of diplomacy and tact.

Fifteens Born in March (third month)

Children with this birth day and birth month combination possess an irresistible urge to experiment and experience as many delights of the mental and physical realms as possible. As they live in a world of multiplicity, their imaginative, physical, and mental restlessness constantly seeks outlets for activity. They could be pulled in all directions at once. Those who by circumstances are confined to a restricted lifestyle will soon rebel against such conditions. As these are highly intelligent, alert, and multi-talented children, parents will be confronted with a real problem if they try to confine them to a special line of development or education. Temptation to constantly try something new is a trait these children need to overcome.

These are children who can talk their way into anything they desire, or talk their way out of any difficulty they may fall into. Fertile minds, self-confidence, and fluency of speech are their most powerful assets. They are brim full of outlets for self-expression. This is confirmed in the chapters on the first, third, fifth, and sixth days of the month. Some time may be needed to do so, but the results will be worthwhile. Any name will suit these multi-talented children.

Fifteens Born in April (fourth month)

The fifteenth birth day provides a combination of individuality and leadership (from the 1), enterprise and adventure (from the 5), and domesticity and community (from the 6). Fifteen personalities born in the fourth month are reinforced in different ways in all three departments of their integral personality. The 4 vibration introduces practicality and down-to-earth values which enhance their 1 attributes. It controls unproductive movement and change in their 5 aspect and most of all, it enhances domestic, community, and nationalistic values. All in all, Fifteen children born in April are mentally and physically strong individuals. Their thoughts and actions are not swayed by impulse or emotion. The 5 vibration functioning without the influence of other major forces can easily release emotion. However, the 1, 4, and 6 vibrations are not emotionally demonstrative forces. These children, therefore, are not likely to be emotionally dependent or emotionally expressive. Deeds rather than words form the expression of their love and loyalty. As these are multi-faceted individuals, reference to the chapters on the 1, 4, 5 and 6 days of the month will be useful. Their personality is formed by a fair share of each of these vibratory forces which operate in positive ways.

These are children who can participate constructively as part of a group and play a strong competitive role in team activity. They will seldom be at odds with their team mates, unless someone tries to push them around. They are easily able to stand up for themselves. They can be trained to abide by normal rules of conduct within the home and in a social environment. They are not by nature rebellious or recalcitrant. Physical chastizement will not help when these children are disciplined. It will only bring out the stubbornness in all the aspects of their personality. With a rich multiplicity of personality traits and talents a name with a special vibration is not needed. Any name will suit them.

Fifteens Born in May (fifth month)

To gain a clear understanding of Fifteen children born in May, the chapter on the fifth day of the month should be carefully read as the attributes of the 5 vibration predominate in their personality. Those of the 1 vibration are not in fact subdued as this is a powerful force. It may not always exercise a firm grip upon the personality because the 5 vibration operates in double strength. It will, however, have a steadying influence on some volatile and changeable 5 characteristics and talents, directing them into positive and clear-cut directions. At the same time, the easy-going and placid 6 attributes may be relegated to the background. These are likely to emerge with maturity.

A prominent feature in these children will be their need for constant physical activity and change of scene. Another observable trait will be their tendency to take control over their environment and change things to suit themselves, as they possess natural skills at manipulating people and situations. They revel in drama. Many things happen with a Fifteen child around. They are popular children who set a tone of vivacity and energy that is quickly picked up by others. Their desire to experience life in as many aspects as possible will continue to increase with age. To the surprise of their elders they will show an unusual ability to extricate themselves from any difficult or compromising situation they may fall into. One way is to talk themselves out of such situations.

They are competitive, physically strong, and alert children who excel in any form of sport. Book learning may not be their chosen pastime. They will be restless and difficult to control when confined to quiet and confined surroundings. They seek outside sources of diversion. Any name except another 5 name will suit these children.

Fifteens Born in June (sixth month)

Children born on the fifteenth day are fundamentally Six personalities. But, the combined forces of their 1 and 5 vibrations represent assertive forces that play a prominent role in their outer personality. Consequently, their more placid 6 attributes are relegated to the background. This condition is altered in children born in the sixth month. As this 6 vibration operates in the birth day as well, its attributes too, combine to confront those of the 1 and 5. As a result, a greater degree of balance between the active 1 and 5 attributes and the receptive 6 forces exist. There is a reduction of the forcefulness of the former and an increase of the effectiveness of the latter. Reference to the chapters on the first, fifth and sixth days of the month will be helpful for a better understanding of these children.

The bold and impulsive actions of the combined 1 and 5 are monitored by many 6 traits of deliberation or quiet mental analysis and cooperation. Their thoughts and actions are creative and purposeful. These personalities emerge as well-adjusted individuals. They are not easily led or misled. They can be argumentative and opposed to anything that does not meet with their strict sense of values. Nurturing these children will be a pleasure as long as they are approached with reason and fair play. In addition, they are unlikely to respond to disagreement by shouting or sulking. The willingness to listen to advice and instructions is a helpful feature of their 6 vibration. Negative characteristics of indolence, boredom, recalcitrance, and ill-temper are not natural traits within the integral personality of these children. Any name will suit these well-balanced children. However, another 1, 5, or 6 should be avoided so that some other vibration will provide another avenue for self-expression.

Fifteens Born in July (seventh month)

Attributes of four dissimilar vibratory forces are within the personality of children born in July. These children are made to cope with a considerable variety of personality traits and talents. The direct result is that the full range of any one trait or special attribute does not enter into their conduct or capabilities. This is by no means a negative condition but one that results in a constant modification as well as an amplification of personality traits. See the chapters on the first, fifth, sixth and seventh days of the month for a full understanding of the complexity of these personalities. Fortunately, these children are, mostly, positive personalities. They are a curious mixture of self-confidence, domesticity, exploration, non-dependence, and self-sufficiency. They may at times experience confusion within themselves but not conflict. They possess all the elements necessary to take charge of their lives.

Their integral personality may be likened to a house with many large doors and windows which broaden their outlook on life. They possess an openness of mind and a willingness to listen and learn, and make up their own minds. The various aspects of their personality do not function independently of each other but blend into a system of mutual benefit. This is their inherent strength. They are children rich in exterior as well as interior resources. Any name will suit them.

Fifteens Born in August (eighth month)

While examining the four vibrations, or numbers (1, 5, 6 and 8), we observe that three of them in different ways contain controlling tendencies. The chapters on the first, fifth and eighth days of the month show that individual decision-making and varying leadership qualities are essential attributes of the 1 vibration. Different forms of manipulation are used by those influenced by the 5 to gain their ends, and a natural propensity to take charge of their environment and the lives of others with whom they interact, is clearly evident in people motivated by the 8. Attributes of the 6 vibration are invariably relegated to the background to emerge intermittently at later stages of adulthood. (The chapter on the sixth day of the month may also be helpful).

While growing up, ambition for high achievement in scholastic studies and subsequently in public life will be the main motivating factors in these children. They are, without doubt, multi-talented children who are capable of entering into any field of study, and in adulthood, into any form of occupation. It is not possible to forecast any special avenues in which they could specialize. They will not be deterred by negative qualities of self-doubt, self-reproach, or lack of self-esteem. They are also capable of outgrowing negative influences suffered during a harsh or neglected upbringing and are not likely to carry too many emotional scars. They could also display a tendency toward pride and insolence, and so they may not be the easiest children to discipline. They would constantly display a strong will of their own. This could be a positive asset in sport and eventually in public life, but may not always act as an asset in family life and in an intimate relationship. The best names for these children will be those that reduce to 2, 6, or 9. Any of these will mitigate to some degree their controlling ways. Other numbers are best avoided.

Fifteens Born in September (ninth month)

Fifteen children born in September are blessed with a balanced personality structure. Over-emphasis or over-action of a particular personality trait is unlikely. The combined operation of two strong mental forces (6 and 9) and two strong physical forces (1 and 5) ensure stability and strength of purpose. (Although the 5 operates on the emotional plane it contains considerable physical features that combine well with their 1 attributes). These latter are essentially acquisitive forces that concentrate on advancement and personal prosperity. The 6 and 9 are vibrations free from self-centeredness and many of the more controlling and enforcing traits. Consideration to the wellbeing of others is combined with that of their own.

These are multi-faceted and super-intelligent children who, with a little guidance, possess the potential to sail through their school days with little effort and subsequently succeed in any profession they choose. They will always hold a positive and broad outlook on life. While paying careful attention to their current course of studies or curriculum they will also be engaged in a variety of other hobbies and interests. Any name will suit these clever children.

Fifteens Born in October (tenth month)

Please refer to the section on Fifteens born in January (first month). There is no difference between children born in January or October. The 1 vibration influences their birth day vibrations. The zero is neutral and therefore does not exercise any influence upon the personality. A first name reducing to 1, 5, or 8 should be avoided. A name reducing to any other number will suit them.

Fifteens Born in November (eleventh month)

Please refer to the section on Fifteens born in January (first month). Fifteen children born in November are not too different from those born in January. However, attributes of the 1 vibration may be emphasized and emotional restriction further restricted. A name reducing to 1 or 4 should be strictly avoided. Any other name will suit them.

Fifteens Born in December (twelfth month)

Attributes of people with this birth day (the fifteenth) are strengthened by the vibrations of their birth month (the twelfth). These are strong, positive children with the potential to demonstrate the best qualities of their birth day vibrations. While any name will suit these children it would be best to avoid one which reduces to a 1. A better choice would be a name reducing to 3, 6, or 9.

Sixteenth Day of the Month

16 reduces to (1+6=7)

Children born on the sixteenth day have the influence of the 1 and 6 vibrations in the outer personality and the 7 vibration functioning in the background. The integration of three different sets of characteristics and talents is nature's gift to children born on this day. This condition will also place them along positive lines of development. Their integral personalities possess the potential to manifest the best qualities of the 1, 6, and 7 vibrations. (These children are, in fact, qualified Seven personalities (1+6=7). All negative aspects of these vibratory forces are counteracted by those that are positive. For instance, self-promotion and egotistic features of the 1 vibration are greatly reduced or even eliminated by even-tempered and balanced aspects of the 6 and 7 without interfering with its self-confident, self-assured, and decisive attributes. The chapters on the first, sixth, and seventh days of the month will be most helpful in understanding these Sixteen children.

At the same time, the tendency of those influenced by the 6 vibration to underrate themselves will be overcome by the non-dependent and self-assured qualities of their 1 and 7 aspects. Extroverted traits of the 1 and 6 will also open out the natural reserve and introspection of the 7. All in all, children born on the sixteenth day are well equipped to develop into stable and successful adults in all aspects of life. As balance in all things is a cardinal feature in these children and adults, they are not likely to fall into any extremes of behavior. Needless to say, intelligent parenting will bring out the best in these multi-faceted children who will display a keen desire to probe into the nature of things.

The need to discipline these well-adjusted children will be minimal.

For the most part they possess an inherent knowledge of the rights and wrongs of conduct. It is, however, most essential that they are treated at all times with reason and understanding. They are certain to resent and reject an irrational approach by parents or teachers based on emotion rather than fact. Loss of trust will be the inevitable result. These children are deep thinkers and keen observers. They do not obediently or passively accept everything that is said to them. In addition they are not types who worry too much about what others think of them. Their natural principles take precedence over society's trends or conventional ideas.

These children can engage happily and successfully in outdoor as well as indoor activities. Attributes of their 6 aspect combine with some of their 7 to create a love for home and domestic attractions, and a quiet and peaceful way of life. Other aspects of the 7 vibration along with the impetus of the 1 respond eagerly to outdoor activities, especially in natural surroundings. They may participate successfully in any form of sport but their egos are not fired by a fiercely competitive or ambitious spirit. Participation and camaraderie are more satisfying. Many Sixteen children and adults are more likely to be attracted to music, literature, and other non-competitive outlets such as fishing, bird watching, mountaineering, canoeing, and other such outdoor pastimes.

They are soft-spoken individuals who do not waste words whenever they have something of importance to say. They soon develop a talent to contain and verbalize their thoughts in precise and meaningful sentences. Emotion and melodrama will not be exhibited in speech or body language. They may at times be regarded as unflappable personalities. They do possess a mixture of extroversion and introversion. They will not be easily influenced by their peers and will always be selective of the company they keep.

Any name will suit these well-balanced children. A repetition of the 1, 6, or 7 vibration in a first name will not cause an overloading or an imbalance but it would be better if they are given a name reducing to 2, 3, 5, or 9. Any of these will open out the personality into additional dimensions of manifestation. The birth month is responsible for variations in the conduct and talents of Sixteen personalities. The following section deals with these variations.

Sixteens Born in January (first month)

Attributes of the 1 vibration are strengthened in Sixteen children born in January. Personality traits such as individuality, decisiveness, determination, willpower, and ego-strength are some special attributes of this vibration that influence the overall personality structure. As a consequence of their 6 and 7 aspects, they favor consideration for the welfare of others before their own (or at least along with their own). But the 1 causes this tendency to be somewhat relegated to the background in ordinary day-to-day living. Personal affairs are given priority. However, they do not remain so because this broader consideration could easily be brought out when circumstances demand.

These are self-reliant and multi-talented children who hold their emotions in check. As a result, their reactions and motives could at times be misunderstood. An outlet for free emotional expression is not present in their birth day and birth month. A first name reducing to 2, 5, or 9 will be ideal. A name with any other number, if given for a special reason will do no harm.

Sixteens Born in February (second month)

There are several genteel and graceful features within the 2, 6, and 7 vibrations that combine to create a personality exhibiting a natural elegance and dignity. The chapters on the second, sixth, and seventh days of the month reveal many such features that contribute to this desirable condition. These features also polish some rough or arbitrary aspects of the 1 vibration, such as egotism, unnecessary self-assertiveness, and self-centeredness. The self-confident and self-sufficient nature of the 1 is not damaged, but rather directed in full strength into the best attributes of their 2, 6, and 7 aspects. These children may be gentle, non-competitive, quiet, and soft-spoken. At the same time, they possess considerable inner strength which is seldom on display until, or unless, someone foolishly attempts to take advantage of their unobtrusive nature.

These are well-rounded and well-adjusted personalities. But their sensitivities are easily touched and harmed in a harsh, noisy, and

123

dysfunctional environment. A diplomatic approach is the only way to gain their attention and obedience. Any name will suit them.

Sixteens Born in March (third month)

There is a partition of sorts in the personality of children born in this month. While they possess the gift of fluent and quality speech, and easy sociability, friendliness, and companionship, another aspect of their personality favors self-reliance, reserve, quietude, and a strict selection of friends and acquaintances. At chosen times they are able to occupy the center of attention, although they may not actively seek to do so. They are exceptionally intelligent and self-assured children with a natural appreciation for art, literature, music, and nature studies.

As a vibration from the emotional plane is not present in their birth day and birth month, emotional expression is limited. They may not like to be touched and cuddled too often by loved ones, and especially not by other relatives, friends, and acquaintances. They are not capable of eagerly responding to these endearments. Their love of nature is deep and enduring, and will often be displayed in artistic expression.

These children can sail through their schooling with ease. They will always be known as a "quick study". Any name will suit these multi-talented personalities. However, a name reducing to 2, 5, or 9 will certainly help with demonstration of emotion when certain occasions demand.

Sixteens Born in April (fourth month)

An orientation toward practical aspects of life will soon be observed in these children. All three vibrations of the physical plane (1, 4, and 7) function within their integral personality. However, there are also other elements that prevent confinement within a purely physical and practical outlook. The 6 vibration from the mental plane will be responsible for the introduction of many aesthetic qualities. In addition, the 7 vibration is not entirely a physical and practical force. It exercises a strong pull toward non-physical aspects of life.

Consequently, these children are motivated by a rich complex of physical, mental, and abstract forces. With the exception of the emotional plane (2, 5, and 8), they are free to manifest all their attributes in positive ways.

Demonstration of emotion will be limited, but will be seen in acts of kindness, consideration, and service. Family members can depend upon them for spontaneous and ungrudging help in good times and bad times. These children are not easily influenced by their peers. They respect an orderly way of life and any wise measures taken to discipline them. As they grow older, self-discipline will also be part of their lifestyle. Although an outlet for emotional expression is not a real problem, a first name reducing to 2, 5, or 9 will be good for them. A name with any other number will also be suitable.

Sixteens Born in May (fifth month)

This birth day and birth month combination offers a widespread abundance of personality traits and talents. These children are gifted with the potential for easy access and expression into the physical (1 and 7), emotional (5) and mental (6) realms. The 5 vibration is a versatile and flexible force. When it operates in conjunction with the 1, 6, and 7 vibrations, all of which operate within these children, a multi-faceted and multi-talented personality is formed. At all ages, and especially in adulthood, they will be known for their multi-tasking skills. In order to gain a better understanding of these children, familiarity with all the vibrations within their personality is important. The chapters on the first, fifth, sixth, and seventh days of the month should be consulted as they are an amalgam of some of the best attributes of these forces.

You will need to provide for, as well as cope with, the plurality of outlets for self-expression which these children need. However, they are not likely to be too demanding, clamorous, or show an inordinate sense of entitlement. Their 1 and 5 aspects may contain some of these qualities, but they are effectively subdued by the well-balanced attributes of their combined 6 and 7 aspects. You must remember that they need variety. Given the right opportunities, there is no avenue of study and future employment that these children cannot undertake and succeed in. Their comprehensive personality structure is such that they do not need assistance from a name vibration. Any name can be given to these children.

Sixteens Born in June (sixth month)

All through their lives these children will be influenced by the attributes of the 6 vibration. It is important to refer to the chapter on the sixth day of the month. Reinforced by the powers of the 1 vibration the best attributes of the 6 will be expressed by these personalities. Very few of its negatives should be expected. The underlying 7 combines harmoniously with the 1 and 6 to provide increased strength and avenues for self-expression. In addition, the home-loving and family-oriented qualities of the 6 combine well with the reserved and nature-loving aspects of the 7. Consequently, these children emerge as well-balanced, introspective, and rational individuals.

They will not be children given to an open display of their feelings. Their love of family and home cannot be questioned, but their love of nature will be displayed in deeds rather than words. Their wellbeing could easily be disturbed by a dysfunctional home environment. Whenever there is turmoil in the home they will make every effort within their power to establish peace and harmony. Ego does not rule their lives. They do not overlook consideration for the needs of others. These children could easily undertake the running of a home in the event of the loss of a parent. A given name with a 2, 5, or 9 will be most suitable. Avoid another 6.

Sixteens Born in July (seventh month)

People born on the sixteenth day are qualified Seven personalities (1+6=7). The 1 and 6 vibrations operate at the forefront of their personality while their 7 aspect functions effectively in the background. The powers of the 7 vibration will be more emphatic in those born in the seventh month. The self-assured, reserved, and nature-loving qualities of the 7 vibration will be evident in these children from an early age. If they have no one their own age to play with they are content to enjoy their own company. They can easily appreciate the freedom that comes with being alone. Love of solitude is a rare state of being generally associated mainly with the 7 vibration. Within reason, non-dependence of outside forces is one of its greatest strengths. The chapter on the seventh day of the month provides more information on this vibration.

While the influence of the 7 vibration exercises a strong influence on these children, it is not in full control. Their 1 and 6 aspects play an important role in forming their integral personality. These children consequently possess a good measure of extroversion, sociability, self-esteem, and self-worth with interference from egotistic tendencies. They also possess a rational, analytical, and probing mentality. Any questions they put to elders should be taken seriously. Ample opportunities should be provided for expansion of general knowledge as well as some form of specialization at a future date. As emotional expression will be limited a name reducing to 2, 5, or 9 will be helpful.

Sixteens Born in August (eighth month)

Sixteen children born in the eighth month are favored with four outlets for self-expression as well as variable personality traits. Differences exist in each outlet or vibration. At the same time, there are certain similarities. Both conditions coalesce to form a strong and capable individual who will invariably assume a role as a leader and decision maker, and never as a follower. They are, by and large, extroverted and competitive children. They also possess attributes that deter them from unfair and ruthless competitive behavior. There is a good balance between self-acquisition and self-advancement, and the recognition of the rights and needs of others. As adults they are likely to be attracted to the business side of life.

To a reasonable degree they should be allowed to make their own decisions and find their own direction. Parents may be assured that they are not likely to fall into extremes of behavior. Nor will they seek outlets for escape from the realities of life. The powers to fight and overcome exist in each vibration comprising their personality, and especially in their combined state. Any name will suit these multi-faceted children.

Sixteens Born in September (ninth month)

There are three vibratory forces in this birth day and birth month combination that manifest in impersonal, altruistic, unmercenary tendencies, and social awareness. But they do so in different ways. The chapters on the sixth, seventh, and ninth days of the month provide

127

much information on this major aspect of all Sixteen personalities born in September.

Community orientation, teaching, and counseling, among other things, are strong elements of the 6 vibration. An innate desire will inevitably drive them to sooner or later probe into non-physical or spiritual realms, and a discussion of their findings with selected associates will emerge from their 7 aspect. A humanitarian and global view of life is a gift of their birth month. At the same time the force of their 1 vibration will provide the impetus and self-confidence to activate these powers.

These are potentially superior children, sensitive to all aspects of life. They can easily develop into elegant, refined speech and body language. A stable home environment is essential for these fine qualities to emerge. Dysfunctional conditions could easily delay their development. You should present these children with ample opportunities for learning on a wide scale as well as encourage them to interact with all sorts of people and social conditions. By nature, they are multi-taskers with wide-open minds that need to be fed. It is not likely that they would take to specialization or conformity to one form of development. Any name will suit these multi-talented children.

Sixteens Born in October (tenth month)

Please refer to the section on Sixteens born in January (first month). There is no difference between these personalities. The zero in the tenth month does not add any fresh attributes.

Sixteens Born in November (eleventh month)

Please refer to the section on Sixteens born in January (first month). These children are in most ways similar to those born in January, but the influence of the 1 vibration is much stronger. They could be more emphatic in speech and action, and a bit more stubborn too. A first name reducing to 2, 5, 6, or 9 will introduce more cooperation and sharing of ideas and possessions.

Sixteens Born in December (twelfth month)

These are children with a kindly, cooperative, and sharing temperament, as well as considerable inner strength. They may readily give of their possessions and services but they do possess the ability to state a firm "No" when they feel that someone may be taking advantage of their willingness to help. They are self-confident and multi-talented with well-balanced personalities. Any name will suit them.

Seventeenth Day of the Month

17 reduces to (1+7=8)

Children born on the seventeenth day have the influence of the 1 and 7 vibrations in the outer personality and the 8 vibration functioning in the background. Children with this combination of vibratory forces will be thinkers, planners, and organizers. The 1, 7, and 8 vibrations do not operate exclusively of each other but blend harmoniously to create a positive and self-sufficient personality. These children are therefore firmly individualistic by nature. They are not easily led or misled. They may admire and follow the example of those they consider more knowledgeable and talented than they are, but they are seldom, if ever, hero worshipers. With a keen sense of discrimination they stand by a self-generated sense of values.

Expect them to develop into down-to-earth, practical, and businesslike personalities with elements of duty, responsibility, respect, and a spiritual connection in their thoughts and actions. This latter feature may be unconscious at early stages of life but brought into conscious knowledge as they grow older. They can also show intolerance and an unyielding attitude toward others who do not measure up to their standards of work and conduct. They can flare up in anger but soon subside. They also possess the potential to take responsibility for their lives as well as show respect for parental authority. They may not be free from an occasional lapse from a strict code of conduct but they do have the capacity to become aware of such conduct and make amends because they possess an inner knowledge of right and wrong. Basically, they possess all the requirements to experience life as they choose to experience it. In other words they may not expect too much parent involvement in their activities.

These children are actors rather than reactors. They can, to a large extent, resist being influenced by negative people and conditions they may be forced to put up with. Many of these advantageous powers will be at an early stage in childhood but progressively increase as their worlds expand and choices increase. They also possess the potential to grow positively out of a home life that is, or has been dysfunctional, especially with a mother or father with poor parenting skills. Having a good attention span they are conscientious students with probing minds wanting to get behind and beyond the surface of things. Taking the initiative to study on their own is a natural feature, and they are unlikely to require assistance outside the classroom. They will not at any stage become a target for bullies. In fact, they will often be admired for the knowledge they possess over and above many of their peers.

These children are sensitive, considerate, and generous by nature, but they do not externalize their emotions. They may find it embarrassing to be openly affectionate. They are most unlikely to display any inappropriate emotions. Fluency of speech is not one of their stronger points, but when they do speak out, they do so in short, meaningful words and sentences. Others take notice of what they say. Although competitiveness is not absent from their general make-up, they cannot be pressured into many sporting activities. They can be quite competitive when they choose to do so, although body contact sports may be avoided.

These are children who do not suffer from an excessive sense of entitlement. Within reason, their natural tendency is to do and get things for themselves. Their need to make their own decisions should not be taken away from them by over-protective or over-concerned parents. A domestic way of life will not be attractive to them as they grow older. They are almost entirely career-oriented, especially in administration, organization, and business. They will also turn out as good money managers. Any name will suit these clever children.

Seventeens Born in January (first month)

Children and adults with this birth day and birth month combination display a natural tendency to take charge of all circumstances in which they find themselves. Exceptions are unlikely as direct leadership is a major aspect of the 1 vibration operating in their birth day and birth month. In addition, as qualified Eight personalities (1 + 7 = 8), they are motivated by powers of organization, method, and administration. Their 7 aspect is not undermined in the face of these assertive forces. It may not possess leadership aspirations as it has other agendas but it does contribute toward a strong individualistic and non-dependent nature.

These children are consequently filled with self-confidence, authority, decisiveness, and self-reliance as well as a strong element of intolerance of others. They expect others to measure up to their high standards of efficiency. In other words, they do not suffer fools gladly. They could rebel against parents and elders lacking in nurturing skills. They may refuse to be mollycoddled and early in life insist on standing on their own feet. Within reason, parents should allow them to do so. However, their independent nature should not be mistaken for disloyalty or self-centeredness. They are, in fact, exceptionally loyal, supportive, and defensive of loved ones. Their emotionally undemonstrative nature may often be the cause for misunderstanding. A first name reducing to 2, 5, or 9 may help them to release their feelings. Names reducing to 1, 4, 7, or 8 may increase their controlling tendencies and are best avoided. 3 and 6 names will release some elements of rigidity contained in their personality.

Seventeens Born in February (second month)

People born on the seventeenth day are qualified Eight personalities (1+7=8) who display a controlling nature. Attributes of their 1 and 8 vibrations are responsible for this condition. They are forces that unconsciously and consciously take charge of the lives of those around them. As children enter into adulthood and are exposed to wider experiences and relationships, their controlling tendencies are certain to be increased. These children are, at the same time, strongly influenced by attributes of the 7 vibration which help people take charge of themselves and improve their own personality before taking responsibility for others. The 7 reduces the controlling tendencies of the 1 and 8 aspects in these children to some degree. Such reduction will be helped by the 2 vibration in their birth month. Qualities of this vibration are directed toward service and helpfulness rather than self-acquisitiveness and self-assertiveness. The chapter on the second day of the month reveals more information on this genteel force.

These children can conduct their affairs with the strength of positive thought, speech, and action, while acknowledging to a fair extent the rights of others as well as their own. In other words, they possess the potential to help themselves as well as others. Ego-centeredness, which is a strong attribute of their 1 and 8 aspects, is reduced by the combined 2 and 7 forces. These are clever, self-confident, and well-balanced children who are not likely to fall into any extremes of behavior. There is a strong self-examining element in their personality. Any name will suit these children.

Seventeens Born in March (third month)

Devoid of other influences, Seventeen personalities are likely to project a thoughtful, businesslike, disciplined, and to some degree, reserved temperament. However, as these people do not stand alone, influences from other areas of their birth date, especially their birth month, either intensify these attributes or extend them into fresh avenues of self-expression. The latter condition is what takes place with children born in March, the third month. The chapter on the third day of the month reveals the reason for this expansion.

These children are blessed with the capacity to take a responsible view of life with its many demands, as well as adopt a joyful and light-hearted approach. They will be talkative, responsive, and inquisitive children who insist on knowing the whys and wherefores of things. They are also gifted with originality and creativity, and the ability to defend themselves. With self-confident egos, their plans and ambitions are not regarded as beyond their reach. They are leaders and organizers, and certainly not submissive followers. Even some degree of compromise could be difficult. They are sentimental and romantic but their emotions are held in check. Give them advice and instructions with caution as they are much too perceptive to be taken in by inaccuracy or deception. Any name will suit these clever children.

Seventeens Born in April (fourth month)

Attributes of the 1, 4, and 7 vibration from the physical plane operate in full force in the personality of children with this birth day and birth month combination. They are, in addition, strengthened by the qualities of the underlying 8 in their birth day. These are, in fact, qualified Eight personalities (1+7=8). Their behavior will soon indicate that they are self-confident, practical, down-to-earth, and well-organized children with a firm sense of purpose.

Self-reliance will be displayed early in life, and these children will not suffer from doubts and fears over their ability to engage in practical and physical tasks and activities. Once a decision has been made by them they cannot be tempted by others or circumstances to change a course of study or subsequently, employment. Parents will observe qualities of loyalty, steadfastness, helpfulness, support, and reliability, as well as concentration and stubbornness. These children are likely to be quite passionate in all they undertake but not emotionally demonstrative. A clear distinction between passion and emotion can be seen in their behavior. Action will always be more important to them than speech. They can speak enthusiastically about their work but not as lively general conversationalists.

Most names will suit these skilful children. But avoid a repetition of 1, 4, 7, or 8. As these children are also of a fairly serious temperament, extroverted vibrations such as 2, 3, 6, or 9 will suit them best.

Seventeens Born in May (fifth month)

This combination of birth day and birth month vibrations produces authentic all-rounders, multi-taskers, adventurers, and originators. Limits can only be placed on the potential of these children by social and economic conditions or by a dysfunctional family life. Manual dexterity, fearlessness, a spirit of adventure, originality, independence, and mental and physical restlessness are some of their natural personality traits. While giving them a reasonable sense of direction in life, parents do not deprive them of the freedom they need to develop in accordance with their own potential and natural disposition.

These children are certain to make their share of mistakes but they are not without the ability to rectify matters. They act for the most part along self-confident and positive lines. They will resent too much parental interference. Parents are not likely to succeed in realizing their own ambitions in these children. If they happen to do so it would be due to the child's choice and not the choices of the parents. A competitive spirit and self-defense, orally and physically, are among their strong attributes. These children will always demand space and opportunities for mental and physical development. Any name will suit these versatile children.

Seventeens Born in June (sixth month)

Attributes of the physical, mental, and emotional planes function in varying degrees of power in this birth day and birth month combination. Sensitivity to ethical, non-physical, and spiritual values is also present. The chapters on the sixth and seventh days of the month will be useful for a better understanding of these children.

These are personalities with rational minds who "think before they leap". Their thought processes are governed by calculation, deliberation, and an awareness of consequences. These children will display a balanced and positive outlook on life. Irrational, impulsive, and extremes of behavior will be exceptional. Emotional demonstration will be under strict control, but passion and earnestness in whatever they undertake will be governing factors.

They are personality types who seek to know and govern themselves before they attempt to lead or influence others. Even at a young age, and certainly in adulthood, others will approach them for help in the proper and efficient conduct of life. One of their special interests will be accumulation of useful knowledge in the art of living. As they are not children who will be tied down in one or two aspects of development, they should be given every opportunity for expansion in physical, mental, and spiritual realms. Any name will suit these adventuresome children.

Seventeens Born in July (seventh month)

Attributes of the 7 vibration will exercise a pronounced influence upon the personality of Seventeen children born in the seventh month. The chapter on the seventh day of the month is recommended.

The 7 vibration contains two sets of attributes – one containing practicality, manual dexterity, down-to-earth values, and financial acumen. The other possesses certain spiritual and mystical traits. The former will mingle and strengthen the 1 and 8 aspects of the personality of these children, while the latter will deflect to a fair extent, self-assertiveness, materialism, strong competitiveness, and a tendency to take control. To a fair degree a detachment from worldliness will develop in these children.

They will certainly display a strong sense of identification with nature. Childhood and adult hobbies, career choices, and occupations are all likely to be directed into natural surroundings for example, gardening, conservation of the environment, and interests in pets, such as birds and other domesticated animals. Directness, honesty, and brevity of speech will stand out as marks of their generally reserved and contemplative temperament. As children, they learn much more by listening and observing, and as they grow older, by investigation and research. These are naturally self-assured and clever children who can be given any name from 1 to 9. But one with a 7 is best avoided. An additional 7 influence is not needed.

Seventeens Born in August (eighth month)

Future business men and women, administrators, organizers and executives are born with this birth day and birth month combination. All people born on the seventeenth day are qualified Eight personalities (1+7=8). Attributes of their fundamental 8 vibration are reinforced in those born in the eighth month. As a result, there will be the inevitable pull toward high achievement in public life. The chapter on the eighth day of the month provides more information on the 8 vibration.

The reinforced 8 nature in these children is also complemented by many attributes in the 1 and 7 forces – especially the originality and leadership qualities of the 1 and the responsibility and financial acumen of the 7. Age will not deter these children from taking charge of circumstances in which they find themselves. Not only will they consciously and unconsciously take charge of their own lives, they will also attempt to control the lives of those close to them. They may use dominant traits of willpower, discipline, and authority for personal gain in adulthood. Having fulfilled their ambitions many such personalities transform into public benefactors and philanthropists, as they are not without an understanding of the needs of others.

Parents with material wealth should not spoil these children with an excess of praise or worldly goods, as they could easily develop an unrealistic sense of entitlement which is certain to conflict with their experience outside family life. Nor should they concern themselves unduly about their ability to succeed in life. All these children need is reasonable guidance. They will eventually get by under their own steam. Names reducing to 1, 4, 7, and 8 are best avoided. Any other name will introduce relaxation and a degree of frivolity into their lives.

Seventeens Born in September (ninth month)

Attributes of the 1, 7, 8, and 9 vibrations are introduced into the personality of these children. The nature of these forces is such that they do not coalesce automatically to form a single united force. They separate into two distinct sets characteristics—one formed by an affinity between the 1 and 8 vibrations, and the other by many similarities between the 7 and 9. The combined features inherent and manifested in the former, provides these children with a confident and positive outlook on life. Willpower, ambition, leadership, competitiveness, a strong ego, and a generally materialistic outlook are some of their contributions. The collective influence of the 7 and 9 creates a desire for study, investigation, and research. Self-advancement along moral, ethical, and spiritual lines is also a significant feature within these vibrations.

This dichotomy may create a degree of confusion and hesitation within immature personalities. But this need not continue as a problem because the two sets of characteristics need not be regarded as mutually exclusive to each other. With self-education and a conscious effort they can be combined to create a superior and successful individual, both in private and public life.

These are intelligent, inquisitive, and intuitive children who will develop an international outlook on life. Their body language will be refined and dignified. Their speech will be modulated and precise. Their natural traits can only be damaged from a badly dysfunctional upbringing. Any name will suit these sensitive yet powerful children.

Seventeens Born in October (tenth month)

The presence of the zero in a birth day or birth month does not indicate that additional attributes are introduced. The zero is a zero and has no assets of its own. Children born on the seventeenth day and the tenth month are no different from those born in January, the first month. Please refer to the section relating to Seventeens born in January.

Seventeens Born in November (eleventh month)

Seventeen children born in the eleventh month possess almost the same temperament as those born in January. However, as the 1 vibration is present in double force in November, its attributes are emphasized in these children. Strength of will, assertiveness, and the tendency to take control are some qualities that are heightened. Names reducing to 1, 4, 7, and 8 are best avoided. Any other number will be suitable.

Seventeens Born in December (twelfth month)

The 2 vibration in December will combine well with the 7 in the birth day of these children. This combination will reduce many assertive and controlling qualities in their 1 and 8 aspects. These will be well-balanced personalities who will not display any extremes of behavior. The best names will be those with numbers 2, 3, 5, 6, and 9. Avoid names with 4, 7, and 8.

Eighteenth Day of the Month

18 reduces to (1+8=9)

Children born on the eighteenth day have the influence of the 1 and 8 vibrations in the outer personality and the 9 vibration functioning in the background. A powerful combination of vibrations operates within this birth day/month. Please refer to the chapters on the first and eighth days of the month, followed by the chapter on the ninth day of the month. You will notice a contradiction between these areas of the inner and outer personalities.. 1 and 8 attributes will be prominent during early stages of life and 9 features will begin to emerge at various stages of adulthood, depending on the degree of self-education the individual has acquired.

These children possess the motivation to do their best in whatever they undertake. As they grow older they will use their motivating attributes to help others. They will also be seen as strongly competitive individuals. But their competitive nature is of a healthy form with a good element of sportsmanship. As their lives expand, and choices and decisions have to be made, these children possess the courage to do things as they see best and not necessarily as others tell them to do. They could revolt against dominant and controlling parents and elders. Many such children could be more advanced in their thought processes than their age would indicate. The fact that they may not always be aware of this condition often leads to confusion when they encounter others with less advanced thoughts. Their confusion gets mixed up with intolerance and frustration.

As these children possess the potential to develop without too much elder interference, they may not choose to live according to their family's set of values. They possess the potential to exceed parental expectations. They are also children who will not submit to peer pressure. Their natural capacity for direct leadership and leading by example will not place them in this position. On the contrary, they may gather around them an admiring group of followers. A good academic education will evoke these faculties to a higher level than would develop naturally. They are born with a heightened capacity to absorb a wide variety of knowledge and gain a comprehensive view of life.

They are individuals who could be demanding and intolerant at early stages of life, but much less so as they grow into maturity. This takes place when the understanding and compassionate aspects of their 9 vibration become more operative. However, it can be safely said that at all stages of their lives their angry selves are not their real selves.

These children do not externalize their emotions in speech or in day-to-day interaction with others. They use sport and other physical activities to express them. Their self-confident nature means they do not feel the need to erect a barrier between themselves and others. They are able to relate to people of all ages and conditions and, at the same time, withdraw when they choose to do so. As they grow into maturity, the concept of the world as a global village will be a reality.

With a great deal of potential waiting to be positively exploited, these children can cope with the power of any name. At the same time, names reducing to 1, 4, and 8 may augment sterner aspects of their personality while those with a 2, 5, 6, 7, and 9 may expand their softer aspects.

Eighteens Born in January (first month)

The repetition of the 1 vibration in the birth month will certainly strengthen its attributes within the integral personality. In doing so, the understanding and magnanimous qualities of the underlying 9 vibration may take a longer time to emerge. Self-interest and the urge to take charge of circumstances in which they find themselves will be prominent features. This condition may last until ambitions are fulfilled. Given a stable upbringing, there is no doubt that these children will do so. Success in public life may, however, be achieved with some degree of sacrifice of togetherness in family life.

These children are seldom unsure of themselves in whatever they undertake due to their self-motivating qualities. They flourish with parents who know when to be involved in their development and when to not be involved. They do not need a name with another 1 or 8. Any other name will suit them.

Eighteens Born in February (second month)

There is a clear division within the integral personality of these children. Attributes of each when applied in proper circumstances will be most beneficial to themselves and others. They can also be combined to act most effectively. Their 1 and 8 aspects integrate well to create a mentality of authority, leadership, ego-strength, willpower, and business acumen. These ensure success during their scholastic years and later in public life. Their underlying 9 aspect (these are qualified Nine personalities 1 + 8 = 9) and the 2 of their birth month possess many features that are opposite to those of the 1 and 8. They are, in the first instance non-competitive, cooperative, and collaborative forces. While their 1 and 8 qualities favor acquisition, influence, authority, and prestige among other things, the 2 and 9 combine to introduce qualities of sympathy, understanding, service, and the capacity to acknowledge and appreciate the point of view of others.

The assertive portion of their personality will be advantageous outside the domestic scene while their compassionate qualities are certain to find fulfillment in family and social life. However, when one aspect is prominent the other is not lost or subdued. It remains effective in the background as a safeguard against development of a one-sided personality. These are well-balanced children with the potential to grow into adulthood as responsible and goodwilled individuals. Any name will suit them.

Eighteens Born in March (third month)

The vibrations within the eighteenth day usually form responsible, ambitious, and often stern personalities. They may be inclined to expend too much of their energies in pursuit of their ambitions, getting entrapped in them, and allowing too little time for relaxation and play. As a result, a fair degree of imbalance is created in their lifestyle. The 3 vibration operating in the birth month corrects this condition by contributing a sense of humor, laughter, light-heartedness, and sociability without diminishing their capacity for the exercise of authority and responsibility. The chapter on the third day of the month will show the 3 vibration's attributes of friendliness, enthusiasm, a creative imagination, a quick intake of knowledge, and attractive forms of leadership. All these attributes, in various degrees, will enter into the integral personality of Eighteen children born in March.

These children are highly intelligent individuals with the potential to succeed in whatever course of study and work they subsequently undertake. Do not underestimate the high degree of enthusiasm and motivation possessed by these children. Their emotions may not be demonstrated openly in person to person contact but they will be channeled into any type of study, play, or work they undertake. Any name will suit these fine all-rounders.

Eighteens Born in April (fourth month)

Willpower, authority, concentration, discipline, method, organization, practicality, manual dexterity, and financial acumen are just a few outstanding features that will develop in children with this birth day and birth month combination. It is a composition of vibrations that often creates workaholics; they provide the stamina to stand up to hard work and stress.

These are children with constructive minds who do not wait for someone to tell them what should be done or how something should be done. They use their initiative and go ahead and perform any task or fix anything that needs to be fixed. They constantly need to be doing something that produces results.

They expect to be consulted in any move that concerns their welfare. They could be adamant and one-pointed in their views. Use subtlety and diplomacy to get them to change their minds or agree with someone else's ideas. As children they cannot be led or misled by their peers or submit to peer pressure. They are much more competitive than cooperative in all their activities. Others may view them as combative by nature but this is not a true expression of their integral personality. The 9 vibration is strong in their birth day. It introduces qualities of sympathy and understanding of the problems faced by others. When they observe others in genuine difficulties they do not hesitate to provide as much help as they can. At the same time, they do not tolerate people who do not attempt to help themselves. Any name will suit these capable children.

Eighteens Born in May (fifth month)

This is one of a few birth day and birth month combinations that produces genuine all-rounders. As children and adults they are strictly individualistic and freedom-loving. In other words they insist on 'doing their own thing' at all times and in all circumstances. This tendency is certain to bring them into conflict with various forms of authority throughout their lives. They may find themselves thinking and needing to act with speed and ahead of those in authority over them. Patience, cooperation, and collaboration are not active elements within their personality.

As children and as adults they need to be the decision makers in their own affairs and often in the affairs of others. They are exceptionally alert and observant. Childhood years may be fraught with disagreements with parents and elders unless a fair degree of allowance is made for self-development. They can be emotionally explosive at times. They possess the capacity to extricate themselves from difficult situations they may fall into due to a degree of impetuosity that is contained in their personality. Any name will suit these multi-talented and multi-faceted children.

Eighteens Born in June (sixth month)

The 1, 8, 9 and 6 vibrations in this birth day and birth month combination divide themselves into two sets of different personality traits and talents. The 1 and 8 combine to provide leadership, control of people and circumstances, ambition, drive, competition, self-promotion, a materialistic view of life, and a good measure of self-centeredness. Sociability, understanding, deliberation, service, extended vision along non-materialistic lines, cooperation, and community consciousness are some qualities introduced by the 6 and 9 forces. A fuller understanding of these two-sided personalities can be gained by reference to the chapters on the first, eighth, ninth and sixth days of the month.

The combined 1 and 8 aspect of the personality of these children will be more prominent at early stages of life. The 6 and 9 portions functioning in unison will emerge gradually as they grow older. The degree to which they reach a balance in their twofold nature will be relative to the degree in which they achieve success in public life and togetherness in family life. Despite an element of stubbornness, they possess open minds that can be reached by wise parents and elders. They cannot be deceived by shallow or insubstantial instructions or explanations. As their emotions are usually held in check, they often suffer from inner frustration when they encounter others who do not measure up to their higher than average standards of work and conduct. This problem will be most evident in adulthood. Any name will suit these potentially powerful personalities.

Eighteens Born in July (seventh month)

The integral personality of Eighteens born in July is divided into two separate and dissimilar sets of vibratory forces. These children are consequently faced with the challenge of identifying, accepting, and making beneficial use of both aspects of their personality. A gradual process of self-study will reap tremendous benefits, as both aspects are powerful in their own fields. Basically, the combination of the 1 and 8 vibrations tend strongly toward personal power and the acquisition of material wealth. These are vibratory forces that represent leadership, ambition, competition, extroversion, control, assertive egos, and success in the world at large. At the same time the underlying 9 vibration in their birth day shares many features in common with the 7 vibration in their birth month, many of which are contrary to those of the 1 and 8. They create an aspect of personality that contains a subdued ego, non-competitiveness, and an orientation toward self-study, introspection, helpfulness, humanitarianism, and eventually a desire to delve into the spiritual aspects of life.

As a result of these sharp divisions, some confusion is likely to enter into the minds of these children until some degree of balance is brought about between these superior sets of vibrations. To a reasonable extent they should be allowed to figure out things in their own way and in their own time. They are not types who will readily accept what others have to say in matters concerning their view of themselves and of life in general.

Eighteens Born in August (eighth month)

Attributes of the 8 vibration exercise a dominant role on the formation of the personality of children born in August. Please see the chapter on the eighth day of the month for more information on this vibration. Personality traits that will be most evident in these children and adults will be a natural urge to take control over people and circumstances. Some clear tendencies that emerge are the love of power, organization, administration, leadership, and good money management.

These children could also be highly competitive, strong-willed, opinionated, stubborn, and self-confident. Many of these traits, which augur well for success in public life, are not always popular in family and social life. These children could be emotionally explosive if they do not get their way in most things. At other times their emotions could be held in check. They may get what they want in life, but in the process they may tread on many toes.

The understanding and compassionate features of their underlying 9 vibration are unfortunately obscured by the strength of their 1 and double 8 aspects. However, it is possible with self-education an earlier policy of "What can I get rather than what can I give" could be overturned. A name with a 1, 4, or 8 should be strictly avoided. Ideal numbers will be 6 or 9.

Eighteens Born in September (ninth month)

The personality of these children who are born in the ninth month is inspired by two sets of characteristics, motivations, and ambitions that are in many respects contrary to each other. Consequently, an element of internal conflict may exist throughout their lives unless an effort is made to gain self-understanding and reconciliation of these differences.

The 1 and 8 vibrations operating in unison form a strong portion of their personality, which is directed toward pursuit of power, influence, leadership, and control. They are supported by attributes of self-confidence, willpower, and assertive egos. The chapters on the first and eighth days of the month provide a good indication of the many effective qualities of these forces. However, in children born in the ninth month, these authoritative tendencies are not permitted to manifest with complete freedom. These are qualified Nine personalities (1+8 = 9). When their underlying 9 traits are reinforced by the 9 vibration of their birth month, another aspect of their personality comes into effect. The 9 vibration is essentially a non-competitive, cooperative, and humanitarian force providing its subjects with a global outlook and a largely impersonal attitude on life.

Their 1 and 8 aspects may be more forceful in their younger years and early adulthood but once they have achieved success in the material world, the generosity of their 9 aspect will emerge, creating a balance between a personal and humanitarian outlook on life. Avoid names with 1, 4, and 8. Any other name will suit these advanced souls.

Eighteens Born in October (tenth month)

The personality of children is no different to Eighteens born in January, (first month). Please refer to that section. The zero does not introduce any fresh attributes. Names with a 1, 4, or 8 should be avoided.

Eighteens Born in November (eleventh month)

Please refer to the section on the Eighteens born in January, (first month). As the month of November contains the 1 vibration as a double feature, its attributes are increasingly emphasized in these children. Names with a 1, 4, or 8 should be avoided.

Eighteens Born in December (twelfth month)

Assertive aspects of the 1 and 8 from the birth day are supported by repetition in the birth month. However, the 2 vibration combines well with the underlying 9 force to introduce a degree of understanding and sympathy into the personality. But the former aspect of the personality may be dominant at early stages of life. Avoid a name with a 1, 4, or 8.

Nineteenth Day of the Month

19 reduces to 1 (1+9=10: 1+0=1)

Children born on the nineteenth day have the influence of the 1 and 9 vibrations in the outer personality and the strength of another 1 vibration functioning in the background. People born on the nineteenth day are motivated by all the positive attributes of the 1 and 9 vibrations. As the 1 vibration appears in the foreground of the personality as well as the background, its qualities will predominate. These children and adults are in fact qualified One personalities (1+9=10 =1). The overall strength of the combined 1 and 9 forces is such that it cannot be weakened or damaged for any length of time by other areas of influence within the integral personality, such as the birth month. It can be expanded and enriched but not weakened. External influences and inevitable reversals in life too, do not alter the overall positive nature of these children. This combination provides tremendous recuperative powers—physically, mentally and emotionally.

Parents may rest assured that a Nineteen child is endowed with the potential to develop as outstanding individuals in all aspects of life. The chapters on the first and ninth days of the month should be combined for a good understanding of these Nineteen children. You will not find mediocrity in any aspects of their behavior. An "I" and "My" mentality found in those directly influenced by the 1 vibration is diminished in these children by the wide horizons and wisdom of their 9 aspect. A fine balance is formed between self-conscious personal desires and an awareness of the presence of others and their needs and expectations. Nineteen children's egos are reduced to a less prominent and dominant role.

These are personalities who will make every effort to live up to their full potential. To start with, a Nineteen child will enter kindergarten with a strong sense of anticipation, and as the years go by, they will never be a target for bullies. Their attention span could vary according to the circumstances in which they find themselves. They will quickly lose concentration in a classroom or social circle that does not measure up to their speed of thought. The problem here is that many Nineteen children are more advanced in their thought processes than their age would indicate. Their emotions are experienced internally and rarely dramatized. They may resist excessive demonstration of emotion from parents and elders. Parents may experience difficulty teaching these children domestic tidiness and attention to other domestic responsibilities. Activities outside the domestic scene will be much more attractive. They do not feel insecure or uncomfortable occupying the center of attention or taking a leading role in any event. They cannot be confined to a limited area of activity or circle of friends and acquaintants. However, their love and loyalty to family cannot be doubted. They will be instantly alert to and available in times of need.

Anything can be obtained from these children when the sympathetic aspect of their nature is approached. But their keen grasp of things may make it difficult for some elders to deal comfortably with them. Parents may be astonished by some of the wise and mature remarks they make. Physical chastizement will certainly be ineffective. The only way to reach these children is to use a mental approach. They are best managed when treated as far as possible as young and responsible adults. Any name will suit these advanced children. Their birth month, especially, could contribute significantly toward the expansion of their personality into other areas of manifestation. The following sections deal with each month.

Nineteens Born in January (first month)

Attributes of the 1 vibration are reinforced in this birth day and birth month combination. Those of the 9 may consequently struggle to exercise a degree of control over some self-centered and assertive aspects of the 1. Their benign, sympathetic, and non-competitive features may take some time to emerge. In the meantime, these children may be wanting and demanding everything for themselves. With strong traits of originality, invention, enterprise, self-confidence, leadership, control, and willpower, they are certain to obtain what they seek. They will effortlessly take responsibility for their decisions and actions, and firmly resist challenge or opposition. Within reason, and in the right circumstances, all these may be taken as positive qualities.

Despite certain willful ways, wise and patient parents may observe that these children possess an approachable opening that can be assessed for creating a balance between self-centeredness and generosity. Their strong sense of individuality has to be taken into consideration. The surest way to alienate them is to downplay this characteristic. Just saying "No" without explanations will not be accepted by them. A name reducing to 2, 6, 7, or another 9 will be best. Any of these will make it easier for them to see the other person's point of view.

Nineteens Born in February (second month)

A good balance between ambition for personal success and an awareness that others possess similar aspirations is an outstanding feature in people with this birth day and birth month combination. Attributes of the 1 vibration operating in strength in their birth day favor the former and those of the latter by the combined effects of the 9 and 2. There are several genteel qualities in the 9 and 2 that serve to round off certain sharp edges of the 1 vibration. Some of these are self-centeredness, egotism, assertiveness, and an acquisitive temperament. While these are considerably reduced, other desirable aspects of the 1, such as decisiveness, leadership, enterprise, and motivation are enriched and expanded. These same 1 attributes, in turn, elicit the positive aspects of the 9 and 2. Without the activating force of the 1, the 2 and 9 are exposed to some of their negative features. The chapters on the first, second and ninth days of the month provide much more information on these forces.

These children possess the dual faculty for experiencing the world, to a reasonable extent, as they choose to do, and to the same degree to sensitively react to certain conditions and circumstances. In both instances they do so with a positive frame of mind. They possess an almost equal ratio of flexibility that relieves them from fixed ideas and arbitrary judgments. They can be directed by circumstances of the moment and a desire to see the big picture. Any name can be given to these strong and open-minded children.

Nineteens Born in March (third month)

These are mentally oriented children who absorb knowledge without effort. With their fertile minds, they display traits of originality, creativity, imagination, and artistry at a very early age. A pleasant voice and fluency of speech are other prominent features. They begin speaking much earlier than average and develop a good vocabulary, with correct pronunciation and accuracy in the use of words. These are also naturally courteous and well-mannered children who need to be told only once to say thank you. They are friendly and considerate children with a good sense of humor. These natural attributes can only be stifled in a dysfunctional upbringing.

They are fond of occupying the center of attention and are quite capable of doing so in intelligent and entertaining ways. As they view the world as a friendly place, they make friends and acquaintances easily. They are generally non-competitive individuals who avoid confrontation and meaningless argument. They use their wit and verbal skills to defend themselves when unable to do so physically. Natural development is speedy, but education will see them develop at a faster rate. Parents should be prepared to cope with their zest for life and swift intake of knowledge. These children need good company. Aloneness and loneliness will interfere with their development.

While the repetition of names adding to 1, 3, and 9 may not be harmful, those adding to 4 and 7 would be best. These will provide more practical skills. A 6 name will add to their mental orientation. 2, 5, and 8 names will help with emotional expression.

Nineteens Born in April (fourth month)

Down-to-earth and practical values are predominant in those enjoying this birth day and birth month combination. While their physical plane vibrations 1 and 4 exercise a strong influence, these children are not without a wide opening into the mental plane of moralistic and humanitarian values and a broad outlook on life. This balance in their personality is provided by attributes of their 9 vibration. These children do not possess a good opening into the emotional plane. Consequently, the deep emotions they do possess are contained and released only on rare occasions. They are not too fond of being cuddled or even touched too often. Their emotions are directed into loyalty, responsibility, dependability, and hard work. Many superior aspects of their 9 vibration impinge upon their speech and actions. The chapters on the 4 and 9 days of the month will be helpful for a better understanding of the personality of these children.

They are essentially positive personalities who seldom fear or doubt their capacity to undertake any task. On the rare occasion they feel inadequate, this would only be an initial barrier that they will soon override. They are not easily led by others but others will often be happy to follow their example. They are certain to turn out as useful little handypersons, both indoors and outdoors. These are naturally strong-minded children who do not need further strengthening from their first name. However, a name with a 2 vibration may soften the tightness they feel in emotional expression.

Nineteens Born in May (fifth month)

Among all Nineteen personalities, the most multi-talented and versatile people are born in the fifth month. Please refer to the chapter on the fifth and ninth days of the month. The chapter on the first day of the month too will reveal the considerable variety of personality traits and talents these children are endowed with. It cannot be denied that this condition results in mental, emotional, and physical restlessness. The urge for frequent change of activity and new experiences are the main motivating factors. Put simply, these are children who cannot keep still for long. They have to be involved in one thing or another. They are certainly capable of extricating themselves from any difficulty that they may fall into. They are not types that instantly look for assistance either.

These are exceptionally alert and courageous children making instant decisions and with quick reflexes. Impatience will always be a prominent trait. Their main personal problem is the vast number of choices that are presented to them by their flexibility, multiple talents, and enterprise. They will be intolerant of others who do not keep pace with their speedy thoughts, speech, and actions. Though not averse to book learning, these children learn more through observation, experimentation, and experience than by instruction. They may lead and influence their peers but will not be lead or influenced themselves. Any name will suit these skilful and entertaining children.

Nineteens Born in June (sixth month)

These children may be qualified One personalities (1+9=10=1) but the attributes of the 9 and 6 vibrations combine sympathetically to form a significant part of their integral personality. They are complementary forces operating on the mental plane with many shared features. For a better understanding of these children please read the chapters on the ninth and sixth days of the month.

One of the first shared features that will be observed is their people-oriented nature. Other desirable personality traits that will develop in these children by virtue of their combined 9 and 6 aspect are compassion, understanding, service, and unselfishness. Personal needs as well as likes and dislikes do not greatly exceed concern for the wellbeing of others. "I" and "My" tendencies of their 1 aspect are changed to a "We" and "Us" approach in family and public life.

The tremendous advantage here is that the self-confidence, willpower, leadership, and originality of the 1 are not reduced but applied successfully in all their relationships and activities. Their egos are refined and leveled out to a degree that ensures success and admiration from people with whom they interact. It would be quite exceptional for these children to incur the enmity of others. They are also children who can form genuine friendships with their parents once the nurturing years have passed. Any name will suit these kindly and broad-minded children.

Nineteens Born in July (seventh month)

The chapters on the ninth and seventh birth days show many sympathetic attributes between the 9 and 7 vibratory forces. Children influenced by either one or the other respond very early in life to the beauty and charms of the natural world. Those influenced by both vibrations feel an even stronger pull toward investigation and contemplation of the inner side of life in natural surroundings as opposed to artificial and materialistic areas. This condition is an early indication of an active spiritual element in both the 9 and 7 vibratory forces. That aspect of their personality influenced by the 1 vibration provides willpower and fearlessness to enter into realms beyond purely physical and mundane activities. At the same time, this vibration along with certain aspects of the 7 will keep these children well-grounded on the physical plane. Practicalities of life will not be neglected but kept separate from their private pursuits.

These are children who can move in and out of social interaction without indecision or fear. They can also enjoy silence and aloneness without feeling negative pangs of loneliness. Occasional contemplative periods should not be mistaken for moodiness. They are never at ease when forced into uncouth and loud-spoken company with superficial values. A dignified posture and refined body language, and a studious mentality will be observed early in life and carried into adulthood. They can remain poised and serene when others display agitation. They are more advanced in their thought processes than their age would indicate. This may create some problems in the classroom. These are generally non-demanding children who do not feel a sense of entitlement. They are also prepared and capable of taking responsibility for their actions. Any name will suit these broad-minded children.

Nineteens Born in August (eighth month)

The chapters on the first and eighth days of the month reveal that the 1 and 8 vibratory forces possess many features in common, and can combine to form a personality with above average willpower, organization, administration, competition, and high ambition. The most obvious trait provided by one or the other of these vibrations is the urge and the ability to take charge of people and circumstances. When they operate in unison the tendency to take control will be more forceful. This characteristic will begin to operate somewhat mildly early in life and strengthen in adulthood. If some of these assertive qualities are allowed free range, certain unsatisfactory aspects of these vibrations may emerge. Pride, self-promotion, egotism, dogmatism, and immediate resentment of any challenge to their views are some of these traits. The forcefulness of these features is reduced in the Nineteen personality by the presence of the 9 vibration. And can be reduced further by a caring upbringing and guidance.

In spite of the expansive and understanding attributes of their 9 aspect, attentive parents may still struggle at times to keep these children under reasonable control due to the overall strength of the 1 and 8 combination. But good nurturing and a proper education can help to create the best version of these children. There is no doubt that they possess the potential for high achievement in all aspects of life. They are well-grounded personalities who can take their stand against anyone who tries to influence them against their will. A name with a number 2, 3, 6, or 9 will be the best. Any one of these will soften the rigidity of some of the 1 and 8 characteristics. A name with a 1, 4, 7 or should be avoided.

Nineteens Born in September (ninth month)

In the course of time, a fine balance of the physical and material side of life and the ethical and spiritual sides will be observed in the words and actions of these children. This condition is the clear result of the interaction between the self-assured and energetic forces of the 1 vibration operating on the physical plane, and the idealistic and open-minded forces of the 9 vibration functioning on the mental plane, with a close affinity with the spiritual. For a better understanding of this combination of birth day and birth month please read the chapters on the first and ninth days of the month.

These children can effortlessly use their high potential for personal advantage without overlooking or overriding the needs and aspirations of others. The relatively equal concern for self-advancement and concern for the wellbeing of others is an outstanding trait. Popularity and success in their studies and subsequently in public life will be certain, due to the respect and understanding of everyone's ideas, while at the same time holding fast to their own. The degree to which these innate attributes of the 1 and 9 attributes are released will certainly depend on family influences, social and economic conditions, and education.

Perceptive parents and elders will not take long to realize that they have the responsibility for nurturing children with high potential for success in all aspects of life. They are extroverted personalities who function at their best in the midst of people of their own mental, physical, and moral levels. Domestic instincts are not strong in these children. They need outside interests that touch the lives of many. They are naturally resilient children with quick recuperative powers from illness or other setbacks of life. Any name will suit these children who will live as receivers as well as givers.

Nineteens Born in October (tenth month)

Please refer to the section on Nineteens born in January, (first month). These birth day and birth month combinations are the same due to the zero in the tenth month, not introducing or taking away any attributes of the nineteenth birth day. A name reducing to the number 1 is best avoided. Any other name will suit these children.

Nineteens Born in November (eleventh month)

Please refer to the section on Nineteens born in January, (first month). The 1 vibration appears four times in Nineteens born in November. Consequently, its attributes are more forceful. Those of the 9 may take a longer time to break through and remain as a contributing force within the personality. The considerate and open-minded features of this vibration are certain to emerge from time to time. Their frequency will depend on the type of upbringing these children receive. A name with the 1 vibration should be strictly avoided. Any other name may be given.

Nineteens Born in December (twelfth month)

In this birth day and birth month combination, the 9 and 2 vibratory forces combine to reduce certain sharp edges the personality may have, due to the controlling forces of the 1 vibration. The 2 and 9 possess many genteel qualities as opposed to the one-pointed thrust of the 1 for self-advancement. A name reducing to a 1, 5, or 8 should be avoided as these are controlling forces which will reduce the generosity and freedom of their 9 aspect.

Twentieth Day of the Month

Please refer to the chapter on the second day of the month. The zero in the twentieth day does not introduce any new features, or take away any existing ones. It may, however, emphasize certain aspects of the 2 vibration.

Twenty-first Day of the Month

21 reduces to 2+1=3

Just as on the twelfth day of each month, children born on the twenty-first day have the influence of the 2 and 1 vibrations in the outer personality with the 3 vibration functioning in the background. The difference between those born on the twelfth and those born on the twenty-first is that in the twelfth, the 1 is the stronger force as it precedes the 2 in sequence. In the twenty-first, the 2 is the stronger force as it precedes the 1. Children of both birth days are qualified Three personalities (1+2=3 and 2+1=3). Twenty-ones are gifted with free access to the physical (1), emotional (2), and mental (3) planes. Their integral personality is therefore a rich combination of the attributes of the 1, 2, and 3 vibrations. Basically, they are endowed with the confidence and leadership of 1 attributes, the adaptability and sensitivity of the 2, and the imagination and optimism of the 3. The chapters on the first, second, and third days of the month give more information on these vibratory forces.

You will see that these are original and clever children, as well as ego-centered personalities. They belong to the "I" and "My" class of personalities as opposed to the "We" and "Us" group. Ego-centeredness is displayed in different ways by their 1, 2, and 3 aspects. The 1 generates a tendency to take charge of people and circumstances. The 3 is a self-conscious and largely dependent force. Those influenced by this vibration expect constant attention. The 3 vibration is essentially a merger of 1 and 2 attributes.

The tendency of these personalities to think firstly of their own needs and ambitions well before they are aware of the needs and desires of others, is a common feature of any of these vibrations. When all three forces are combined in a single personality this tendency is naturally enhanced.

However, self-centeredness in these children should not be equated with selfishness as all three vibrations also contain qualities of generosity, helpfulness, loyalty, and support. These remain as underlying qualities that need to be awakened from time to time by exterior agencies. Good nurturing and a sound general education will bring out a fine balance between concern for self and concern for others.

Parents and elders will soon discover that these children are independent thinkers who are likely to resent excessive parental control. Parents may succeed to some degree in directing their activities but not their thoughts and dreams. They will insist on putting their own thoughts and dreams into action in their own way. Inception of this inherent trait will be most evident when these children reach their teens. They may possess strong willpower but they are also endowed with equal elements of good manners and accessibility. They are open to instruction as long as it is given with tact and consideration. Beneath their sometimes over-confident façade, they possess a friendly, sensitive, and sociable nature. There is certainly a fair degree of complexity within their integral personality structure. These children could also feel a sense of entitlement which leads to a tendency to be demanding. At the same time, when making their demands they are seldom disrespectful.

Their original and imaginative qualities are such that they do not accept as inevitable the circumstances in which they find themselves. Rarely given to boredom or moodiness, they constantly look out for outlets for self-expression. They do not suffer from anxieties usually felt by people unable to live up to the expectations of others. Tendency toward individual action may be stronger than attraction to group activity. In the event of membership with a group or association, they soon find their way into a role of leadership or decision-making. They display very little or no shyness during their interaction with their peers or in communication with older people. Their school days will be happy and successful. Seldom, if ever, will they be at odds with their teachers or schoolmates. Being very much self-directed personalities, they will never remain content in secondary or subordinate roles. Any name will suit these gifted children. The only aspect of their personality that needs strengthening is the awareness that others need attention as much as they do. A name with a 6 or 9 will be ideal. The number or vibration of the birth month is responsible for significant variations in the integral personality. These are now given in the sections below.

Twenty-ones Born in January (first month)

The repetition of the 1 vibration in the birth month results in reinforcement of its attributes at the expense of the 2 and 3 aspects of the personality. The 1 vibration may emphasize self-interest and stifle, to some degree, the gentle qualities of the 2 vibration and the light-hearted and generous qualities of the 3. These changes may strengthen the personality in many ways, but children with this birth day and birth month are likely to take a longer time to realize that the needs of others are as important as their own, and on certain occasions, more so.

There is no doubt that these personalities, in childhood, in their teens and as adults, possess the initiative, self-confidence, optimism, and intelligence for rapid self-development and fulfillment of their ambitions. They do not hesitate to take a stand against people and conditions that may interfere with their own ideas and plans. To say an emphatic "No" is never a difficulty. They do not falter under pressure. They may even use stress as a motivational condition. They prefer to acquire knowledge more through self-motivation, experimentation, and observation than by direct instruction from others. Parents and elders receive a better response from these children if they listen to their opinions. Parents who foolishly look down upon their ideas and ambitions get nowhere near them. Wise parents know when to be involved with these children and when not to be involved. The best names for these children will be a repetition of 2, 5, 6, and 9. The numbers 1, 4, 7, and 8 should be avoided.

Twenty-ones Born in February (second month)

Although these children are qualified Three personalities (2 + 1 = 3), the attributes of the 2 vibration will exercise a good deal of influence upon their personality. They will also be displayed in positive ways. None of the negative qualities of this vibration, such as shyness, self-consciousness, and sensitivity will be allowed entry into their general conduct. The strength and self-confidence attributes of their 1 and 3 aspects will ensure that this does not happen. The effectiveness of these latter forces is not in any way reduced by the prominence of positive 2 qualities. In fact, they may be enlarged by the 2 qualities of cooperation, compromise, and companionship. This interaction makes these children more willing to spend time and energy helping others, and especially to perform their share of domestic duties. The 2, among other things, is a vibration of care and service. It is also the vibration of attraction. People under its influence attract many good things in life that others have to strive for. It is also a physical force that gives its subjects occasional glimpses into the higher dimensions of life. This faculty may confuse many children but will soon be forgotten as they grow older. They could always be resuscitated in adulthood. The presence of the 2 also contributes toward the formation of a fluid, rhythmic, and supple physical body. These children are performing artists, especially in dance and gymnastics. They will be equally skilled with the written word, the spoken word, and numbers. Any name will suit these clever children. A repetition of any of their birth day or birth month numbers will do no harm.

Twenty-ones Born in March (third month)

The repetition of the 3 vibration will result in an amplification of artistic talents in these qualified Three personalities (2+1=3). Another result will be the creation of sensitive egos that expect acknowledgment of their presence in any company as well as praise and attention. Deprived of the company of their age group or admiring adults, much of these children's initiative and wellbeing will be inhibited. One of their greatest fears will be social exclusion. They are never at ease in a quiet place.

These are mentally restless children who need constant mental stimulation and outlets for self-expression. To them the world is a friendly and beautiful place. Quite early in life they will turn out to be great talkers, as fluency and accuracy in speech, as well as a lively sense of humor, are some of their strong points. They will not hesitate to correct anyone who may use incorrect words or phrases in their speech. They do not mean to be rude; but their high sense of accuracy prompts them to do so. Parents and elders need to be alert to their sharp wits and instant retorts. Twenty-ones may not allow slow or deliberate talkers to finish their sentences due to their speed of thought, and may finish their sentences for them. Their emotions are directed into artistic creations and entertaining behavior; they are not physically demonstrative with frequent embraces and cuddles. In the classroom they are likely to find themselves ahead of their age group, which may result in restlessness and boredom. Avoid a name with another 3 vibration.

Any other name will suit them.

Twenty-ones Born in April (fourth month)

There are several outstanding attributes in this birth day and birth month combination. Originality, a creative imagination, practicality, artistic talents, and manual dexterity are just a few. These children are simply overloaded with a multiplicity of potential in several directions.

The originality and thrust of the 1 vibration, the fantasy and fertile imagination of the 2 and 3, and the practicality and perseverance of the 4 combine easily to make their dreams come true. And they are certain to entertain many varied dreams. It is not possible to suggest a particular course of study best suited to them as any direction is open to these versatile and multi-faceted personalities. Decisions may depend upon social, economic, and family conditions. They will be successful in whatever course of study or work they undertake. They are mentally and physically active children who need to engage in a variety of activities in order to satisfy their natural creativity. There is nothing dull or predictable in their behavior.

These are not children who suffer from highs and lows in their conduct. Expect balanced development. They are self-confident and self-sufficient children who are not easily led or misled. Parents may rest assured that, within reason, they are able to look after themselves. In interaction with family members, they can be won over but not ordered about, when requested to undertake their share of domestic responsibilities. The best way to gain their cooperation is to treat them as intelligent and responsible personalities. Any name will suit these all-rounders.

Twenty-ones Born in May (fifth month)

The chapter on the fifth day of the month shows the extraordinary impact the 5 vibration makes on the 1, 2, and 3 forces of the twenty-first birth day. All the active and extroverted features of this birth day and month combination are intensified and extended into additional areas of self-expression.

These children are exceptionally alert, active, experimental, and changeable. Life will be an adventure to be experienced with optimism, courage, and curiosity. Their days will be filled with a variety of activity and change of scene. They will be delightful and entertaining personalities who are certain to create problems if their parents are possessive or fearful. Busy parents and teachers will find their mental and physical restlessness rather exhausting and often disrupting. Their demand for attention and outlets for self-expression will be more than that of an average child. They are also great talkers who take command of conversation, using a variety of stories and anecdotes, mainly relating to their own interests.

They possess ample energy and resources needed to get what they want out of life. As change and the ability to cope with change brought about by other forces is a natural characteristic, they do not stop long enough to enjoy and appreciate what they have acquired. They need some degree of stability or steadfastness. A name reducing to a 4 or a 7 will be ideal. Avoid names with 2, 3, 5, or 9. A 6 or 8 will be fine.

Twenty-ones Born in June (sixth month)

Family attachment and social consciousness are prominent among the many attributes of the 6 vibration. The principal effect of this orientation is an unconscious shift from a self-centered "I" and "My" consciousness to one of a "We" and "Us" mentality. The powerful forces of 1, 2, and 3 will be used for personal benefit as well as to the advantage of all those with whom these children interact. Please see the chapter on the sixth day of the month.

The degree and speed by which 6 attributes are used will depend on an ethical upbringing. These attributes are not totally lost in a child who has suffered a dysfunctional home life, but rather, may take some time to emerge. These are children who can be called upon to help in domestic chores, and when required, to care for younger brothers and sisters. Any task allocated to them will be accepted dutifully and performed responsibly. They also need a good deal of time tending to their own devices. These are also children with rational minds who are confident and outspoken in disagreement and controversy. They choose their friends and acquaintances wisely, not easily submitting to peer pressure. They are not open to a full expression of their emotions, choosing to demonstrate more in deeds rather than words. Any name will suit these loyal children.

Twenty-ones Born in July (seventh month)

The chapter on the seventh day of the month shows how the 7 vibration contains many features that are contrary to those of the 1, 2, and 3 of the twenty-first day. This is a vibration that pulls its subjects away from excessive attachment to things of the material and physical worlds, and introduces them to the world of nature and spirit. Manifestation of the spiritual nature of the 7 vibration may take various forms; the most widespread being a comprehensive love of all things of the natural world. Inquiry into abstract or esoteric realities of life develops later, subject to family life, and social and cultural conditioning.

Though the 1, 2, and 3 vibrations forming the fundamental personality tend toward material and physical wellbeing, they are not without a spiritual element. The problem here is that these personalities may be overwhelmed by outer forces at the expense of their inner nature. The 7 qualities of their birth month need to be awakened. Various factors can be responsible for this happening. The extrasensory perception of the 2 vibration and the deep intuitive nature of the 7 will be responsible for much self-awakening. These children may need to withdraw from time to time into quiet, private spots for contemplation. They should be introduced very early in life to a wide variety of music and literature which will expedite their development toward becoming knowledgeable and perceptive human beings. Any name will suit these clever children.

Twenty-ones Born in August (eighth month)

The aspect of people born on the twenty-first day that tends to take charge of their own affairs and, if allowed, the affairs of others, will be intensified and expanded in Twenty-ones born in the eighth month. Essential attributes of the 8 vibration are control, administration, and organization. When this force is coupled with the combined strength of the 1, 2, and 3 vibrations, it will be almost impossible to prevent or hold back the budding tendencies in these children toward willpower, leadership, control, and insistence. These may be, to a degree, admirable and rewarding attributes in certain conditions, especially in adulthood. But they may be difficult to cope with in childhood and adolescence. However, parents will derive the advantage of these children's independence and self-sufficiency.

Given reasonable opportunities, the potential for these personalities to combine academic achievement with success in any form of sport will be evident early in life. Competition, motivation, and pride of achievement are among many contributing factors. It is not in their nature to believe that some ambition is out of their reach. Well-meaning parents, who have their own ideas about what these children should or should not study, or what sport they may enter, could be disappointed. These children would rather make up their own minds. Domestic instincts are not strong. It may not be easy to get them to abide by a share of personal and domestic responsibilities. They are essentially outdoor personalities. Avoid choosing a name with the numbers 1, 4, 5, or 8. These numbers may increase these children's controlling tendencies. Any other number will suit them.

Twenty-ones Born in September (ninth month)

Refer to the chapter on the ninth day of the month to see how the 9 vibration is essentially an outward-looking force as opposed to the inward, or largely ego-centered forces, symbolized by the 1, 2, and 3 vibrations. People born in the ninth month are not entirely removed from self-interested thought processes and actions, but they are certain to experience promptings from within themselves that as well as their own needs, consideration should be given to the presence and needs of others. They may also pay more attention to reminders from others of this need.

Opportunities for self-expression will be expanded. The 9 vibration provides the potential to develop a strong sense of identification with life as a whole. Parents may not need to frequently explain too many facts of life. These children have an instinctive understanding within the integral personality. They are extroverted personalities with evenly distributed personality traits. It is most unlikely that they will fall into extremes of behavior. They will be eager to make friends and enliven their friendships with laughter and humor, and they will entertain friends with mental flexibility. As their 9 aspect introduces a rare touch of wisdom, they are likely to come out with comments and opinions not expected of their age. Any name will suit these popular children.

Twenty-ones Born in October (tenth month)

Please refer to the section on Twenty-ones born in January (first month). The zero in the tenth month does not introduce any new features. The most it may do is to emphasize certain 1 attributes. A 1 name should be avoided. Any other name will suit them.

Twenty-ones Born in November (eleventh month)

Please refer to the section on Twenty-ones born in January (first month). All aspects of the 1 vibration are intensified within the integral personality of people born in November. Ego-consciousness and individuality especially, are prominent features. A name reducing to the number 1 should be avoided. Any other name may be given.

Twenty-ones born in December (twelfth month)

The repetition of the numbers 1 and 2 in the birth month has the effect of strengthening the willpower of the 1 aspect and at the same time increasing the genteel and polite qualities of the 2 and 3 vibrations. Consequently, a fine balance is formed in the behavior of these children. They may still remain ego-centered but their conduct will not be assertive and demanding. Names with the numbers 1, 2, 3, and 8 should be avoided. The numbers 5, 6, 7, or 9 will be best.

Twenty-second Day of the Month

22 reduces to 4 (2+2=4)

Children born on the twenty-second day have the strong influence of two 2s in the outer personality and the 4 vibration functioning in the background. The number 22 symbolizes a 'power-plus' vibratory force, considered as a Master Number (along with the 11). A Master Number is one that is not reduced to a single digit as is the practice with all multiple digits. Its merits may be considered in its full potential or at a considerably reduced rate, as not many of us possess the soul maturity or are given the opportunity to reach up to its elevated heights. Most children will be influenced predominantly by the 4 vibration until they have greater opportunities to draw from the powerful 22.

In a few children, some exceptional qualities may appear for brief periods during their developing years. The unique nature of the 22 vibration is found in two sets of vibratory forces. One operates on an elevated plane of moral, ethical, humanitarian, and spiritual values; the other, on a down-to-earth plane of physical and material values. The latter force precedes the former at early stages of life, and the degree to which the former begins to emerge, intermittently depends on conditions of growth. Some children may begin to experience certain stirrings that lead to their questioning things other than the purely physical and material. Either way, these children are born with a heightened capacity for understanding the complexities of life.

These children will invariably live up to what is expected of them with qualities of reliability, steadfastness, and loyalty. They are also gifted with hands containing extraordinary strength as well as delicacy of touch. This condition enables them to undertake the most arduously heavy work as well as the most minute and delicate. They are certainly all-round handypersons. Until these Twenty-two personalities reach their higher levels of potential they operate as powerful Four personalities. The chapter on the fourth day of the month may be helpful for a better understanding of these children. However, unlike the regular Four personality, most Twenty-two children who connect with their higher potential are forward thinkers who need to constantly break out of conventional values and practices. There is little that is commonplace or predictable about their thought processes and ambitions.

An anomaly in the personality of the Twenty-two is that they can appear quite unyielding in their convictions and conduct, but at different times soft, gentle, and flowing. The best way to control a degree of inconsistency in their moods is to keep them occupied. Provide them with things to build, put together, or repair. Their minds are geared along constructive lines. Thoughtful parents may observe the gradual emergence of a deeply intuitive nature and a desire to reach out beyond family life into social and humanitarian problems. These children will develop a desire to play an active role in solving such problems. Most Twenty-two children are practical idealists. This condition will reach its maturity in those who eventually merge the earth-bound and spirit-bound aspects of their personality.

The number or vibration of the birth month is responsible for certain significant changes in the personality of Twenty-two children. Not all Twenty-twos act as a single or standard type. These differences are listed in the following sections.

Twenty-twos Born in January (first month)

The vibration symbolized by the number 1 is known as the activator. Its presence in the birth month ensures a positive application of the vibrations of the birth day. The Twenty-two personality therefore receives a tremendous boost through a selective choice of the most advantageous qualities of the 1 vibration, such as self-confidence decisiveness, willpower, and consistency. Ego-centered qualities of the 1 do not exercise a strong influence upon the personality due to the wide horizons of the 22. What the 1 vibration actually does is to add strength to an already strong personality.

These children can complete and succeed in anything they set out to do. While staying well-grounded on the physical plane with all its practical demands, they can also reach out into higher cultural and spiritual realms without losing a sense of balance. An even balance may not be realized for some time as they need to gain knowledge and experience on physical levels before entering into esoteric realms. Any name will suit these extraordinary children.

Twenty-twos Born in February (second month)

An obvious feature in this birth day and birth month combination is the excess of the number 2 or the 2 vibration. This vibration is a giving and receiving force. The chapter on the second day of the month provides more information on this genteel vibration. It does not provide the active energy or thrust needed for fulfilling the full potential of the Twenty-two birth day. In fact, its presence in the birth month may act as an obstructive or defeating force as many negative aspects of the 2 vibration are likely to engage the personality. Some of these qualities are hypersensitivity, extreme self-consciousness, low self-esteem, and concern for and dependence on the opinion of others. Despite these self-defeating attributes, the practical talents these children are gifted with are not lost. It is their general lack of self-belief that may prevent them from reaching their full potential.

Talent with the written word is much stronger than with the spoken word. These children possess a powerful imagination, applied more often than not along negative lines. They are also open to psychic phenomena. This may create some confusion in their minds and set them apart from other children. They may suffer considerably in a dysfunctional family atmosphere and withdraw into a fantasy world of their own. A name reducing to the number 1 is most essential. A 7 may help. Another 2 should be strictly avoided. Other numbers too, are best avoided.

Twenty-twos Born in March (third month)

Children with this birth day and birth month combination are able to access the physical, emotional, mental, and spiritual planes. However, mental and physical activity will be displayed almost immediately. Their emotions may be held back and released on special occasions in outbursts of joy or temper. Entry into spiritual realms may be delayed until their late teens or early adulthood, or not at all. A great deal depends on family upbringing, teachers, friends, and other social influences.

There is no doubt that these children will be well behaved, courteous, and well- spoken individuals. Music is likely to be one of their best outlets for self-expression. A fertile, creative imagination combined with exceptional manual dexterity will invariably place them at an advantage over fellow students. Teachers may find them restless and inattentive when they are made to follow a standard syllabus. Parents too, will find that these children demand a good deal of attention and opportunities for advancement over and above their age group. These are children who go through the process of unlearning much of what they have been taught, and introducing fresh ideas and knowledge through self-study and their deep intuitive nature. They are genuine inventors, multi-taskers, and actors. Any name will suit these versatile children.

Twenty-twos Born in April (fourth month)

Although the number 22 is known as a Master Number, most of its attributes will not be manifested until a certain degree of maturity has been reached. It is then viewed at a secondary level as a powerful 4 vibration. The 4 vibration as explained in the chapter on the fourth day of the month is a down-to-earth, physical, and practical force. Mental habits such as fantasy, dreaming, and imagination are not associated with people influenced by this vibration. In other words, their feet are firmly planted on Mother Earth and not in the clouds. Seeing is believing with all genuine Fours.

As these children are heavily influenced by the 4 vibration they will exhibit characteristics such as, efficiency and diligence in all practical tasks as well as reliability and level-headedness. Their spiritual nature will be displayed in a job well done and in service to others, but not in effusive language or demonstrations of emotion. They may not be bubbly and entertaining, but can always be called upon for help in any practical task.

Certain negative qualities may creep into children with this birth day and birth month combination. These are usually laziness, resistance to change, and stubbornness. In order to overcome them a name reducing to 2, 3, 5, or 9 will help. A 4 name should be strictly avoided.

Twenty-twos Born in May (fifth month)

An exceptionally dynamic and magnetic collection of vibratory forces operate within this birth day and birth month combination. The chapter on the fifth day of the month gives a better understanding of these electric vibrations. Do not expect tranquil and placid behavior from these active and extroverted children. They cannot be confined to narrow boundaries of thought and action either. They thrive on exploration, experimentation, and advancement. Although they may contribute a good deal toward their own wellbeing and the welfare of others, not all their varied schemes may be valid or fruitful.

The attributes of the 5 vibration enhance all the active and outgoing features of their 22 birth force, especially on the emotional and physical planes. A normal range of emotion may be disturbed by a sensitive and volatile nature. They may unknowingly experience an inner battle between a need for quietude and a need for activity. The latter may prevail until well into adulthood.

These children are most certainly multi-talented, adaptable, and versatile. But they can also be changeable and unpredictable, and not always available when needed. Preoccupation with a great variety of thought and activity will be a problem for them and for their parents. They are also courageous, curious, and resilient. They could be troublesome if not kept constantly occupied. Avoid names reducing to 4 or 6.

Twenty-twos Born in June (sixth month)

Love and service to humanity at large is an elemental force within both the 22 and 6 vibrations. When these forces act in combination, as they do in this birth day and birth month, a compelling urge to contribute toward the welfare of all people will develop in the minds of these children. The degree in which it is allowed to manifest will inevitably depend on the circumstances in which they are nurtured.

In childhood they are certain to demonstrate qualities of love, helpfulness, non-violence, non-competition, togetherness, and peacefulness. They are able and willing little helpers within the home and at school. Even at an early age they may act as guides and confidants. As adults, they will be naturally attracted to the medical, helping, and teaching professions. They may, at times, indulge in a touch of self-deprecation. Their egos are not self-centered but extend outwards in efficient performance of whatever task they undertake. They are steady learners and workers. As they are not motivated by speed or impulse, they seldom make mistakes. They prefer to remain within their comfort zone. Sudden changes upset their sense of balance. A 2 or 6 vibration should be avoided when a first name is chosen. Any other name will be suitable. Consult the chapter on the sixth day of the month for a better understanding of these children.

Twenty-twos Born in July (seventh month)

The chapter on the seventh day of the month shows that the 7 vibration is a curious mixture of practicality and abstract thought. You will see that this dichotomy, in many ways, is similar to the one that exists within the 22 Master vibration. The result of this mingling of these sympathetic forces is a 'power-plus' personality structure. Its greatest strength is derived from the quality of self-sufficiency and comes from within personalities themselves and not from outside agencies. The degree of self-assurance within children born with this birth day and birth month combination will develop progressively as they enter their teens, early adulthood, and maturity. However, you may notice early signs that they wish to be left undisturbed while engaged in their chosen pastimes. They are likely to be drawn into nature studies and activities within natural surroundings. Exceptional manual dexterity will be displayed in the competent ways they handle all practical tasks. They will also display a lifelong interest in esoteric literature, history, music, and other related matters. Their personality will be a balance between practicality and spiritual enquiry. Not only are they born with a heightened understanding of life as a whole, but they continue to enlarge their knowledge with study and practice.

Any name will suit these multi-dimensional children.

Twenty-twos Born in August (eighth month)

Reference to the chapter on the eighth day of the month will indicate that the 8 vibration is essentially a businesslike, materialistic, practical, and constructive force. People who put these qualities into effective and progressive use invariably reach the peak of their careers, professions, or business ventures. Many characteristics are shared by the 8 and the materialistic and practical side of the 22.

The potential to serve and contribute to the welfare of humanity at large, or to selfishly use people for personal gain are alternatives these personalities are faced with. These children could be demanding and controlling. A sense of entitlement which lies dormant in the 22 will be aroused by the 8. They may struggle to contain and channel the powerful forces that begin to emerge. They may be young in body but mature in authority and general manner. Expect occasional self-serving and unpredictable conduct. They may not exercise full control over their emotions and could be petulant and disagreeable at times, but cooperative and helpful at others. Avoid names that reduce to 2, 4, and 8. Any other name will suit these powerful but unpredictable personalities.

Twenty-twos Born in September (ninth month)

When all single-digit vibrations are taken into consideration we find that the 9 is the force that is most akin to the Master vibration 22. Both are internationally-oriented, humanitarian, and spiritually alert forces. These are their fundamental qualities. All others that follow are secondary. The degree to which these qualities extend to their full potential depends entirely on opportunities provided. Please see the chapter on the ninth day of the month for more information.

These children may entertain thoughts that are far in advance of their peers and often their elders. This condition may often lead to frustration and unsettling reactions when they encounter disbelief and opposition to their elevated thoughts. Their feelings could be easily hurt until they gain an understanding that all people, including themselves, are at different points on the path of enlightenment. They are, for the most part, self-stimulated children. There is no need to provide too many toys or other superficial distractions for their entertainment. Rather, these may endanger inspiration and creativity. The gifts these children would appreciate the most are books, music, and entertainment at cultural centers. They need openings and reminders of knowledge they already possess. They are naturally non-competitive children who choose to participate or display leadership by example. Any name will suit these evolved children.

Twenty-twos Born in October (tenth month)

Please refer to the section on Twenty-twos born in January (first month). The zero does not introduce any new features. Any name will suit these children.

Twenty-twos Born in November (eleventh month)

Please refer to the section on Twenty-twos born in January (first month). The influence of 1 vibration characteristics will be stronger in this combination of birth day and birth month numbers. Any name will suit these children.

Twenty-twos Born in December (twelfth month)

The softer features of the 2 vibration may enter the personality as a result of its repetition in the birth month. But the presence of the 1 vibration as well, will prevent any of the 2's negative features from taking hold of the personality. The chapter on the second day of the month may be of interest. Any name will suit these children.

Twenty-third Day of the Month

23 reduces to (2+3=5)

Children born on the twenty-third day have the influence of the 2 and 3 vibrations in the outer personality, and the 5 vibration functioning in the background. This birth day is an agreeable combination of sensitive, alert, imaginative, and extroverted vibrations. These attributes, and more, are explained in the chapters on the second, third, and fifth days of the month which will help with a better understanding of these pleasant and animated children. It is unlikely that one aspect of their multiple personality will be more noticeable than the other. All three numbers interact to form a multi-talented and multi-faceted personality. The considerable variety of personality traits and aptitudes possessed by these children need to be harnessed and directed along productive lines. If not, a scattering of talent is a likely result.

Everything these children say and do is infused with energy, enthusiasm, and spontaneity. They make decisions according to the circumstances of the moment and how they may be feeling at that time. Acting and reacting are not always separate conditions. They are easily receptive to change and frequently initiate change. Do not leave them to their own devices, as they are socially-oriented personalities needing constant interaction with people. It is in such situations that they display the best version of themselves as genuine entertainers. Others look out for their company as an enlivening influence. They are easily accessible and responsive. They possess the capacity to enjoy life and meet its ups and downs with a good sense of humor. They are often unconventional in their habits and may lose their way from time to time when they get off the beaten track. They use all ways to acquire general knowledge and experience. Observation, experimentation, adventure, questioning, and oral communication are some of their principal methods. They do not live in a specific comfort zone.

These children will begin speaking and articulating their speech accurately earlier than others in their age group. Speech will always remain one of their most effective assets. They can be fluent, flexible, and also insightful when necessary. They are not easily cornered in argument. However, their natural tendency is to avoid serious argument. They can also talk their way out of any difficult situation due to their impetuous nature. They do not hesitate to promote themselves as they do possess a good sense of self-admiration. They are certainly natural actors.

Twenty-threes are not easily led or disciplined as the need for independent thought and personal freedom are fundamental characteristics. They may emulate some of their peers but not submit to their influence. They can relate to their parents and elders on a courteous, respectful, and friendly basis as long as they are given credit for their individuality and capacity to look after themselves. They are modern, up-to-date, and fashionable children who effortlessly move with the times. Clothing them may be costly. It will be difficult to hold them down to routine duties in the domestic scene. Punctuality will also be a problem. Too many distractions lead them away from regularity and consistency. For them, the grass is always greener on the other side of the fence.

Their changeable tendencies will be curtailed but not eliminated in children born in the first, fourth, seventh, tenth, eleventh and twelfth months. The following sections indicate the various changes the vibration of the birth month can make in the personality of children born on the twenty-third day.

Twenty-threes Born in January (first month)

A knowledge of the powers of the 1 vibration will be useful for a better understanding of this birth day and birth month combination. Please refer to the chapter on the first day of the month. The principal function of this vibration will be the introduction, in varying degrees, of steadfastness, of a sense of direction, and control over impulsive behavior. Then the creative talents of the 2, 3, and 5 vibrations of the birth day can be used more productively, and will not be scattered through lack of cohesion. The 1 acts as the cohesive force.

These children can accomplish whatever they set out to do. Their changeable nature will not be entirely altered as their birth day vibrations are much too energetic and forceful. They acquire the capacity to efficiently perform the many tasks they undertake and see to the completion of these tasks. As multi-taskers they cover a wide field of experience. They maintain good self-esteem and enthusiasm in whatever they undertake. They are certainly conscious of their individuality and variety of talent. Their egos are healthy and strong but not necessarily abrasive or self-centered. Their sociability is increased and expanded by the confidence they gain from their birth month. They demand recognition of their presence and of their achievements. Any name will suit these amazing children.

Twenty-threes Born in February (second month)

As seen above, the vibratory structure of the twenty-third day provides a considerable variety of personality traits and talents. At the same time, many of these splendid attributes may be incompatible with the balancing attributes of firm decisiveness, consistency, concentration, and a strong sense of direction. These essential needs are usually found in a suitable birth month. The 2 vibration in this birth day and birth month combination, unfortunately does not provide this balance. It, in fact, emphasizes the volatility of the combined birth day vibrations. The power to harness the charms and talents of the lively personality of these beautiful children, and to use them constructively, is reduced. Parents and others responsible for their nurturing and education will need to constantly remind these clever children to maintain a steady course until their studies and whatever else they may undertake are successfully completed. This will not always be an easy or rewarding task. Please see the chapter on the second day of the month for more information.

These children possess a beautiful, loving, and entertaining nature, but they are certain to lack adequate self-confidence to act on their own. They will need a boosting of self-esteem from time to time. Chastizement will seldom be needed as they do not intentionally create serious problems for themselves or others. A first name reducing to 1 will be the best. Names reducing to 4 or 7 will also be suitable. All other names are best avoided. These children need grounding on the physical, realistic, and practical realm.

Twenty-threes Born in March (third month)

The repetition of the 3 vibration in the birth month will certainly emphasize this aspect of the personality of these children, despite the fact that they are qualified Five personalities (2+3=5). The chapter on the third day of the month provides more information on the 3 vibration.

The abundance of 3 attributes will expand their artistic talents, especially the urge for oral self-expression. All people governed partly or wholly by the 3 vibration ensure, in various ways, that others are aware of and appreciate their presence. If they do not receive the attention they expect they do not hesitate to create situations whereby others are forced to pay attention. This is usually due to a lack of adequate self-confidence and their incapacity to live without interaction with others. This need, and the urge to hold the center of attention, will be increased in children born in March. They are chatterboxes who are not easily silenced. They possess exceptionally fertile and imaginative minds. Imagination may often overtake practicality. They need stability on the physical plane to reduce mental and emotional unease. The speed at which they speak and move can be bewildering. Names reducing to 1, 4, or 7 should be chosen. Avoid all other names.

Twenty-threes Born in April (fourth month)

This birth day and birth month form a very advantageous combination of vibratory forces. The chapter on the fourth day of the month shows that the 4 vibration is a physical, and pragmatic force. These are exactly the qualities that a person born on the twenty-third day needs. They help combine versatility and a vivid imagination with practical application. These children therefore possess the ability to put their ideas into practice. And most importantly, the 4 vibration reduces their desire for constant movement and change for change sake. It makes a valiant attempt to effect a balance between changeability and stability. It may not always succeed as it is only a secondary force, but it does constantly try to do so. The eventual result is an exceptionally clever and productive individual.

Investment in the education of these children in whatever direction they choose will certainly pay dividends. With wise guidance they could be persuaded to complete a task or course of study before moving on to something else. They need to be kept mentally and physically occupied, and freedom of choice is important to them. At the same time they are not averse to some form of guidance. They may not be as confidant of their multiple talents as they should be. However, self-assurance will develop when they keep proving themselves in whatever they undertake. With quick reflexes, alertness, physical courage, and a fast intake of knowledge, their talents as students and sports people will be displayed early in life. Most names will suit these clever children, but one with a 1 or 7 will be most advantageous and will help with self-confidence.

Twenty-threes Born in May (fifth month)

Children born on the twenty-third day are qualified Five personalities (2+3=5). Those born in the fifth month are over-charged with attributes of the 5 vibration. As seen in the chapter on the fifth day of the month, this is an unpredictable force that resists containment or direction into regular forms of conduct and activity. Thought processes and emotions are active as well as reactive well above normal. Physical needs are varied and changeable.

When the 5 vibration takes control over the personality, as it will do with these children, change for change sake will be their major problem. It is difficult to hold them down to routine, timetables, or regular domestic tasks. They are exceptionally alert, alive, and restless children. Nothing escapes their notice. They are never at ease in quiet places. They need to entertain and be entertained. To remain silent, inactive, or enjoy their own company are conditions wholly against their temperament. More often than not, they do not know what they want, unless its excitement. They can be enthusiastic starters but unreliable finishers. They can be incessant talkers with a talent for foreign languages. They can be accident-prone due to their impulsive and adventuresome nature. Anything that offers a challenge arouses their keen interest. A first name reducing to 2, 3, 5, or 9 should be avoided. Names with 1, 4, 6, 7, or 8 will introduce some balance between unrestrained activity and quietude in these vivacious children.

Twenty-threes Born in June (sixth month)

A tendency toward unrestrained activity and speed will be curbed to some extent in children born in the sixth month. The chapter on the sixth day of the month shows that people influenced by the 6 vibration prefer deliberating before speaking and acting. As this vibration is only a secondary force it may help, but it will not be, the driving force. This is taken over by the combined powers of the 2, 3, and 5 vibrations of their birth day. However, as the 6 vibration is essentially a domestic force, its limited influence will make it easier for parents to train these children into a degree of order, regularity, and punctuality. Rebellious reactions may be exceptional as long as parents approach them with reason and fair play. If they do not do so they are likely to face the formidable powers of speech and rationalizing force of these children. They are not easily defeated in a verbal contest.

Basically, these are friendly, loving, good humored, and sociable children. Their artistic talents will be expanded by the 6 vibration. It combines with the 3 aspect of their personality for a heightened appreciation of form and beauty. Underestimating themselves may be a minor problem. Their mild egos mean they do not push themselves forward and make maximum use of their multiple talents. In other words, these children are much smarter than they think they are. A name with a 1 or 7 will be best as these children can do with a boosting of self-confidence.

Twenty-threes Born in July (seventh month)

July is a most fortunate month for Twenty-three children to be born in to. The 7 vibration contributes many desirable attributes that are missing, or, perhaps, not quite evident in the individual or combined forces of the 2, 3, and 5 vibrations. The 7 is an unusual force in the sense that it is a mixture of practicality and realistic values, as well as esoteric and spiritual elements. The former is observed by conscientious, dependable, responsible, and down-to-earth characteristics in these children; the latter by their love of nature and periods they enjoy in their own company. The personality of July children is therefore enriched by a fresh set of attributes. The mobility of their birth day vibrations is controlled to a fair degree and is also directed into productive channels. A scattering of talent is prevented. The chapter on the seventh day of the month helps with a better understanding of the 7 vibration.

The 7 vibration also helps its subjects penetrate into the inner or hidden side of things. It is a fearless force that does not hesitate to carry its subjects into areas other than the physical. It also expands and deepens the artistic talents of these children. Their nature is likely to contain mild enigmatic attributes. Their actions and reactions cannot be taken for granted. They are neither followers or leaders, but free and independent thinkers and actors. Most names will suit these intriguing children. But it may be better to avoid another 2, 3, or 5.

Twenty-threes Born in August (eighth month)

The 8 vibration governing the month of August contains attributes that may be weak, or lacking, in the individual or combined forces of the twenty-third birth day. This is essentially a businesslike vibration related to ambition and success in public life. Real success cannot be achieved without talents in organization, administration, competition, and dedication. The 8 vibration contains all these qualities. When they act in conjunction with the multi-talented, multi-faceted, and extroverted forces of a Twenty-three personality, much can be expected of these children and adults. Of course it will depend on how much they have been encouraged to exercise their high potential. Although self-awareness is a prominent feature, it is quite possible that they may not make maximum use of their talents unless properly directed.

As the 8 vibration is a secondary force, these children will need to make some effort to open out to its much needed attributes, in order to reach their full potential. They can be helped in this process by a first name that reduces to the number 1. This vibration has the power to reduce or eliminate any feelings of inadequacy or uncertainty. Names with the numbers 4, 6, or 7 are good alternatives. Other numbers are best avoided.

Twenty-threes Born in September (ninth month)

The 9 vibration governing the ninth month broadens the horizons of these children. It will be of considerable help in personal development as well as in their interaction with others. The humanitarian qualities of the 9 vibration will extend their consciousness beyond self-interest and remind them of their interconnectedness with all life. The Twenty-three personality's tendency to emphasize personal views and needs while remaining oblivious of the views and needs of others will be reduced. The chapter on the ninth day of the month will help with a better understanding of these alert and enlightened children.

While introducing wisdom, compassion, and high principles, the 9 vibration does not slow down the speed of their birth force. It not does provide practicality, financial acumen, tenacity, and a businesslike mentality. These children need to be instructed in down-to-earth values, thriftiness, and steadfastness. These are exceptionally intelligent children, but they may suffer from insufficient self-confidence despite the fact that they succeed in whatever study or project they undertake. They are extroverted children who can mix with, and provide entertainment to, any age group. A first name reducing to 1, 4, or 7 will provide a booster in their physical and practical affairs. Other names are best avoided.

Twenty-threes Born in October (tenth month)

Please refer to the section on Twenty-threes born in January (first month). The zero in the tenth month does not add or take away personality traits or talents. Any name will suit these clever children.

Twenty-threes Born in November (eleventh month)

Please refer to the section on Twenty-threes born in January (first month). Attributes of the 1 vibration will be emphasized in the personality of these children. Any name will suit these potentially very successful children.

Twenty-threes Born in December (twelfth month)

Emotional expression will be made easier in children born in December. Their powers with the written word will also be extended. The repetition of the 2 vibration in the birth month will be responsible for the extension of these attributes. The presence of the 1 vibration will provide direction and self-confidence. Any name will suit these well-balanced children.

Twenty-fourth Day of the Month

24 reduces to (2+4=6)

Children born on the twenty-fourth day have the influence of the 2 and 4 vibrations in the outer personality and the 6 vibration functioning in the background. The fundamental personality of children born on the twenty-fourth day of the month is formed by a sympathetic interaction of three even numbers, or receptive vibrations. An interesting condition is that each of these three operate from different planes of expression; the 2 from the emotional, the 4 from the physical, and the underlying 6 from the mental. This distribution is an assurance of a well-balanced personality structure. All three vibratory forces contain many similar and agreeable attributes in addition to individual features. The great advantage enjoyed by these personalities is that they are free from conflicting elements as they do coalesce into a single unified force. Basic attributes that create this fortunate condition are the sensitivity of the 2, the practicality of the 4, and the rationality of the 6.

Emotional expression is held in check. As a consequence, they are generally unflappable children who do not lose control of themselves. One aspect of their personality does not act independently of the others. Therefore, expect balanced growth or development. Speed, impulse, and frequent change will not be parts of their lifestyle. As they do not act out of character they are purposeful and for the most part their actions are predictable. More information about their integral personality can be obtained by reference to the chapters on the second, fourth, and sixth days of the month.

Awareness of family and community responsibilities will develop early in life as these are essential attributes of all three vibratory forces of this date. Love, loyalty, and duty to family will certainly come first with the latter not far behind. Their nature is such that they choose to connect with people rather than see their own interests as apart from others. They are not types that will engage in the frivolities of society. They need to interact productively with others as their outstanding attributes are service and constructive action in any form. This is also an avenue through which their spiritual nature is manifested, consciously or unconsciously.

Children born on the twenty-fourth day will perform many acts of kindness and self-sacrifice. Some respond to life's events and associations with elements of caution, deliberation, and uncertainty. The presence or absence of these slightly negative features depends on the vibration of their birth month. More information is given below. Cooperation, togetherness, conciliation, harmony, and peacemaking are some other motivating factors within the personality of these children, while control, rivalry, dominance, egotism, and self-centeredness are alien features.

They may not be as optimistic, jovial, adventuresome, and flexible as children governed by odd numbers or active vibrations. But these are substituted by strength of purpose, loyalty, dependability, punctuality, contentment, and a generally non-demanding temperament. Safekeeping, safeguarding, nurturing, and domesticity are some other positive qualities. They possess the potential to rescue loved ones or others from physical dangers, as well as from emotional and mental difficulties. These special traits will be displayed early in life, especially if they are called upon to look after younger siblings or a disabled parent.

These are children who cannot be enticed into unsocial or any other type of unethical behavior. Most Twenty-four children are quite able to think for themselves and act independently. All three vibrations forming their personality favor close family life, home, and domestic responsibilities. They are certain to maintain close family connections after they have left home. During their childhood and teen years all domestic chores will be performed willingly and efficiently.

They usually know what has to be done without being told. They are happy to follow routine and home rules without argument and do not feel they are confined to boundaries in a domestic scene. They are also capable of challenging a system or practice that is unfair or unproductive by suggesting something better. Parents should not expect them to be fiercely competitive as participation is more enjoyable to these children than constant winning; any form of aggression is not a true expression of their nature. The following sections relating to their birth months indicate some important differences in these Twenty-four children.

Twenty-fours Born in January (first month)

The vibratory force symbolized by the number 1, is known principally as the activator, creator, and energizer. These basic attributes create a positive attitude toward life in Twenty-four children born in January. They possess the potential to make maximum use of the several benign, helpful, and caring attributes of their birth day vibrations. This can be done not only for the wellbeing of others but also for their own. A fine balance can be established between helpful and obliging ways and a good measure of discipline, steadfastness, and authority. They do possess the power to say 'No' in circumstances that do not meet with their approval. They will not be taken advantage of by people who are only takers and not givers. They possess a very advantageous combination of vibratory forces that ensure success in whatever they undertake.

These children will mature into adults who will be respected and admired by all those with whom they interact. The beginnings of this trend will be seen from their early teens onward. As children, they will be loved and valued by family members for the contributions they willingly make toward the peace, harmony, and efficient running of their home. Their opinions and decisions will be based on practical values and fair play and seldom open to question. They may not be talkative children because they prefer action to speech, and concentration on what they are doing prevents too much speech. But when they decide to verbalize their thoughts, others are prepared to listen to them. Members of their age group do not hesitate to approach them for help on practical and other personal matters. Nurturing and educating these receptive children will be a pleasure for parents and teachers. Any name will suit these well-balanced children.

Twenty-fours Born in February (second month)

Children born in February gain an intensification of all the sensitive, helpful, obliging, and genteel attributes of their birth force. The repetition of the 2 vibration in their birth month may act in two ways. While talents, especially those of the 2 vibration are enriched, certain negative aspects of the 2 vibration may enter their thoughts and actions. The ability to assert themselves in certain circumstances or to say "No" when necessary may be weakened. They may allow others to take advantage of their kindly and obliging ways. They also depend on others when firm decisions have to be made. They will need to be advised that life will present constantly increasing situations in which they will have to rely on their own decisions and not be led by others.

These are truly loving and beautifully-natured children who need a frequent injection of self-confidence so that their multiple talents can fully emerge. The written word will be stronger than the spoken word. Shyness is a minor problem which interferes with speech but not with writing. They worry that anything they say may not be entirely correct and therefore open to criticism. These children flourish in group activity and in non-competitive work and sport. Participation is more fulfilling than keen efforts to win. Their sense of self-worth can be harmed by parents who push them into competitive activities or too frequently into the spotlight in social scenes. They are most effective and productive within their comfort zones. Venturing into unfamiliar territory upsets their sense of order and regularity. These are domesticated children who will be a delight to have around the home. No domestic task will be beyond their capacity. In order to strengthen their self-confidence a first name reducing to the number 1 will be most helpful. Another 2 should be strictly avoided. Other numbers will be suitable.

Twenty-fours Born in March (third month)

The comfort zone created by the coalition of three complementary receptive vibrations is invaded by the active forces of this birth month. The chapter on the third day of the month will help with a better understanding of this condition. Attributes of this additional force are in many ways different to those of the 2, 4, and 6. The introduction of these differences creates certain advantages as well as certain disadvantages. The powerful imaginative qualities of the 3 will certainly expand the thought processes of children with this birth day. At the same time they are likely to create a degree of uncertainty between the basic sense of caution and stability of their fundamental personality and the 3 vibration's attraction to novelty, extroversion, extended sociability, and youthfulness. In other words some conflict may arise between conservatism of their birth day vibrations and modernism of their birth month. As the former is the primary and stronger force, and the latter a secondary and a contributory force, the eventual result will be advantageous. To begin with, these children's voice and vocal powers will be enriched along with their appreciation for art, literature, and music. As a mental force the 3 will also contribute fresh and innovative ideas which expand their practical talents.

Adults should note that these children are, in fact, practical idealists and multi-faceted personalities who could do with a greater degree of confidence in their abilities. Any of these very capable children may underrate themselves. A first name reducing to the number 1 will be of considerable help in this regard. It will certainly boost self-confidence. Names with 2, 4, or 6 are best avoided. Other numbers will not do any harm.

Twenty-fours Born in April (fourth month)

The repetition of the 4 vibration in the birth month is a guarantee that the solid attributes of the 4 vibration exercise a major influence over the personality of these children. They combine well with the mental 6 vibration to produce a system of order, routine, reliability, and punctuality. Nothing is left undone by these children. Any task or responsibility undertaken is completed before they move on to another. They take pride in their accomplishments. But a boastful ego does not follow their achievements or their relationship with others. They can be stubborn but not rebellious, and are not easily dislodged from the firm opinions they hold. Flexibility and adaptability are not strong points in their nature. They do not welcome sudden changes, but they do not display agitation or nervousness when faced with a sudden change. Unflappability is a noticeable personality trait.

These children are seldom interested in playing a prominent role in a social scene, preferring to be active and productive in the background. They may not possess the confidence to mix freely with all types of people. These children can certainly be relied upon to shoulder any form of domestic responsibility without demur. Anything to do with building or repairing will instantly attract their attention. The chapter on the fourth day of the month indicates that manual dexterity is one of their chief assets. The best names for these children are those that reduce to 1, 3, 5, 7, or 9. Another 4 should be strictly avoided.

Twenty-fours Born in May (fifth month)

The chapter on the fifth day of the month shows that the general attributes of the 5 vibration contrast sharply with those of the 2, 4, and 6 that make up their fundamental personality structure. Their dynamic qualities will inevitably create some form of disturbance within the harmonious condition formed by their birth day forces. They may create a degree of uncertainty or confusion but they can also act as a positive influence.

The 5 vibration will help these children out of a comfort zone which would otherwise delay speedy progress on their outlook on life and interaction with others. They will also be relieved of a natural bashfulness when meeting people for the first time. Qualities of the 5 vibrations will also help them assert their individuality and prevent others taking advantage of their helpful ways. Objection to sudden changes will be lessened and the capacity to cope with them will be increased. This birth month will be responsible for forming a greater degree of roundness and balance by introducing flexibility and adaptability. These children are certainly multi-taskers who can be called upon to help in any domestic task. For the best expression of their talents they could do with an injection of self-confidence from time to time. A name with a 1 vibration will be perfect. A 7 name will also help. It would be best to avoid all other numbers.

Twenty-fours Born in June (sixth month)

All people born on the twenty-fourth day are qualified Six personalities (2+4=6). The addition of another 6 vibration increases the effectiveness of its attributes. The chapter on the sixth day of the month is essential reading for a better understanding of the personality of children born in June. The presence of strong 6 attributes does not necessarily create an overloading and the consequent entry of certain negative features of this vibration. It may, however, emphasize attachment to domesticity and family life. Possessiveness of loved ones may interfere with freedom of expression for themselves and their loved ones. Anxiety for their own wellbeing and safety, as well as their loved ones, may remain a constant problem. Lack of sufficient ego-strength and self-confidence may delay speedy progress despite the fact that they are well equipped to handle any task they choose to undertake. They may also be too concerned that they may upset the feelings of others if they assert themselves. All the above conditions can be corrected to a large extent by a first name that adds up to the number 1, or if the total of their birth date, which includes the year as well (known as the Life Path or Destiny number), adds up to number 1.

There is no doubt that these are home-loving and domesticated children. Housekeeping and cooking will be among their special interests and skills. Caring for the physically sick and mentally and emotionally troubled will be another talent that will emerge early in life. At the same time, these children need to be nurtured with love and harmony themselves. Their sense of wellbeing and high potential for doing good will be seriously affected in a dysfunctional or harsh home environment. If the number 1 is not chosen for their first name the number 7 will be a good alternative. Another 2, 4, 6, or 8 should be strictly avoided. Other numbers should be harmless.

Twenty-fours Born in July (seventh month)

The chapter on the seventh day of the month shows that this birth month contributes a rich parcel of attributes. Some similar features and others that are new will be added to the fundamental personality created by the birth day. The most advantageous quality introduced by the 7 vibration will be individuality and inner strength. Children and adults influenced by this vibration do not, for the most part, depend on others for their wellbeing, as they are able to summon inner resources that help them meet life's experiences.

The contemplative nature of the 7 vibration will merge naturally with the shared peaceful qualities of the 2, 4, and 6 vibrations. Other aspects of the 7, such as practicality, integrity, down-to-earth values, and love of nature add to the overall strength of personality. These are graceful and multi-talented children with an attractive and kindly disposition. They do not advertise their talents but simply await recognition of their competence in anything they undertake. If not given adequate acknowledgment, they keep going in their own inimitable fashion. Their loving and sensitive nature may not be displayed in external demonstrations of sentiment. Love and loyalty will be observed in unassuming service to others. All these attractive qualities will be seen in children nurtured in a peaceful and loving family environment. In a dysfunctional environment these qualities are easily inhibited, causing personal distress and disillusionment. A name reducing to 1, 3, 5, another 7, or 9 will open these children to more extended fields of interest and experience.

Twenty-fours Born in August (eighth month)

The urge to take control over their own lives and the lives of others is a characteristic of the 8 vibration. The chapter on the eighth day of the month gives more information on the attributes of this vibration. To control is not a feature common to the 2, 4, or 6 vibratory forces, or a combination of all three. Their natural qualities are cooperation, togetherness, partnerships, and participation. As the 8 vibration is a secondary aspect it does not interfere to an appreciable degree with the receptive qualities formed by the birth day vibrations. It does, however, add strength and effectiveness in the exercise of these qualities. The extraordinary organizational and orderly powers of the 8 interact advantageously with the systematic qualities the 2, 4, and 6.

These children choose to live efficiently and comfortably within confined boundaries. They show little or no interest to most things outside their comfort zone or chosen field of activity. They are known for their strength of purpose but not necessarily for curiosity, adventure, flexibility, and adaptation to change. Their emotional displays could vary from obstinacy and outbursts of anger to feelings of remorse and conscience. As adults they are certain to develop into responsible money managers with a broad streak of parsimony in their dealings with others. They can look forward to success in any form of business.

These children can profit from a name that opens out their personality into wider fields of thought and action, such as 1, 3, 5, and 9. The numbers 4 and 8 should be avoided as these will increase their controlling and circumspect nature.

Twenty-fours Born in September (ninth month)

The mental orientation of these children will be amplified by the 9 vibration of this birth month. Their horizons will be extended from family and community consciousness, relative to their birth day vibrations, into a national and global outlook. The extent to which this is taken will certainly depend on the cultural levels of the society and family in which they are nurtured. But the potential for opening into wider realms through self-education will always remain at their disposal. The desire to be of service to others, which is a fundamental quality of their birth day vibrations will be increased and extended by 9 qualities. The comfort zone created by their birth day vibrations will be abandoned and replaced by the extroverted qualities of the 9. Please refer to the chapter on the ninth day of the month for more information on the 9.

These children are known for their sensitivity toward the feelings and needs of others. Egotism is an alien characteristic. At the same time, they may need some strengthening of ego when the need arises for assertiveness in certain circumstances. Also, they should be reassured that they have the capacity to handle life's situations and hold their own with all people, especially classmates and peers. A tendency to underrate their potential can be overcome through good nurturing by parents and elders, and a given name that adds up to the number 1, or the number 7.

Twenty-fours Born in October (tenth month)

Please refer to the chapter on Twenty-fours born in January (first month). The zero in the month of October does not make any real difference. These are well-balanced personalities. Any name will suit them.

Twenty-fours Born in November (eleventh month)

Please refer to the chapter on the Twenty-fours born in January (first month). The presence of the 1 vibration in double strength will increase the effectiveness of all individual and combined attributes of the birth day vibrations. Any name will suit these children, but it would be best to avoid a name that reduces to the number 1.

Twenty-fours Born in December (twelfth month)

The 1 vibration in the birth month adds considerable strength to the attributes of the birth day vibrations. Please refer to the chapter on the first day of the month. The 2 vibrations which also operate in the birth month will increase the effectiveness of the 2 attributes to the advantage of the integral personality. Please see the chapter on the second day of the month. Any name will suit these generally confident children.

Twenty-fifth Day of the Month

25 reduces to (2+5=7)

Children born on the twenty-fifth day have the influence of the 2 and 5 vibrations in the outer personality and the 7 vibration functioning in the background. The considerable variety of personality traits and talents contributed by the 2, 5, and 7 vibrations are comparatively uncongenial forces. People born on this day are faced with the task of becoming aware and accustomed to their complex personality. The chapters on the second,, fifth and seventh days of the month explain more about this condition.

These children are essentially qualified Seven personalities (2+5=7). Attributes of the 7 vibration can be seen, functioning obscurely, but firmly, in the background, while those of the 2 and 5, especially the 5 will be prominent in the foreground. Due to this dichotomy and the diversity of their vibratory forces it is not easy, or even possible, to assign them to a particular personality type. Too many enigmatic qualities deter classification. This condition is not likely to change in adulthood. Gaining some degree of familiarity with them will not be easy. The process may take some time and understanding.

The 2 and 5 aspects of their personality operate from the emotional plane with certain similarities and an equal number of dissimilarities. Adaptability to change and movement is present in both. The major difference, however, lies in the calm and receptive nature of the 2 and the energetic and outgoing nature of the 5; in other words, right brain energy and left brain energy. Affecting a balance between the two will remain a constant need. These forces also provide free outlets for emotional expression. The 2 portion demonstrates emotion in sentimental ways while the 5 displays it in explosive ways. The next challenge facing these personalities will be reconciliation with their fundamental 7 vibration. As this force operates on the physical plane it does not favor spontaneous demonstration of emotion. The differences in their emotional nature are likely to create uncertainty in regard to proper expression of their feelings in these children. Outbursts of emotion followed by embarrassment or guilt may not be infrequent. However, good emotional control can be gained by education and their cultural status. A unique quality shared by all three vibrations is enthusiasm. It is not in the nature of these children to do things half-heartedly. As multi-taskers they concentrate on study or any form of work they undertake. This habit will be carried into adulthood.

Their strong 7 aspect reveals the contemplative side of their nature. It may find a degree of affinity with the 2 but not with the 5. Herein lies another challenge. They need to divide their time between time for themselves and time for interaction with others. They are certainly selective of the company they keep. They will avoid loud-spoken and frivolous people. These are not constantly talkative children, but when they choose to say something it is well considered and worth listening to. They are not always keen listeners; they are easily put off by conversation that does not interest them. Their attention can be gained when conversation turns to knowledgeable and productive topics. They can listen without being critical or losing self-confidence as the gathering of knowledge is another common feature in all three of their vibratory forces.

These personalities experience an inner conflict that they must face and overcome— a desire to control and arrange things to suit themselves, which is typical of their 5 portion, and allowing others independence and freedom of choice, natural to their 2 and 7 aspects. There is also a spiritual element underlying surface behavior which will be seen in their love of nature, their occasional contemplative moods, and the need to withdraw themselves from prolonged interaction with people. From early adulthood onwards they are certain to enter into various esoteric studies, especially if they have been nurtured in a family with similar interests. All these attributes are derived from the 7 aspect of their personality. This aspect also helps them stay grounded and prevent their emotional nature taking control of their speech and action. Their multi-faceted nature often provides too many choices. They may be genuine multi-taskers but the 7 prevents them from scattering their talents.

These children develop with greater ease through self-motivation, experimentation, and investigation than by instruction and book learning. They need to be involved in life and explore and expand their boundaries. They need to work things out for themselves and not submit to peer pressure. Also, they may not choose to follow their parent's system of values or ambitions. Parents and guardians will be faced with quite a challenge when nurturing these fascinating children.

The best names for these children will be those that reduce to 1, 4, or 7.

Another 7 will do no harm but 2 and 5 are best avoided. These children need to be well-grounded, and only a physical vibration can do this. The birth month of these children is responsible for certain changes in their personality. The following sections deal with each month and the changes they introduce.

Twenty-fives Born in January (first month)

Children with a twenty-fifth birth day who are born in January are in a position to make maximum use of their many-sided nature. The willpower and ego-strength natural to the 1 vibration can help them employ to their advantage and to the advantage of others, each aspect of their personality in appropriate circumstances and conditions. One will not be allowed to overlap the other, causing concern and uncertainty. The degree to which they separate these different powers and make effective use of them will depend on good nurturing and self-education. The latter will eventuate as a voluntary exercise as they grow older.

These children develop speedily when opportunities are provided for setting free their curious and exploratory nature. For the most part they need to be left alone to indulge in their hobbies. These are not domesticated children. Almost all their interests will be outdoors. However, there will be some who naturally include book learning; a habit that will continue for the rest of their lives. Keen observers will not fail to note considerable depth of character and potential. These are personalities who cannot be treated lightly. Pay attention to their current store of knowledge and their desire for on-going improvement. They certainly cannot be used as a target for inane jokes. They are not without a subtle sense of humor, but they usually take life seriously and they expect to be taken seriously by others.

These children may adopt the habit of communicating at certain times without the use of words. They speak when they have something to say that is worthwhile. Any name will suit these self-sufficient children.

Twenty-fives Born in February (second month)

The repetition of the number 2 in the birth month clearly indicates greater influence of the qualities of the 2 vibration. This condition is not necessarily an advantage as it reduces stability and strength of purpose. The 2 is a fluid force. Certain negative aspects of this vibration may interfere with full use of their high potential. Indecision, procrastination, uncertainty, sensitivity, self-consciousness, and the need for more self-assertiveness may be some problems introduced by an excess of 2 attributes. Their 5 aspect may not help much as this is also a vibration of change and unpredictability. However, their fundamental 7 force operating on the physical plane will make valiant attempts to introduce some down-to-earth and practical values. To what extent it succeeds will depend on good nurturing and education.

The united force of the strong 2, 5, and 7 are most likely to expose psychic attributes in these children. They may be subject to flights of fancy, imagination, and contemplation. They will use the power of the written word to express themselves. Their precognitive faculties are often stifled by parents, elders, and social conditions. These children do not lose any of the powers of their 2 aspect, or of their 5 and 7. What may be lacking is a firm belief in themselves. Inadequate self-esteem needs to be replaced by self-confidence. These are loving and lovable children who are free from egotism and demanding habits. A first name reducing to the number 1 will help them overcome many of their uncertainties. Also, if the total of their birth date (day, month and year) reduces to the number 1, self-confidence will be a natural outcome. A 4 or 7 name will also be helpful. What these children need is a name from a physical vibration so that an excess of sensitivity can be reduced by an objective force such as the 1, 4, or 7. Names with 2 and 5 should be strictly avoided. Other numbers too are best avoided.

Twenty-fives Born in March (third month)

A careful study of the chapters on the second, third, fifth and seventh days of the month will reveal that the personality of these children contains two distinct areas of expression. One is governed by similarities between attributes of the 3 and 5 vibrations and the other, by certain affinities between the 2 and 7. These conditions exist despite the fact that the vibrations operate on different levels of expression (the 2 and 5 emotional, the 3 mental, and the 7 physical). There is a noticeable difference between the extroverted, spontaneous, imaginative, adaptable, flexible, freedom-loving, and impulsive attributes of the 3 and 5, and the calm, introspective, reserved, sharing, serving, and intuitive nature of the 2 and 7. Another thing that can be observed is the absence of a strong self-governing or self-restraining force that could harness and direct the multiplicity of personality traits and talents within the integral personality of these children. The 7 aspect of their nature is able to answer to these needs but it will be constantly faced with the problem of overcoming the mercurial nature of their 2, 3, and 5 aspects.

These children may take time to understand their complicated nature. Their biggest problem will simply be choice. Life may often be bewildering as there are so many choices open to them. They may not, as a habit, follow advice and instructions, choosing instead to experience life as they choose to experience it. Their choices may often be of short-term benefit. The number 1 vibration will keep them to a fair extent on the "straight and narrow" and halt a scattering of talent. If the total of their birth date (day, month, and year) reduces to the number 1, they will experience an inner urge to control their thoughts and actions. If not, a first name reducing to the number 1 will help them to do so. Numbers 4 and 7 will also help, but not as effectively as the 1. Other numbers are best avoided.

Twenty-fives Born in April (fourth month)

The practical and sensible temperament of these children will be evident early in life. The sympathetic interaction of physical 4 vibrations of their birth month and the 7 of their birth day will be responsible for their down-to-earth values. In addition, the 2 and 5 aspects of their personality operating on the emotional plane form a good balance. The latter vibrations favor movement, experimentation, and spontaneity, while the former are emotionally contained and of a "stay put" nature. These children are not likely to submit to change for change sake or display extremes of behavior. There is a fine balance in the overall personality structure. For a fuller understanding of these well-balanced children, please read the chapters on the second, fourth, fifth, and seventh days of the month. Their integral personality is formed by a good portion of each vibration.

It is not possible to foretell the direction into which these multi-faceted and versatile children will be attracted in relation to study and occupation. They are blessed with the potential to succeed in anything they choose to do. The only difficulty they face is one that is experienced by all multi-talented people, and that is eventually having to make choices. Many of their talents and even their personality traits may never be put to use, but they will be there all the same. These could be rather costly children to entertain and educate as their interests will be spread over so many areas. A name reducing to the number 1 will be best as it will provide a firmer sense of direction and decision.

Twenty-fives Born in May (fifth month)

The repetition of the 5 vibration in the birth month is a clear indication that its attributes have a greater hold on the personality of these children than the 2 and the underlying 7. Although they may be qualified Seven personalities (2+5=7), attributes of the 7 vibration are subdued by the dynamic nature of the 5. The genteel qualities of the 2 also struggle to keep up with the excessive powers of the 5. The chapters on the second, fifth and seventh days of the month will help with a better understanding of the changeable nature of these children.

Due to the prominent show of 5 attributes and the obscure position of the 2 and 7, these children could often be classified as Five personalities with a more than desirable share of its negative attributes. Emotional expression could be one problem; these children are easily swept away by their feelings, despite attempts by their 7 aspect to exercise control. They need to learn how to express their emotions without being controlled by them. Addiction to change for change sake, restlessness, unpredictable actions, and responses may be other problems. Despite these possible drawbacks these children do not lose their innumerable practical talents. They need regulation of thought, speech, and action to perform at their best. Their underlying 7 force can help but it also needs to be aided by outside influences, such as understanding parents and teachers.

External interests will always be much more attractive to them than domestic responsibilities and home-based hobbies. A first name reducing to 2 or 5 should be strictly avoided. The best names will be those reducing to 1, 4, or 7. These will help them develop self-control and steadfastness.

Twenty-fives Born in June (sixth month)

The vibration governing the sixth month adds a range of talents and personality traits not clearly evident in the birth day vibrations 2, 5, and 7. There may be some similarities between the 2 and 6, but very few, if any, between the 5 and 7. The introduction of the 6 vibration creates a fine balance or roundness to the integral personality structure of these children. They possess vibratory forces or powers from the physical plane (7), the emotional plane (2 and 5) and the mental plane (6). At the same time, the twofold nature of the 7 vibration creates an attraction toward spiritual and abstract values which may develop as they grow older.

The capacity to "think before they leap" is the advantage derived from their balanced personality structure. The rationality of their 6 aspect and the caution of the 7 prevent impulse, emotionalism, and changeability, natural to their 2 and 5 aspects, from taking a grip on the personality. At the same time the 2 and 5 provide qualities of spontaneity and extroversion not found in strength in their 6 and 7 aspects. They are, consequently, sensible children with the capacity to exercise self-control. They can easily be approached with reason and fair play.

Apart from impressive qualities of logic and rationality, the 6 vibration introduces love of home, family life, and domestic responsibilities. These children may not be all-out domesticated personalities as the 6 vibration is only a secondary force, but they will not need to be coerced into a fair share of domestic chores. All they need is gentle direction and good example set by parents and elders. As these are well-balanced children who can get by without too much aid from a name vibration, a first name with any number can be given. However, a name that reduces to the number 1 will certainly help strengthen self-esteem and self-confidence. Their integral personality could be slightly wanting in these areas.

Twenty-fives Born in July (seventh month)

As qualified Seven personalities (2 + 5 = 7) there is no doubt that these children will be influenced for the most part by the practical as well as the qualities of mystique in the 7 vibration. Please see the chapter on the seventh day of the month for a better understanding of this personality.

Children with this birth day and birth month are likely to experience some degree of inner conflict between the extroverted and social attributes of their outer personality (2 and 5) and the reserved, contemplative, and studious nature of their inner personality (7). Reconciling these differences will be a challenge as they grow older and are faced with more demands from exterior influences. In the meantime, their outer nature may be more prominent. At any stage of life they will be genuine nature lovers who resort whenever possible to solitary enjoyment of natural surroundings. City-dwelling children may experience an inner loss of this experience. As an alternative they may take to artificial outlets such as books and electronic entertainment. Curiosity is not only a strong element in the 5 vibration but it is as strong and even more widespread in the 7. While their 5 aspect may be concerned with physical realms, their 7 moves through the physical into metaphysical realms. Their interests will be spread in relatively equal proportions over the past, present, and future. Very little escapes their attention as they are exceptionally observant personalities. If opportunities for extended study and specialization are not provided in childhood and teen years they are certain to use their initiative for advancement in early adulthood. Any name will suit these highly intuitive children.

Twenty-fives Born in August (eighth month)

Vibrations from the emotional plane predominate in the outer personality of children with this birth day and birth month combination. Their combined force results in sensitivity, reactivity, self-consciousness, and frequent demonstration of emotion. At the same time, their inner person is governed by the emotionally restrained 7. These children will consequently be faced with the need to establish some form of emotional balance. This may not be an easy task due to the combined strength of the 2, 5, and 8. They may use their emotional nature to take control of their lives more often than their rational nature. A better understanding of their emotional complexity can be gained from the chapters dealing with the second, fifth, seventh, and eighth days of the month.

Nurturing these children may be a delicate task. Sensible advice and correction will do much to help them use their rational and discretionary powers, but good example, good role models, understanding, and encouragement will help much more. These children are, without doubt, intelligent and multi-talented personalities. All they need is a bit more grounding on the physical plane. A name with a 1 vibration will be ideal. This will not only join their inner 7 nature in practical values and self-control, but will also instill more confidence. Those whose complete birth date (day, month, and year) adds up to the number 1, will develop these qualities naturally as there will be a strong pull in these directions. A name with a 4 or 7 will also help. Avoid other numbers.

Twenty-fives Born in September (ninth month)

All people born on the twenty-fifth day are qualified Seven personalities (2+5=7). In this birth day and birth month combination, the 9 vibration of the birth month acts as a strong ally to the 7 inner personality. The 7 and 9 possess cultural, humanitarian, and spiritual forces that cannot be overshadowed by egotistic and materialistic forces.

Quite early in life these children will display a desire for acquisition of wide-ranging knowledge as their mental powers are not confined to academic study only but expanded into wider horizons. They are prompted by the high sense of curiosity inherent in their 2 and 5 aspects for experience and investigation into emotional and physical aspects of life. Their 7 and 9 aspects go further into spiritual and metaphysical realms. They are, in short, perennial students. In order to reach this high potential all these children need is moderate or normal nurturing. Most of it will emerge naturally. Reference to the chapter on the ninth day of the month will be helpful. The egos of these children do not block their efforts toward self-advancement. They keep open minds. Attributes of the 9 vibration also expand the extroverted qualities of their outer personality in positive ways. These are naturally charming, winning, wise, and knowledgeable children. Everyone will find it a pleasure to entertain them and be entertained by them. A boosting of self-confidence will draw out more of their potential than they may be prepared to use. A name reducing to the number 1 will be most beneficial. A 5 or 7 will also be helpful. 2 and 5 names are best avoided. 3, 6, 8, and 9 names will also be helpful.

Twenty-fives Born in October (tenth month)

Please refer to the chapter on Twenty-fives born in January (first month). The zero in the tenth month does not change the personality one way or another. Names with 2 and 5 are best avoided. Any other name will suit these children.

Twenty-fives Born in November (eleventh month)

Please refer to the chapter on Twenty-fives born in January (first month). In this instance the personality is strengthened by the presence of the 1 vibration in double strength. Any name will suit these self-confident children.

Twenty-fives Born in December (twelfth month)

Please refer to the chapters on Twenty-fives born in the first and second months. The personality is strengthened in two ways by the presence of these active and receptive forces. Names reducing to 2 and 5 are best avoided. Any other name will suit these versatile children.

Twenty-sixth Day of the Month

26 reduces to (2+6=8)

Children born on the twenty-sixth day have the influence of the 2 and 6 vibrations in the outer personality and the 8 vibration functioning in the background. Three even numbers or receptive vibrations intermingle within the personality of these children. Readers who are familiar with the attributes of the 2 and 6 vibrations, which operate at outer levels of the personality, are aware that these are genteel, considerate, peace-loving, and helpful forces. The chapters on the second and sixth days of the month are recommended to those who are unfamiliar with these vibrations. Other obvious characteristics displayed by people influenced by the 2 and 6 are the love of home, diplomacy, tact, service, and, avoidance of noise and disharmony. Their other even number 8 operates as an inner force. These children are qualified Eight personalities (2+6=8). Attributes of the 8 vibration are in many ways opposed to those of the 2 and 6. They contain qualities of ambition, assertiveness, control, competition, and acquisitiveness. These may conflict with those of the non-assertive 2 and 6, but they provide strength of purpose, self-protection, and self-assurance. When these opposing qualities are successfully intermingled, expect a higher degree of success in all their ventures.

Although these personalities possess two vibrations from the emotional plane (2 and 8), they are not open to a full expression of their emotions. The mental 6 holds emotional demonstration in check and the 8 aspect has a tendency to suppress emotion and release it in outbursts of joy or anger. There is also an interconnectedness between the 2, 6, and 8 forces. You might notice this in their need for order, system, regularity, organization, and stability. These personalities are capable of establishing a balance between activity and rest. Their responses are usually predictable. Ego activity and self-interest are usually subordinated by family loyalties, concentration on schoolwork, as well as helpfulness at school and work. They will carry out domestic responsibilities conscientiously. In adulthood they will be capable of undertaking a dual role of homemaker and breadwinner, or at least a part-time worker. Attachment to family will never be loosened by outside interests.

These children will accept advice and correction without resentment, provided they do not take the form of criticism, rudeness, or excessive demonstration of authority. Their feelings are easily hurt, and although they may not show the harm they may receive from others, it does go deep into their personality. Despite inner turmoil they are able to remain poised and serene in circumstances that would agitate others. These children may also respond resentfully to teasing even though it may be done without intention to hurt. They may suffer from varying degrees of anxiety which is easily intensified in those exposed to faulty parenting. They will be cautious in all their dealings; they do not see the world as always a safe and friendly place.

These children would rather involve themselves in some form of productive activity than an excess of play and sociability. At the same time, they will not neglect interaction with all age groups. They favor a team spirit, group activity, and group entertainment to solo performance. They are conciliators and negotiators rather than agitators. They are not inclined to question authority. They cannot be hurried in study, play, or work but rather having an innate need to work at their own pace. They are well-balanced children who are not likely to do anything out of character. They will always benefit from frequent reminders that they are capable of undertaking and successfully completing any task presented to them. They need these reminders as their self-esteem and self-confidence are not as strong as they should be. They should be reminded that any apparent failure is actually a learning process and not an indication of inadequacy of talent. A first name reducing to the number 1 will be most helpful in this respect. The numbers 2, 6, and 8 are best avoided. Names with other numbers will open out their personality into other dimensions of self-expression but they may not help with an increase of self-confidence.

Twenty-sixes Born in January (first month)

Children born on the twenty-sixth day of January are endowed with the additional vibration they need for confident expression of all the attributes of their birth force. As the above section indicates, people born on the twenty-sixth day tend to suffer from inadequate self-confidence, and consequently underrate their capabilities. They may not always display this problem outwardly but they may entertain inner feelings of hesitancy and self-doubt. The 1 vibration influencing the month of January dismisses and overcomes these drawbacks. It injects a positive approach to all their undertakings. Willpower and strength of purpose helps them withstand and overcome people and circumstances that prevent them from making maximum use of the powers of their birth force. Decision-making is made much easier.

These children will be valuable helpmates in all domestic duties, especially the kitchen. Cooking will be one of their natural talents. In needy circumstances they will be prepared to take care of younger siblings, with family loyalties taking precedence over their own welfare. They will also turn out as conscientious students with the potential to be elevated to the position of school captains. This position will be gained and held by virtue of the admiration they receive from their peers and their own sense of responsibility. Any name will suit these responsible children, but the numbers 2, 6, and 8 are best avoided.

Twenty-sixes Born in February (second month)

The repetition of the 2 vibration in the birth month means that many of its attributes succeed in influencing the personality to a greater degree. Its impact is not of a forceful or easily perceptible nature but rather one of a tactful and subtle quality. It may be overshadowed by the rationality of the 6 and the assertive nature of the 8 but it stays effective in the background of the personality. As a result, sensitivity, self-consciousness, and indecision may be increased. Also, extra sensitive perception (ESP), which is a surface attribute of the 2 vibration, is likely to be triggered. You may see these children talking to fairies and other non-physical elements. They quickly lose this faculty as they grow older, but it could be activated at any stage of their lives, both consciously and unconsciously. The chapter on the second day of the month should be consulted for a better understanding of the influence of this vibration.

These children may be subject to imaginary and fantasy-making pastimes and yet, these practices are not permitted to take over their lives by the rationality of their 6 aspect and the practicality of their 8. They possess a beautiful and gentle nature with a good balance of imagination and down-to-earth values. The strong receptive and caring nature of the 2 vibration will be seen in their desire to collect things. This may range from responsible collections to the hoarding of all sorts of material from which they may never benefit. They are cooperative and helpful at home, in school, and at play. They need company in order to give out their best, and loneliness may have an inhibiting and destructive effect on their personality. Due to their powerful fantasy-making qualities they could be subject to imaginary fears. They do need strengthening of self-confidence and decisiveness. They have a tendency to underrate or undervalue themselves which is often a drawback. This can be overcome with a first name that reduces to the number 1. Names reducing to 2, 6, and 8 are best avoided. Names with other numbers will open out the personality into fresh areas of self-expression but they will not provide the ego-strength that is present within the 1 vibration.

Twenty-sixes Born in March (third month)

The 3 vibration governing the month of March contains assets that expand the personality with active and enthusiastic characteristics and talents. These are, however, secondary traits that contribute but do not take control over the personality formed by the combined forces 2, 6, and 8. Some fresh benefits derived from the youthful 3 vibration are, an enlargement of their social life, the introduction of an optimistic view on life, extroversion, and an increase of artistic appreciation and talents. Higher quality speech and an increased vocabulary are other significant additions. However, Twenty-sixes need sufficient confidence in their abilities or faith in themselves. Their personality does not possess this in strength nor does the 3 vibration provide it. The 3 vibration may introduce a false sense of bravado but not real self-assurance. This certainly does not mean that these children are not equipped for success in all their undertakings. They are resourceful, intelligent, adaptable, and pleasant personalities. All they need is greater strength of purpose and firm decisiveness. These can be gained to a fair extent with a first name that adds up to the number 1. The 1 vibration provides ego-strength and the ability to concentrate on one thing at a time. A 4 or 7 name will provide stability on the physical plane and provide roundness to the personality as a whole. Other numbers are best avoided.

Twenty-sixes Born in April (fourth month)

It is interesting that the personality of these children is formed by the full range of even numbers or receptive vibrations (2,4,6, and, 8). This provides them with the potential to take charge of their own lives as well as the capacity to take responsibility for the lives of others, when circumstances warrant. The interconnectedness of these forces results in solid attributes of balance, loyalty, steadfastness, practicality, and above all, willingness to be of service whenever needed. Tension created by contrary forces does not exist. Their movements are invariably calm and purposeful. The Twenty-six personality's penchant for order, system, and regularity is increased by the 4 vibration of their birth month. This habit may at times be taken to extremes, much to the annoyance of more easy-going people.

These children do not do anything out of character. It will not be easy to entice them out of their comfort zone. Conservative by nature, they conform to, as well as uphold, rules and regulations set within the home, school, and society. It is not in their nature to do things half-heartedly. Early in life they are certain to develop into enthusiastic handypersons in and around their home, and with friends and neighbors. They are family and community-oriented personalities. They give more and gain more out of life from cooperation than by competition and rivalry. The most suitable names for them will be from vibrations they do not already possess, such as the numbers 1, 3, 5, 7, and 9.

Twenty-sixes Born in May (fifth month)

The fifth month contributes a vibratory force that is different in most respects to the three vibrations comprising this birth day. The 5 can be said to be the most active of all active vibrations represented by odd numbers. Although, in this birth day and birth month combination, where its attributes are of contrary nature to those of the birth day, they do not take control over the personality. They act as secondary forces that are beneficial rather than disruptive. While deliberation, calculation, forethought, and caution are usual features of these people's birth day vibrations, impulse, fearlessness, experimentation, change, flexibility, and enthusiasm are normal attributes of the 5. The presence of these 5 qualities serves to stimulate the personality as a whole. Comfort zones are extended. None of the less attractive or less useful attributes of the 5 will be allowed to emerge. The chapter on the fifth day of the month has more information for a better understanding of the influence of this vibration upon the Twenty-six personality. The 5 vibration also gives them the ability to stand up under pressure, especially when they need to uphold their rights. More emotion is also introduced into their speech and body language, which usually adds to their attractiveness.

Although these children are blessed with a multi-faceted personality structure they could benefit from a vibration that gives them more willpower and a clear sense of direction. This can be easily supplied from a first name that reduces to the number 1. Names that reduce to 2, 4, 6, and 8 are best avoided. A 7 name will be a good alternative to the 1.

Twenty-sixes Born in June (sixth month)

The chapter on the sixth day of the month should be read for a better understanding of these children. Many attributes of the 6 vibration will be observed in their behavior. Love of home and family will figure largely in their lives. The 2 aspect of their personality combines well with the 6 in this respect, as both are loving, serving, and compatible forces. These children are happiest in the company of family members and a few intimate friends. They can relate to and enjoy the company of all age groups. It is possible that an element of possessiveness and dependency may enter into their relationship with some people. Until these children mature somewhat, they may show reluctance to open out to people outside their family circle or close friendships. The 8 vibration controlling their inner personality is a family-proud force which emerges in adulthood. All adults influenced by this vibration work hard for the welfare of their families.

These children can easily be trained to perform simple domestic tasks and this increases as they grow older. They will accept these responsibilities with pride and satisfaction. Culinary arts will eventually become one of their favorite pastimes. Some may suffer moods of despondency or poor self-esteem from time to time. How long they last depends on positive or negative conditions prevailing in their home environment. They need a good deal of peace, tranquility, and togetherness to live up to their full potential. These are certainly loving and lovable children who should be treated with love and caring. They could do with more optimism and self-confidence. These qualities can be obtained from a first name that reduces to the number 1. Names reducing to 2, 6, and 8 should be avoided. Other numbers will be suitable but they may not provide the ego-strength of the 1 vibration.

Twenty-sixes Born in July (seventh month)

The vibrations of the birth day and birth month combine to form a well-balanced personality structure. The physical (7), the emotional (2 and 8), the mental (6), and the spiritual (7) planes are easily accessible. A notable feature of the 7 vibration is the existence of physical, practical, and spiritual qualities that prevail side by side. The chapter on the seventh day of the month shows this dichotomy.

Spiritual values exist nearer to the surface in people influenced by the 7 vibration than other forces. It has the potential to awaken or release those in the Twenty-six personality. In addition, it merges easily with the 2 and 6. All three forces call for peace and tranquility in their environment. While not interfering with social interaction, the 7 introduces a need for occasional periods of solitude or private time. These children use this time for contemplation, analysis, dreaming, and wondering. They can indulge in romance but not be carried away by impracticalities. Any name will suit these dependable children.

Twenty-sixes Born in August (eighth month)

Children born on the twenty-sixth day are qualified Eight personalities (2+6=8).

Attributes of the 8 vibration are operative at fundamental levels, or as the inner personality. However, these children cannot be classified as pure Eights as their outer 2 and 6 forces modify the strength of their 8 by introducing attributes of their own. The chapter on the eighth birth day provides useful information on the nature of the 8 vibration.

The 2 and 6 are calm, peaceful, non-competitive, and not-assertive forces. Mingled with ambitious, competitive, and assertive 8 qualities these aspects of the personality may be subdued. Some other common attributes of the 8 vibration are the urge to take control of people and circumstances, and use their authoritative nature to do so. The additional 8 vibration may also result in the personality being too meticulous in their demand for order, method, and proficiency in their own lives and in the lives of others. The quality of their productivity may increase but it will take place at the expense of pleasantry and popularity. They may be inclined to take life too seriously. These idiosyncrasies can be overcome to a fair degree by a first name which reduces to 3, 5, or 9. Any of these will open out the personality into fresh dimensions. 4, 7, and 8 names should be avoided as these may increase the controlling tendencies of these personalities.

Twenty-sixes Born in September (ninth month)

The chapter on the ninth day of the month explains how the 9 vibration has the potential to extend its subjects into broader horizons or fields of vision—broader than other forces symbolized by the single digits 1 to 8. Family and community orientation of children born on the twenty-sixth can therefore be expanded into a national and international outlook. In other words they can gain a stronger sense of identification with life as a whole. The degree in which all this takes place will depend to a large extent on family and cultural values. But the receptivity and capacity to do so on their own initiative is always present through the influence of the 9 vibration of their birth month. Another contribution will be dignified body language with the absence of self-promotion and self-assertiveness.

These children will lead by example rather than through controlling or domineering habits. They are also too rational and wise to be led by others. They use diplomacy and tact to get out of tricky situations.

Two strong mental forces, 6 and 9, control their thought processes. They are motivated by a combination of rationality and wisdom, as well as good emotional balance. As they grow older, it is likely they will not be entirely absorbed in how they are being treated by the world but in how the world is being treated by them—less self-centeredness and greater concern for the wellbeing of others. Self-examination and self-motivation will be disciplines that guide their lives. The ordered nature of the Twenty-six personality will be more relaxed and flexible.

Although the 9 vibration introduces many superior attributes it does not necessarily provide an increase in self-confidence. These children are far more capable than they think they are. Self-confidence will be strengthened by a first name that reduces to the number 1. A 7 name may also help.

Twenty-sixes Born in October (tenth month)

Please refer to the chapter on Twenty-sixes born in January (first month). The zero does not change the personality in any significant way.

Twenty-sixes Born in November (eleventh month)

Please refer to the chapter on Twenty-sixes born in January (first month). Due to the presence of another 1, the influence of the 1 vibration is much stronger in these personalities.

Twenty-sixes Born in December (twelfth month)

Please refer to the chapter on Twenty-sixes born in January (first month) as well as the chapter on Twenty-sixes born in February (second month). The extra 1 and 2 in the birth month will strengthen their influence in the personality of these children.

Twenty-seventh Day of the Month

27 reduces to (2+7=9)

Children born on the twenty-seventh day have the influence of the 2 and 7 vibrations in the outer personality and the 9 vibration functioning in the background. Vibrations symbolized by the numbers 2, 7, and 9 interact harmoniously to form the integral personality of children born on this day. The sympathetic blending of these numbers creates a personality free from inner conflict or distress that might be otherwise caused by a clash of contrary forces. The inner and outer aspects of their personality are relatively the same. Usually, this is not a natural condition. If traces exist, living conditions may be responsible. Twenty-seven children do not feel the need to make out that they are something other than what they are. Their greatest strength lies in the fact that they do not need to compromise their beliefs and ideals to satisfy others. These superior qualities may not normally be related to children, but they will be observed developing as the years pass.

Characteristics of egotism and active self-promotion, if they exist at all, are eventually overcome. Twenty-sevens do not habitually relate life's experiences to themselves. Others are included in their reactions. Their independent spirit is neither compliant nor assertive. The 7 and 9 aspects of their personality indicate that they have emerged from a small circle of self-centeredness of an "I" and "My" mentality into one of "We" and "Us". Awareness of all forms of life is now in the foreground of their thoughts, speech, and actions. The potential and urge to abide by ethical and spiritual principles can be reached by these children and adults.

As these children possess interior and exterior resources that help them balance material and physical impulses with those of the spiritual, consciously and unconsciously, they stand out as wise and understanding personalities. Without displaying traits of assertiveness, competition, and authority, they are leaders by example. Self-serving ambition is an unnatural characteristic. There is nothing that is uncouth, vulgar, or strident in their body language and oral expression. Many of their thought processes could be more advanced than those of their elders. Their opinions should not be impatiently dismissed whenever they decide to give them, and this will not be too often. With open and curious minds they do not hesitate to venture into uncharted mental realms that the average child may not attempt. Anything to do with historical, cultural, and spiritual aspects of life will sooner or later attract their attention. All they need is a slight nudge in order to develop a lifelong interest in classical music, especially sacred music. They cannot be influenced or led astray by others who do not share their ideas and ideals.

These children are never at ease in unsettled and turbulent conditions as peace and tranquility are conditions needed individually and collectively by their 2, 7, and 9 forces in order to live up to their full potential. On the rare occasion when some form of mild chastizement is warranted it should be carried out in private with soft-spoken words. This approach will have a deeper effect on them than harsh language, which will only alert these wise children to their parents' own inadequacies. As these are very understanding children they do not possess an unrealistic sense of entitlement. In the long run they develop into givers rather than takers.

They are not incessant talkers. Preferring to work things out by themselves, they do not ask too many questions or explanations. Early in life they will be able to distinguish right from wrong. They could display a degree of introversion. This is a positive quality related to their contemplative nature. They do experience hesitancy when sudden decisions have to be made. Their compassionate nature and widespread thought processes see too many sides to an issue for immediate decisions to be made. Finally, these children are genuine nature lovers. The more time they spend in natural surroundings the greater their sense of wellbeing will be. The best name for these children will be one that reduces to the number 1. This will provide them with stronger motivation to pursue their ambitions in public and private life. However, any other number will do no harm to these wise children.

Twenty-sevens Born in January (first month)

A twenty-seventh birth day and a January birth month is almost a guarantee that the full potential of these children can be positively exploited. Attributes that ensure success are certainly present in the twenty-seventh birth day but particular ones, such as, motivation, self-belief, and assertiveness are not as strong as they should be. The 1 vibration covering the month of January not only provides strong motivation but also the willpower to complete whatever they undertake. When this vibration is allied with those of the twenty-seventh day, the personality gains a non-competitive form of authority and self-assuredness. When any form of assertiveness is needed and used it is not disputed by others as they are aware that it is not for personal advantage or power but for the exposition of reason and facts.

These superior characteristics can be expected to develop gradually in these children and blossom in adulthood. However, there is a definite proviso that applies to all children, especially to thoughtful and susceptible ones such as these. Their progress could easily be hindered by a faulty upbringing. However strong in potential, young children could be scarred by the speech and actions of uninformed and inattentive parents and elders. Future relationships may be tainted by behavior not natural to the elevated thought processes of these children. Any name will suit these wise and compassionate personalities.

Twenty-sevens Born in February (second month)

For a good understanding of this birth day and birth month combination please see the chapters on the second, seventh, and ninth days of the month. Pay special attention to the chapter on the second day of the month, as the 2 vibration has a heightened influence upon these children due to its presence in the second month. You will see that a close affinity exists between the 2, 7, and 9 vibratory forces. These children, and subsequently adults, are not disturbed by conflicting forces that cause inner turmoil. They also possess the advantage of outlets for expression through emotional and physical (2), physical and spiritual (7), and mental and spiritual (9) planes. Their essential nature is one of gentleness and refinement, and they have a tendency toward contemplation, dreaming, and fantasy. They broadcast these tender characteristics through their general conduct rather than speech. Allied with their non-competitive and non-aggressive temperament, their behavior elicits the admiration and affection of all people known to them.

These children's elevated thought processes could easily be smothered in a harsh environment. Many people they meet, may not possess the capacity to appreciate the depth of their nature. They could be forced to retire into themselves and, as a result, deprive others of their wisdom and compassion. These are children who need a degree of strengthening in order to face and overcome boisterous, disorderly, and inconsiderate individuals. The extra 2 vibration in their birth month does not provide this reinforcement. In fact, while enhancing their insight into the inner side of life, it weakens their efforts to engage in the harsher aspects of life. This problem may not exist if their birth date (day, month, and year) adds up to the number 1. This vibration will provide all the strengthening they need. A name reducing to the number 1 will certainly help. A name with the number 2 should be strictly avoided.

Twenty-sevens Born in March (third month)

Vibrations operating within the twenty-seventh day are inclined to create a thoughtful and serious outlook on life. The mental energies of these children may be concentrated on study, research, and investigation at the expense of sufficient attention to the lighter side of life. This condition will be altered to a fair degree by the youthful, optimistic, and extroverted attributes of the 3 vibrations of their birth month. The chapter on the third day of the month provides more information on their vibratory force.

This vibration also complements and activates many existing characteristics. Extroversion and sociability are extended. Optimism is increased. Artistic appreciation and expression are enhanced, and there is an increased capacity to absorb new facts. Therefore, these children are quick learners who are unlikely to "burn the midnight oil'", attempting to keep up with their studies. They will not need private tuition. As multi-talented and multi-faceted individuals they are capable of involving themselves in more than one task at a time.

If the total of their birth date (day, month, and year) reduces to the number 1, they are quite capable of emerging as brilliant students. This vibration reinforces strength of purpose, willpower, and self-confidence. A first name which adds up to the number 1 will be a good alternative. Any other name will suit these highly intelligent children but it will not provide the strength of purpose as the 1 vibration would do.

Twenty-sevens Born in April (fourth month)

These children are endowed with a well distributed set of vibratory forces. There is, however, an emphasis on the physical plane. The 4 vibration covering their birth month allied with the physical aspects of the 7 creates a down-to-earth and practical mentality. At the same time, a fine balance is formed between this aspect of their personality and their spiritual nature. In adulthood, among other things, they will display expertise in all money matters without surrendering their ethical and spiritual values.

Attributes of the 4 vibration also reinforce these children's love of nature. They are attracted to rocks and stones, plants and trees, and all animals. A cautious approach to humans is often a contribution by the 4 vibration. The only real extroverted aspects of their personality are derived from the underlying force of their 9 vibration. Their 2, 4, and 7 aspects could be described as leaning more toward being very selective of the company they keep. Generally, these children will gain the respect of all people by their unassuming and often unconscious manner in which they disclose the vast amount of philosophical and practical knowledge they possess. They make every effort to avoid egotistic, competitive, loud-spoken, and aggressive individuals. Forced into such conditions, they retire into themselves or resort to their private hobbies. Parents will discover that the best way to keep these children happy and contented is to take them on holidays to mountains, creeks, and waterfalls. Their love of the countryside filled with fauna and flora is usually greater than their love of the sea shore. In other words, the bush is more attractive to them than the ocean. They possess the potential to enjoy life by paying close attention to what they see and experience. A name reducing to the number 1 will help them withstand any negative influences they may encounter and help them interact with greater freedom with all people. Any other name will also suit these all-round personalities.

Twenty-sevens Born in May (fifth month)

One of the prominent characteristics of children influenced by the 5 vibration is curiosity. The chapter on the fifth day of the month shows how they apply this attribute to all their activities. The 5's curiosity is for the most part confined to the emotional and physical realms. In this birth day and birth month combination, it is merged with attributes that are generally partly attracted to mental and metaphysical realms. The inevitable result is a child's need to know the whys and wherefores of things. Parents and elders may not always be able to satisfy their questioning minds. The 5 vibration of their birth month increases courage and initiative to pursue their quest for knowledge in physical and metaphysical realms. It also enhances extroversion, vivacity, and emotional expression. Impulsiveness may also be activated.

These are knowledgeable and exceptionally perceptive children. Very little can be hidden from them. They are multi-taskers capable of undertaking and succeeding in any course of study, and eventually, in any form of work. They may decide to change courses but this will not be too often. They can cope with change and not allow it to affect the eventual outcome of study or work due to their probing nature and quick intake of knowledge. Any name will suit these physically, mentally, and spiritually energetic children. But a name reducing to the number 1 will be the best. It will slow down a temperament that may move too fast at times.

Twenty-sevens Born in June (sixth month)

The mental orientation of these children will be emphasized with the addition of another vibration from the mental plane. The 6 is known for characteristics of balance, reason, and deliberation. Combined with the steady 7 aspect of their personality, the actions and reactions of these children will not be allowed to fall out of control. Allowed free rein, it is always possible that the emotional content of their 2 and 9 aspects could resort to impulsive and emotionally charged behavior. This will be prevented in these children by their 6 and 7 aspects, as a fine balance exists between heart and mind.

These are children who think of others as much, or sometimes more, than they think of themselves. Self-centeredness is at a minimum. They are natural helpers and counselors who can be called upon for help at any stage of their lives. People are attracted to them for their tendency not to flaunt their knowledge or promote their egos. Feelings of "me" and "mine" are balanced with those of "we". Despite their good reasoning powers they may often suffer from unreasonable feelings of anxiety and worries that do not eventuate. They may continue to do so even after they have proved to themselves and others that they are capable of succeeding in any course of study or task they undertake. Optimism is not a strong attribute. There is invariably an initial hesitancy when they are faced with a new undertaking. However, faith in themselves and optimism can be gained with a first name that reduces to the number 1. Names with the numbers 2, 4, 6, and 9 are best avoided.

Twenty-sevens Born in July (seventh month)

The 7 vibration has a powerful influence upon the personality of children born with this birth day and birth month combination. To appreciate the full impact of 7 attributes on their personality, please refer to the chapter on the seventh day of the month. Additional information can be found in the chapters on the second and ninth days of the month, as the 2, 7, and 9 vibratory forces contain many shared and sympathetic attributes.

These children are richly endowed with qualities from the emotional and psychic 2, the physical and spiritual 7, and the mental and spiritual 9. There is a strong emphasis on the spiritual. Spiritual qualities are so varied that their appearance is seen in different ways and at different times and circumstances. These will naturally be observed at an emerging stage in children. The first indication will be their fondness for quietude and their own company. They are deep thinkers who try to figure out life's conditions by themselves. They may occasionally ask pertinent questions and give out equally pertinent opinions. They seek every opportunity to do their thinking and relaxation in natural surroundings. They need no encouragement to seek knowledge from books and the company of knowledgeable people. Forced into company not of their own choosing, they withdraw into themselves and enjoy their own thoughts. These are not unfriendly or unsociable children but they cannot put up with rudeness, uncouthness, egotism, competition, and excessive frivolity. They do possess an inner desire to share their wide-open minds with those of similar temperament. They may not find too many. This will not unduly disturb them as their greatest strength lies in their personal search for knowledge. Their generally reserved nature can be improved with a first name that reduces to the number 1. Any other name will also suit these deep thinkers.

Twenty-sevens Born in August (eighth month)

The chapter on the eighth day of the month discusses how the 8 vibration is essentially one of practicality, order, organization, and administration. These attributes combine effectively with the practical sides of the 2 and 7. The eighth month forms a fine balance between intellectual and esoteric values on the one hand, and realistic and practical values on the other. These are children who will not be caught up in dreams and unproductive contemplation. They can dream and not make dreams their master. Nor will they be easily led or misled by the thoughts and fantasies of others. They can think for themselves.

The combination of the 7 and 8 vibrations introduces an element of intolerance of people who do not measure up to their standards of efficiency and conduct. However, this can be held in control by the kindly and understanding qualities of the 2 and 9. There will be occasions when one aspect of their personality takes over from the other.

These children possess inner resources that help them mature early in life. The sooner they are treated with consideration and respect, the sooner their advancement in their studies and in self-development will occur. Some of their opinions may appear dogmatic and unyielding while others may be wise and sympathetic. These children are multi-taskers who are capable of undertaking and completing any task. Any name will suit them.

Neil Koelmeyer

Twenty-sevens Born in September (ninth month)

All people born on the twenty-seventh day are qualified Nine personalities (2+7=9). Attributes of the 2 and 7 vibrations are prominent in the forefront of their personality but those of the 9 remain firmly in the background. Children and adults influenced by the 2 and 7 are generally reserved in manner. They are observers more than actors. Those influenced by the 9 are extroverted performers. The natural tendency in children with this combination of vibratory forces is to submit to the 2 and 7 aspects of their personality and open out only when they receive a nudge from others or circumstances. This condition is altered in those born in the ninth month as the 9 vibration provides a boost by its repetition in the birth month. These children are therefore moderately extroverted personalities who can interact with others whenever they choose to do so. Due to many similarities between the 2, 7, and 9 vibrations, their sociability is confined to carefully selected company. All three vibrations introduce refinement in speech and body language, emerging from their genteel and spiritual nature. These children instantly recoil from crudeness, excessive noise, over-keen competition, boastfulness, and egotism in others. Their own egos are used for positive expression and not for self-promotion.

They should not be pushed into entering body contact sport or any other activity that does not meet with their sensitive nature. They see life in a larger context than the average child and blossom in the company of knowledgeable people. They promptly retire within themselves in the company of people with no interest in acquiring worthwhile knowledge. Any name will suit these open-minded children, but a name reducing to the number 1 will be best.

Twenty-sevens Born in October (tenth month)

Please refer to the section on Twenty-sevens born in January (first month). The zero in the tenth month does not introduce any fresh talents or personality traits. These are strong personalities. Any name will suit them.

Twenty-sevens Born in November (eleventh month)

Please refer to the section on Twenty-sevens born in January (first month). These are very strong individuals. Their personality greatly benefits from the presence of the 1 vibration in their birth month in double strength. Any name will suit them.

Twenty-sevens Born in December (twelfth month)

The presence of the 1 vibration in the birth month is an indication that these children take a positive attitude toward life in general. They can make the best use of all the attributes of their birth day vibrations. The presence of another 2 will certainly enhance their precognitive and other psychic powers. Any name will suit these intuitive children.

Twenty-eighth Day of the Month

28 reduces to (2+8=10=1)

Children born on the twenty-eighth day have the influence of the 2 and 8 vibrations in the outer personality and the 1 vibration functioning in the background. Because children born on the twenty-eighth day are qualified One personalities (2 + 8 = 10 = 1), attributes of the 1 vibration would normally be effective in the background as in most double digit birth days, allowing those in the foreground freedom of expression. For instance, in a birth day such as the twenty-sixth, qualities of the 2 and 6 are more obvious than those of the underlying 8. This not quite the condition in a twenty-eighth birth day as the 8 and 1 vibrations contain many similar features. Attributes of the 1 emerge effortlessly to join the 8 in creating a personality exhibiting characteristics of authority, control, decisiveness, and willpower. These children do not suffer from conflicting forces that pull them into different directions, creating uncertainty. They know what they want and proceed to get it by direct means. Ambition and self-confidence are their motivating forces.

The 2 vibration serves to mitigate excess of assertiveness and the urge to take control over people and circumstances. Advancement in public life followed by the acquisition of material wealth and power are essential qualities of the 1 and 8 vibratory forces. When they act in unison as they do in the twenty-eighth day, the capacity for success in any undertaking is considerably strengthened. The chapters on the first and eighth days of the month should be consulted. The full force of these vibrations can be applied in public life. The gentle 2 aspect can be used in relationship with loved ones and close friendships. Their need to remain in charge should be reserved for public life and a more democratic attitude adopted in private and social life. This is a lesson people born on the twenty-eighth day need to learn.

These children will display their natural leadership and organizational talents as soon as they are old enough to interact with their age group. They will be fierce competitors and natural team leaders. They are most likely to begin school with a strong sense of anticipation. Friendships and other relationships will sooner or later be placed in proper perspective as they do not, for the most part, depend on others to provide them with decision-making and strength of purpose. Children and adults who do not have proper channels to manifest their authoritative nature in public life direct it into their private life. Family members become victims of an excess of authority.

These are children who need to and are capable of making their own decisions. Within reason, they should be allowed to do so. They are certain to resent too many decisions being made for them. Despite their positive temperament they are also sensitive personalities who take pains to safeguard their sense of self-worth. They do possess prominent egos which in many ways contribute to success in public life but should be subdued in family, school, and social environments. They do not as a rule dramatize their emotions, but they could on occasions burst out in anger and frustration. Their thoughts are positive and constructive, and clearly reflected in their speech and opinions.

These are not domesticated children. They are usually drawn into outside activity. They excel in any form of sport due to their competitive nature. Their strong sense of method and organization may not always be applied to their private life. In other words, their bedrooms may not be kept in as neat and tidy condition as they should be. They will always be in some sort of hurry to get going, leaving no time and inclination for necessary domestic chores. These are children who learn more by paying close attention to the conduct of parents and elders than from advice and instructions they receive. As they are generally personalities who are young in body but mature in command, parents and elders should be careful not to "talk down" to them. Attempts to argue with them usually result in heated feelings and inconclusive results. The major portion of their personality, controlled by the 1 and 8 vibrations, does not allow much flexibility and open-mindedness. Names reducing to 1 and 8 should be avoided. Any other name will suit these strong-minded children.

Twenty-eights Born in January (first month)

The repetition of the 1 vibration in the birth month inevitably emphasizes its attributes. On the positive side this condition strengthens the capacity of these children to resist and deal with the ups and down of life. They are fortified with enhanced characteristics of stubbornness (in positive ways), concentration, persistence, vital energy, originality, loyalty, and self-reliance. An aspect of their personality that may not sit well with others will be a boosting of an "I" and "My" mentality. The pronoun "I" will be prominent in their conversation. Others may not be able to enter into a reasonable expression of their own views. However, their "I" consciousness may not increase or lessen their chances of success in public life. A good deal will depend on circumstances. It cannot always be regarded as a negative quality.

Their "I" or "Me" first mentality may certainly lead to stubbornness (in negative ways), self-interest, and expansion of ego. These characteristics will not help in cooperative living and working, or in equal partnerships. Forced into any group activity at school, these personalities will prefer to work alone or occupy a position of leadership. Their sense of self-protection is so strong that they could brazenly refuse to admit or deny an error or misdemeanor. These children usually insist on taking responsibility for their lives. They are quite capable of doing so.

Normal emotional expression is restricted by the repetition of the 1 vibration. These are, however, exceptionally loyal and protective children whose love nature is demonstrated by action rather than words and outward displays of sentiment. They will be fiercely protective of younger siblings. A first name reducing to 1, 4, or 8 should be avoided as these will increase their naturally disciplinary nature. Any other name will suit them.

Twenty-eights Born in February (second month)

The 2 vibration operating within the month of February has a salutary effect upon the integral personality of people born on the twenty-eighth day. Reinforced qualities of the 2 vibration are now able to exercise an effective influence upon the combined 1 and 8 forces. Authoritarian and egotistic attributes of these forces will not be allowed free rein. The personality is given the capacity to see the points of view of others and their needs and wishes. Cooperation is made easier. This condition makes their interaction with loved ones and all others much easier. At the same time it does not reduce their extensive powers of competition and ambition. It removes certain sharp edges created by their assertive 1 and 8 aspects with qualities of politeness and consideration.

These children are able to release emotions of joy or sorrow. They are not likely to suffer the ill-effects resulting from suppression of emotional expression. Their thoughts are not entirely confined to physical and material aspects of life. Fantasy and imagination extend their thoughts beyond these issues. They may not be carried away by full-time study or work. They can apportion some time for family and personal interests. Their 2 aspect controls the heart and emotions while their 1 and 8 aspects controls the mind, so a reasonable balance can be achieved. Names reducing to the numbers 1, 4, and 8 are best avoided. These will reduce the influence of the 2. Any other number will be suitable.

Twenty-eights Born in March (third month)

The chapter on the third day of the month will reveal that the 3 vibration contributes characteristics and talents that are either lacking or inadequate among the vibrations operating within the twenty-eighth day. The personality of these children is enriched by attributes of optimism, a sense of humor, a creative imagination, extended sociability, adaptability, and versatility. These are, therefore, all-round personalities with the capacity for self-expression in the physical, mental, and emotional realms. As children, they are already proven multi-taskers. Oral expression is also expanded and refined. Self-consciousness, the desire for attention and the urge to lead are also enhanced, and they make sure that they are not overlooked in any company. They do possess the power to hold the center of attention whenever they choose to do so, and this will be quite often.

Their interactions with all people, along with their form of leadership, are improved by a flavor of youthfulness, friendship, and humor. These latter qualities will not diminish any position of leadership they may hold, but will increase the admiration from others for the practical knowledge they possess and the manner in which they display their knowledge. These are mentally and physically active children who need to be kept occupied in study, sport, and other outdoor activities. They will not be attracted to domestic interests. While any name will suit these clever children it would be best if names reducing to 1 and 8 are avoided, as they are likely to increase the authoritarian nature of these personalities.

Twenty-eights Born in April (fourth month)

The practical nature of children born on the twenty-eighth day receives a tremendous boost when the 4 vibration is part of their integral personality. The chapter on the fourth day of the month provides a good understanding of the attributes of this vibratory force. The 4 complements the 1 and 8 aspects of the personality and enhances the desire for material wealth and comfort, as well as the capacity to acquire these. That part of their personality influenced by the 2 vibration also provides faculties that combine well with practicality. Basically, these are sensible children with loads of common sense. They are firm believers in self-help and do not hesitate to take responsibility for their lives at an early age.

These are children, and subsequently adults, who can only be influenced by people of similar temperament. They possess the strength and determination to develop self-discipline and eventually employ discipline in others. They are sure to show intolerance and impatience of laxity in speech and action in others, and even in themselves. In youth and adulthood they will display astuteness in all money matters. They will spend pocket money carefully and save a portion. Impulsive speech and action are exceptional. They may be inclined to take life a bit too seriously. First names reducing to 2, 3, 5, 6, 7, or 9 will be very suitable. These will open out the personality to dimensions other than the material and physical. 1, 4, and 8 names are best avoided.

Twenty-eights Born in May (fifth month)

Many attributes of the 5 vibration covering the month of May complement and strengthen those of the twenty-eighth day. In addition, they contain certain features that are lacking or weak in the birth day. Consequently, this birth day and birth month combination creates a multi-faceted personality. Characteristics and talents that are reinforced are initiative, courage, enterprise, enthusiasm, and competitiveness. Fresh features that are introduced are adaptability, flexibility, alertness, emotional expression, curiosity, and willingness to venture into unexplored territory. Conformity with social standards will also be relaxed; a feature that is common with most Twenty-eight personalities. Attention span will be expanded.

Controlling and leadership characteristics are also augmented. People influenced by the 5 vibration quite unconsciously take control of people and circumstances. When this characteristic is allied with the 1 and 8 vibrations, the urge to do so can hardly be controlled. This is likely to show up as a prominent feature in children and subsequently in adults. It is left to the individual to use it in positive or negative ways.

With all these self-sufficient attributes these are generally non-dependent children. As they mature, they will insist on making their own decisions and resist intrusion on their freedom to do so. These children do not need a name vibration to strengthen an already strong personality structure. However, a name that will open out their personality toward consideration of the needs and welfare of others, along with their own, would be advisable. Such names are those reducing to the numbers 2, 4, 6, 7, and 9.

Twenty-eights Born in June (sixth month)

The genteel aspects of the 2 portion of the Twenty-eight personality are, to a large extent, subdued by the assertive thrust of the combined 8 and 1. Their receptive influence can hardly be recognized. However, with the advent of the 6 vibration in their birth month this sphere of their personality is strengthened, and therefore able to play an active role. Although the 2 and 6 operate on different planes (emotional and mental), they share many features in common. Peacemaking, service, togetherness, cooperation, non-competitiveness, tact, courtesy, and domesticity are some of these. As these attributes are not natural to the 1 and 8, their introduction moderates the assertive, controlling, and one-pointed habits of the plain Twenty-eight. The personality becomes more sensitive to others and their right to be regarded as individuals. This results in an increase in popularity in the classroom, social, and public life, and a greater increase in family life. They are still able to fulfill all their ambitions, but they now do so without treading on the toes of others.

These are well-balanced children able to use qualities of heart and mind in their interactions with others. They can also relate to life in the domestic scene as well as the public arena with an equal degree of fulfillment. Their approachability will be one of their endearing features. Others learn from them and they learn from others. Any name will suit these self-controlled children.

Twenty-eights Born in July (seventh month)

Attributes of the 7 vibration operating during the month of July are of a different quality to those of the collective forces of the twenty-eighth day. The chapter on the seventh day of the month confirms this fact. Attributes of the 2 vibration which are normally subdued by the 1 and 8 can be evoked and strengthened when 7 characteristics enter the personality. The 2 and 7 have many features in common, such as non-competitive, non-assertive, and contemplative habits. These children experience adverse reactions to excess of noise, and crude and uncouth speech and actions in their environment. However, as they grow older, the passive and preoccupied part of their personality takes second place to realities and practicalities of life, so favored by the combined 8 and 1 aspects of their personality. There are also elements in the 7 vibration that contribute to their businesslike and practical temperament. The 7 is a dual force with its curious mixture of earthiness and spirituality.

These are essentially self-confident and multi-talented personalities with the potential to develop and express a fine mixture of empirical and charismatic power. This combination will gain the admiration and respect of almost all people they come into contact with. It also opens wider fields of study and opportunity. These children are doers rather than talkers. An element of non-material aspects of life will also enter into their speech and actions. They will not display too much emotion as the 7 vibration adds emotional restraint to the 1 and 8. Any name will suit these well-balanced children. However a name reducing to 3, 6, or 9 will contribute to a further expansion of their personality.

Twenty-eights Born in August (eighth month)

The conspicuous position held by the 8 vibration in this birth day and birth month combination is evidence that 8 attributes have the strongest hold on the personality of these children throughout life. They are also fundamentally One personalities (2+8=10=1). 1 and 8 forces do not conflict, but rather merge happily to create a personality of considerable strength and presence.

Attributes of the 1 and 8 that are strengthened in these children, are willpower, decisiveness, leadership, high ambition, organization, administration, strength of purpose, and an urge to acquire power and fame in all aspects of life. These are essentially adult characteristics but they can be observed in children from their tendency to take control of others of their age group and almost all circumstances in which they find themselves. Their attitude toward adults will also be one of self-assurance, independence, and self-determination. They can be quite unyielding in their demands, decisions, and opinions. They will be reluctant to open out to ideas and opinions other than their own. Early in life, they need to be taught that everyone is entitled to express their own individuality.

These children will eventually turn out as career-oriented and business-oriented adults. What will distinguish them from others will be the absence of pessimism in their thoughts, speech, and actions. A first name reducing to 1, 4, or 8 should be strictly avoided. Other numbers will help reduce their controlling nature.

Twenty-eights Born in September (ninth month).

The 9 vibration operating within the month of September contains many attributes that are contrary to those of the 8 and 1 that control the major portion of the Twenty-eight personality. It does, however, have an affinity with their 2 aspect. While peace, cooperation, tact, and diplomacy are essential attributes of the 2, wisdom, wide perspectives, compassion, and access to spirituality are natural qualities of the 9. These forces combine to mitigate to a fair degree the controlling characteristics of the 8 and 1. This will not be an easy task due to their unyielding nature. However, in the course of time, definite inroads will be made into the integral personality creating an individual acceptable to all people and successful in all their endeavors.

These are children who are capable of mastering any course of study they choose or any form of outdoor activity. Given reasonable opportunities they are capable of expressing their multi-talented personality to the fullest. Their competitive spirit is not diminished by the genteel qualities of their combined 2 and 9 aspects, but is tinged with acceptance and fair play. While paying attention to advice and suggestions from adults, they are imbued with the courage to do things as they see best and not always as others instruct them. Any name will suit these children who possess a fair balance between heart and mind. However, it may be best to avoid names reducing to 1 and 8.

Twenty-eights Born in October (tenth month)

Please refer to the section on Twenty-eights born in January (first month). The zero in the tenth month does not create any change in the personality.

Twenty-eights Born in November (eleventh month)

Please refer to the section on Twenty-eights born in January (first month). Attributes of the 1 vibration are strengthened in this birth day and birth month combination due to the frequency of the 1.

Twenty-eights Born in December (twelfth month)

The personality of children with this birth day is enriched by the strengthening of their 1 and 2 aspects. Any name will be suitable; however, a name reducing to a number other than 1 or 2 will open the personality out to wider influence.

Twenty-ninth Day of the Month

29 reduces to (2+9=11, 1+1=2)

Children born on the twenty-ninth day have the influence of the 2 and 9 vibrations in the outer personality and the 2 vibration functioning in the background. Due to the 11 being a Master Number (as is the 22), the powerful 11 force in this birth day will surface as the child grows and matures. It will be most unusual (but not impossible) for a child to live up to the elevated levels of a Master Number when very young. Notable features within the twenty-ninth day are attributes from the physical, emotional, mental, and spiritual planes. For an examination of this birth day the number 29 is reduced as follows: $2 + 9 = 11 = 2$.

The proportion in which attributes of one or two of these planes are more effective than the others is not easy to foretell. Age, upbringing, and circumstances will be responsible for the outcomes. A merger of all four planes can also be expected. However, the spiritual element is always present and most likely will increase with age. Children may be unconscious of their spiritual nature but sooner or later they begin to become aware of its presence. Family conditioning may expedite or slow down the process.

Wisdom and understanding revealed by these children will be well beyond their years. They are individuals who develop wide horizons and a global outlook on life. They are, in fact, an even mixture of idealism and pragmatism. Egotism and self-centeredness do not hinder their development or their popularity in whatever area of activity they find themselves. They are sensitive, non-competitive, and non-demanding children. Without a strong sense of entitlement they display a fair degree of non-attachment to material goods. Greater satisfaction is gained in giving rather than taking or grasping. They admire and easily acquire the beautiful things of life without becoming slaves to them.

The pursuit of knowledge on a wide scale and interaction with knowledgeable people will always remain a strong motivational force. Having a predisposition for good behavior they could be confused when they encounter some of the harsh realities of life, especially when their kindly attitude to others is not reciprocated. Expect a degree of inconsistency in their conduct until they gain a better understanding of their own complex nature and the differences in others. They may not always remain in full control of their emotions, and be subject to variations of mood. They may take some time and encouragement to develop a strong self-image and overcome a tendency to underrate themselves. These are children who have the potential to succeed in any form of study or task. There are no halfway measures with them. Gentle encouragement by parents and elders will not go amiss. A dogmatic approach will not succeed. The truth is that many of these children can be more insightful than their parents.

These are extroverted and open-minded personalities with no inherent prejudices and fears. When they meet these negatives, they possess the capacity to resist them. They approach strangers with curiosity and without fear. Their choice of intimate companions, however, will be from the genteel and cultural sections of society as they possess a flair to seek out people who can contribute toward their development, not detract from it. Being non-competitive by nature, they participate in sport or any other activity with a strong team spirit. They are mentally and physically fluid and flexible. These qualities are reflected in their relaxed body language. From an early age they will develop naturally as lively and knowledgeable conversationalists. Egotistic views and the pronouns "I" or "My" do not taint the quality of their speech. They are prepared to listen to others without interrupting. Their non-assertive nature abides by rules and regulations, although they would resist interference in their own personal development. When they receive arbitrary commands they are more likely to ignore them than challenge them.

Twenty-nines are generous with their possessions and often over generous. Others could take advantage of them, especially when their compassionate nature is aroused. As they grow old enough to handle money they will use it for responsible spending and not for saving or hoarding. There is an innate faith in these personalities that they will get what they need when the time comes. They possess a reasonable balance between domesticity and outside activity. These are personalities who can look beyond the surface of things.

Twenty-nines Born in January (first month)

Vibrations symbolized by the number 1 strengthen the integral personality formed by the twenty-ninth day. The chapter on the first day of the month provides details of the powers of this vibratory force. Among other things, the 1 injects positive thought processes, self-confidence, decisiveness, and a clear sense of purpose. To a large extent, children born on this day do not have doubts and fears about their ability to succeed in whatever course of study or activity they may undertake. They pursue self-development with confidence. The addition of positive attributes of the 1 vibration also increases their courage to express their views on life, while also influencing and motivating others. They will be known for qualities of leadership by example as well as by direct means. In other words, a strong team spirit is combined with leadership.

These are children who attract a host of admiring followers. When this takes place they do not lose their sense of balance or sense of comradeship. Stability in all practical affairs is strengthened by the powers of their birth month without reduction of mental, emotional, and spiritual attributes. They enter life on a blueprint that does not contain characteristics that detract from positive expression of thought, speech, and action. Progress is faster than others in their age group and even faster than many of their elders. They are equipped with the potential to live life deeply and fully. As these children are gifted with an exceptional combination of birth day and birth month vibrations, any name will suit them.

Twenty-nines Born in February (second month)

The 2 vibration figures largely in this birth day and birth month combination (29 = 11 = 2). Consequently, attributes of this vibration will remain an influential force in children and adults. Refer to the chapter on the second day of the month for a better understanding of these children.

Extraordinary sensitivity is a quality that already exists in the Twenty-nine personality. When another 2 vibration, which is responsible for this condition, is present in the birth month the personality becomes the basis for extra sensory perception and other psychic openings. Perceptive parents will observe this in young children in their speech and conduct, especially when they are by themselves. Usually these qualities are stifled or relegated to the inner personality in the course of their upbringing. They may or may not return at a later age.

The 2 vibration is a genteel, receptive, non-competitive, and non-assertive force. People influenced by it thrive in conditions of cooperation, companionship, peace, quietude, and helpful service—given and received. They are always appreciative of little things done for them. Certain negative characteristics can enter the personality due to an overloading of the 2 vibration. These are inadequate self-confidence, indecision, and an underselling of self. The 9 aspect of this personality, despite its wisdom, does not help in strengthening the personality. These children can be helped by frequent boosting of their confidence and never by criticism of any faults or failings imagined by others. Their loving and compassionate nature is easily hurt by the speech and actions of judgmental and uninformed people.

These children possess flexible, fluid, and supple bodies. Their body language expresses these qualities. They make natural dancers and acrobats. They are also natural water babies who learn to swim effortlessly. A name with a 1 vibration will be most helpful. It will greatly strengthen their personality.

Twenty-nines Born in March (third month)

The extroverted nature of these children will be apparent in those born in the third month. The good speech they already possess will be further improved in quality and quantity. Sociability and a sense of humor are some other traits that will be expanded. These are mentally oriented personalities with a quick intake of facts and figures. In a classroom they may be distracted by a multiplicity of thoughts and a vivid imagination, yet they will not lag behind. They are clever children who stay ahead of their age group. If they are placed in one class above their age, they will not struggle. As they are easily bored, their days need to be filled with opportunities for self-expression. They are certainly in their element in music, song, and other artistic activities.

Confidence in their abilities is not necessarily a strong feature. They are likely to look to others for interaction and appreciation. Because of the 3 in their birth month, they may demand more attention than others born on the twenty-ninth day of other months. They are well-mannered and well-behaved children who can easily be taught the particulars of acceptable social conduct. They are also easily offended by coarse speech and uncouth behavior in others. The youthful and optimistic attributes of their birth month prevents them from falling too frequently into feelings of uncertainty. These are fascinating children who can be a real joy to their parents, siblings, and classmates. Any name will suit them, but a name reducing to the 1 vibration will be best. It will provide greater strength to the personality. The chapters on the first and third days of the month may also be helpful.

Twenty-nines Born in April (fourth month)

April is one of the most advantageous months for a Twenty-nine child to be born in. It equalizes practicality and physical aspects of life with those of the emotional, mental, and spiritual. They are, consequently, well-balanced personalities. Wide variations in conduct will be most unlikely. Impulsiveness in thought, speech, and action is held in check by the down-to-earth and pragmatic attributes of the 4 vibration. The chapter on the fourth day of the month can be consulted for more information.

These are truly multi-faceted and multi-talented children. A combination of mental and physical creativity is their strongest asset. Using their mental and spiritual attributes they will also develop the ability to give themselves reality checks from time to time. In other words, they can be their own teachers.

Self-seeking and self-important characteristics are not strong in any of the vibrations that comprise their integral personality. They are readily receptive to guidance and instruction. If their natural characteristics are not inhibited or twisted into negative forms by a dysfunctional home life, they will be a boon to their parents and a teacher's delight. They do not shy away from hard work; nor do they entertain high expectations from others, relying on their own skills and aptitudes instead. Self-sufficiency is another strong characteristic. They are not easily led astray. There is a certain atmosphere about these children that prevents others from attempting to lead or take advantage of their obliging ways. These are personalities who can choose any line of study and eventually any line of work. Their options are wide open. Despite their superior talents they may take some time to become aware of their full potential. They need to be reminded from time to time that they are capable of succeeding in anything they undertake. A name with the 1 vibration will be best. Any other number will also suit them.

Twenty-nines Born in May (fifth month)

The 5 vibration within the month of May introduces similarities and dissimilarities into the fundamental personality formed by the numbers of the twenty-ninth day. The 5 is a powerful emotional force. Consequently, children born in this month express their emotions with little restriction. The 5 also contains strong physical attributes such as fearlessness in all activities within the physical realm. Alertness, observation, sensitivity, and their span of attention are all sharpened by the 5 vibration. These children are natural adventurers along all paths of life. They are also actors and dramatists. Flexible thought processes are reflected in quick-witted speech and animated body language. Being mentally and physically active children they gain popularity by their ability to motivate others. They make their presence felt in whatever situations they find themselves. They easily adapt to changes in their life.

These children need more freedom for self-expression than those born on the twenty-ninth day of other months. Competitiveness will also be stronger, but not to a degree that obscures their essentially cooperative nature. They are also children who enter adulthood with the potential to live life to the fullest. They are able to bounce back after illness or other negative experiences. They are subject to changes in mood, but they do not entertain gloomy and distressing thoughts for long periods of time. While any name will suit these talented children, those reducing to1, 4, or 7 will be best. These will ensure greater stability in the physical realm.

Twenty-nines Born in June (sixth month)

The potential to direct thought and action into humanitarian activity exists in all children and adults with this birth day and birth month combination. Most personalities will be compelled by inner urges to extend their thoughts and activities beyond attachment to family and domestic responsibilities. However, the extent of their outer interests will not endanger family welfare. The 6 vibration is strictly a family-oriented force. Their primary concern will be love and devotion to family. The 6 is also a strong community-oriented force. These children will not, therefore, be confined to home and family. They will develop a responsible balance between private life and public life. These are loving children with the potential to develop into loving parents, and successful and respected public figures. When the keen social conscience of the 6 vibration is combined with the international outlook of their Twenty-nine personality, a strong humanitarian outlook is the inevitable result.

From an early age they will turn out to be little helpers in and around the home, classroom and playground. Parents can safely entrust younger brothers and sisters to their care. Care of older siblings too will not be beyond them. They gain greater satisfaction by helping and serving than by expecting care and attention themselves. They will be sought after by their age group for friendship, confidentiality, advice, and counseling. The reason for this attraction is an aura of trustworthiness and an absence of self-promotion.

Despite these many superior attributes these children may not be aware of the strength in their personality. In course of time experience will strengthen their self-confidence. The best name for them will be one that reduces to the number 1. Others may not help as much in strengthening self-knowledge.

Twenty-nines Born in July (seventh month)

The vibrations controlling this birth day and birth month combination, each in their own way, express active elements of sensitivity, intuition, psychic awareness, and spirituality. Consequently, the personality of these children contains an extensive range of non-physical attributes. However, as they are born into a material and physical world these non-physical or metaphysical traits recede into the background as they grow older. But they are never far from the surface, and are likely to emerge at any time at any age. They are children young in body but old in wisdom.

They are quiet thinkers and contemplatives with open minds and a willingness to listen to what others have to say. Their minds contain much more knowledge than they are prepared to or able to put into words. Usually, they speak when they have something worthwhile to say. Parents and elders should not fail to pay attention to their opinions and enquiries. If ignored, they are not likely to repeat them or insist on being heard. Much of their knowledge is gathered from observation and, sooner rather than later, from books and knowledgeable people they meet. Learning will be extended into the world of nature. They need to spend time by themselves and this is done whenever possible in natural surroundings.

They will always be very selective of the company they keep. There is an inbuilt knowledge of when to get involved and when to stay out of things. Their comfort zone is more extensive in their thought processes than in their interaction with others. Their natural traits of gentility and refinement revolt against ill-mannered, rough, and inconsiderate people. These children will be a delight to teach and instruct at home and in school as they possess an intuitive knowledge of right and wrong, and an eagerness to learn. They should always be handled with care and consideration. Any name will suit these open-minded children.

Twenty-nines Born in August (eighth month)

The chapter on the eighth day of the month shows how attributes of the 8 vibration function in contrast with those in the twenty-ninth day. They are indeed of an opposite nature. The advantage in this birth day and birth month combination is a good balance between idealistic and practical values. These are children, and subsequently adults, who can actualize their high-minded thoughts and ambitions. With the aid of the 8 vibration's strength of purpose, organizing talents, a determination to succeed, and competence in whatever they undertake will be the hallmark of these personalities. The strengthening of opposites rather than the tension of opposites can and should be applied.

These are not children who submit to peer pressure. They are teachers, as well as leaders, who use a combination of wisdom and common sense in forming opinions and making their decisions. The 8 vibration also introduces a fair degree of competitiveness which strengthens the personality without damaging genteel traits. A sound secondary education and subsequent specialization in whatever they choose will allow their considerable faculties to develop higher than if they are deprived of these opportunities. At the same time, these are individuals who possess the mental and physical energy to pursue higher education as adults if they have been deprived of it as children and teenagers. Using their abstract and concrete powers interchangeably, these children possess the potential to carve out a successful life for themselves, as well helping and influencing others to do so. Any name will suit these well-balanced children.

Twenty-nines Born in September (ninth month)

The chapter on the ninth day of the month discusses the extended worldwide outlook of individuals with this birth day and birth month combination. Attributes of heart and mind are amplified by the repetition of the 9 vibration in the birth month. Superior characteristics that will appear in these children and then blossom in adulthood are generosity in both goods and services provision, compassion toward humans and animals, and above all, an unfolding of a spiritual way of life. The clash between the spiritual and material will exist but the spiritual will always remain as a guiding force. A dysfunctional environment is bound to create a great deal of inner turmoil and interfere with natural development. These are children whose minds are agitated by a great variety of thoughts. They will need time, effort, and maturity before they sort out and establish emotional and mental stability.

These are children (and subsequently adults) who are givers much more than takers. Others may take advantage of their kindly nature. They find it difficult to say "No" when their compassionate nature is touched. Their emotions are easily aroused and just as easily subsided. Their highs and lows are released in demonstrative body language. They are good listeners and perennial students. They acknowledge any mistakes they may make and profit by learning from them. Ego does not stand in the way of development. Generally extroverted children, they also need short periods of time to commune with themselves. Names reducing to 1, 4, or 7 will make them stronger in the physical world. A name reducing to 9 should be avoided. Other numbers will be more suitable.

Twenty-nines Born in October (tenth month)

Please refer to the section on Twenty-nines born in January (first month). The zero in the tenth month does not affect any appreciable change in the personality.

Twenty-nines Born in November (eleventh month)

Please refer to the section on Twenty-nines born in January (first month). The influence of the 1 vibration is much stronger in November due to the repetition of 1s in the birth month combining with the 1s in the birth day.

Twenty-nines Born in December (twelfth month)

This personality is strengthened by attributes of both the 1 and 2. Please refer to the sections on Twenty-nines born in the first and second months.

Thirtieth Day of the Month

Please refer to the chapter on the third day of the month. The zero in the thirtieth day does not introduce any new features or take away any of those already existing. It may, however, emphasize certain aspects of the 3 vibration.

Thirty-first Day of the Month

31 reduces to (3+1=4)

Just as on the thirteenth day of each month, children born on the thirty-first day have the influence of the 3 and 1 vibrations in the outer personality with the 4 vibration functioning in the background. The difference between those born on the thirteenth and those born on the thirty-first is that in the thirteenth, the 1 is the stronger force as it precedes the 3 in sequence. In the thirty-first, the 3 is the stronger force as it precedes the 1. Children of both birth days are qualified Four personalities (1+3=4 and 3+1=4).

Creativity is a quality that stands out individually and collectively in the vibratory forces that comprise the thirty-first day of the month. Mental creativity containing a vivid imagination is the hallmark of the 3 vibration. Originality and inventiveness are conspicuous features in the 1, while practicality and manual dexterity are fundamental attributes of the 4. People influenced by the 1 and 3 are creators of blueprints, while the 4 follows through by building upon the blueprints. A more talented and versatile combination of vibrations can hardly be found.

In addition to these combined natural aptitudes, the birth day provides a valuable mixture of youthfulness, optimism, enterprise, ambition, confidence, caution, steadfastness, and level-headedness. These are also children with a strong sense of identity. Quite early in life they begin to make their own decisions with an inner knowledge that they are capable of standing on their own feet. They are certain to resist excessive attempts by others to instruct and guide them, being gifted with the confidence to choose their own directions in life. At the same time, they will not refuse to fall in with a parent's choice of a course of study and subsequent career, if it offers scope for use of their multiple talents. They refuse to be restricted to monotonous work or narrow fields of expression, however profitable they may be.

Although they are certainly multi-talented personalities they need to do one thing at a time, and do it well. Concentration is one of their assets. Everything they do is infused with abundant energy and enthusiasm. They are loving, lovable, and entertaining children but physical expression through touch and embrace is limited. These are children who cannot be overlooked. While their presence draws the attention of others, they also consciously make sure that attention is paid to them. They are natural entertainers and versatile conversationalists. They excel in any form of sport though natural skills and a friendly form of competition. They are motivators of any form of activity—productive, mischievous, or otherwise.

There is an unmistakable element of ego and self-centeredness in their personality. However, their quality of ego is accompanied by a positive, friendly, and obliging manner that people find attractive. Parents, elders, and close friends are happy to feed their ego and, in turn, enjoy their vibrant and optimistic temperament. All these children need is an occasional reminder, kindly put, to come out of themselves and pay attention to others around them.

As quick learners these children will be found at the top of their class as soon as they begin school, and will continue to remain so. More often than not they could be in advance of their curriculum. As natural all-rounders, they will also be drawn as leaders, into extracurricular activities without interference in their studies. Parents may find them costly to educate. Besides the costs involved in the classroom and other activities, these children fancy and demand the good things of life. They may develop expensive tastes with their own system of values. However, the investment parents make in these children will pay ample dividends. The fashion and entertainment industries could attract both sexes. As these are multi-talented personalities it is just not possible to forecast what line of study and work they may undertake. Their potential is extensive and opportunities are unlimited.

These children may eventually strike out on their own but they are certain to maintain close family connections. Boys could develop real friendship with their fathers, and love and respect their mothers, and girls vice versa. Any name will suit these gifted children.

Thirty-ones Born in January (first month)

The self-confidence allied with mental and physical creativity provided by the vibrations of the thirty-first day are enlarged and emphasized by the addition of another 1 vibration in the birth month. Ego-consciousness and willpower are also increased, along with the determination to abide by their own decisions. For good or ill, these children have become harder to influence due to their leadership talents being strengthened by the 1. Elements of pride, self-indulgence, and self-centeredness, which already exist in a milder form, may be increased in various degrees. Cooperation and equal partnerships will be made more difficult. These children (and subsequently adults), will expect others to follow their lead. Many people may do so, but certain others will challenge their self-assured and managerial manner.

These children and adults may not be popular with everyone they meet but there can be no doubt of their capacity to succeed in anything they undertake. Parents can expect a good deal of stubbornness, but they will also receive an equal degree of loyalty and support which will be given voluntarily in time of need. Emotional demonstration will be limited. Their constitution is such that they avoid being touched or hugged too often. As they grow older they outgrow any need to be kissed and embraced. This does not mean that they are cold personalities. Their sentiments are deep and abiding and demonstrated in good deeds and other tokens of love and loyalty. A first name reducing to 2, 5, or 9 will help them to some extent to release their emotions. It will be helpful if the numbers 1, 3, and 4 are avoided. Apart from some help in emotional release, these children do not need an additional vibration to strengthen their personality.

Thirty-ones Born in February (second month)

The number 2, or the 2 vibration, provides these children with a personality structure that covers the physical, emotional, and mental realms. It completes the personality by supplying an emotional outlet that is not present in the thirty-first birth day. However, it will always remain a secondary feature which will assist in emotional release. The chapter on the second day of the month will be of interest.

Certain attributes of the 2 vibration such as cooperation, quietude, diplomacy, negotiation, sensitivity, and unselfishness will certainly enrich the personality. Self-centeredness will still be a powerful force. But all these children need is a gentle nudge to awaken them to the presence and needs of others. Selfishness is not an aspect of their nature. They are actually generous individuals—especially in service and helpfulness. To get the best out of them, acknowledge their abilities and willingness to help. They look for recognition of their talents. They need to be included in family discussions and activities. The contributions they make will always be fresh and worthwhile. Parents should remember that these children are not loners and definitely need interaction with people. Personal popularity and high academic achievement are well within their reach. Expertise with the written word as well as the spoken word is one of their talents. A tertiary education will see an immediate release of their multiple talents. Anything less will delay but not diminish progress. Any name will suit these well-balanced children.

Thirty-ones Born in March (third month)

As the number 3 is repeated in the birth month, attributes of this vibration will maintain a major influence upon the integral personality. Artistic appreciation and creativity may override other considerations. A constructive imagination, sociability, quick wit, a keen sense of beauty, design and color, and a high sense of accuracy are essential attributes reinforced by the 3 vibration. These children are also natural entertainers and performing artists. They are certain to exhibit a vibrant, youthful, and optimistic outlook on life. They are natural trendsetters, always involved in the latest fashions in dress, music, dance, and other accomplishments.

Do not be surprised if these children begin speaking earlier than others of their age group, and making maximum use of their power with words and fluent oral expression. They are likely to develop a habit of talking about their own likes and dislikes, and not paying attention to what others have to say. In other words, they are impatient listeners. Despite this element of self-absorption, they are attractive and enjoyable company. They are happy children who can easily lift the spirits of people with whom they interact. Following their high sense of accuracy, they do not hesitate to correct or even pick on anyone who falls into the slightest error in speech or deed. They do not mean to be offensive; they just cannot help correcting something they see as inaccurate. This trait may lead to misunderstanding by people who do not know them intimately. Any name will suit these versatile children.

Thirty-ones Born in April (fourth month)

People born on the thirty-first day are qualified Four personalities (3+1=4). The vibratory force symbolized by the number 4 is an exceptionally strong aspect of the physical plane and its attributes will be clearly evident in these children due to the presence of another 4 in the birth month. With the combination of their mental and physical powers, it is easy to believe they can do anything. The originality and imagination of their 1 and 3 vibrations, combined with the practicality of the 4, now appearing in double strength, provide unlimited potential in all departments of practical living. Although they are articulate, these children are doers more than talkers. In other words, they would rather be doing something constructive than engaging in prolonged conversation. Convinced of their ability to do anything they undertake and do it well, they may not welcome interference from others. Once they have decided upon a course of study, they are not driven by temptation or impulse to change course.

These are exceptionally loyal children with a high sense of duty. Parents can confidently entrust them with domestic responsibilities at various stages of growth. With qualities of determination, staying powers, and versatility, expect success in any form of sport, including body contact sport. Emotional displays will be rare as they do not possess an outlet for easy emotional release. They do not feel the need to be frequently touched, nor do they feel the need to touch others in order to assist communication. They display their love and loyalty in deeds rather than in words and demonstration. There may be occasions, however, when they resort to outbursts of temper when their expectations are not met. Any name will suit these versatile personalities. Emotional release can be helped with a name reducing to a 2 or a 5.

Thirty-ones Born in May (fifth month)

These qualified Four children who are born in the fifth month, inherit an amplification of personality traits and talents. See the chapter on the fifth day of the month for a better understanding of their expanded personalities. The 5 vibration, among other things, is a powerful emotional force. Its presence in this birth day and birth month combination creates a rounding off of the overall integral personality. Emotions that are held back in their birth day vibrations can now be released when necessary. Access to the physical, emotional, and mental planes provides these children with unlimited opportunities for living life to the fullest. Unless restricted by a harsh upbringing, they seldom fail to do so. They are exceptionally alert and active personalities who quieten down only when they are physically exhausted. But their recovery is always speedy.

They have no time to indulge in negative feelings of melancholy and boredom. Parents will be pressed to constantly find them a variety of outlets for self-expression. They are able to interact with all types of people and age groups. Their spirit of adventure is very much alive, and their vibrant and imaginative nature attracts a host of admirers and followers. They are genuine multi-taskers who involve themselves in a variety of activities with equal competence. With sharp minds, alertness, flexibility, and adaptability, they succeed in whatever they undertake. They do not experience problems adapting to changes in their lifestyle, such as a change of school or a change of residence.

As these children are driven by speed of mind and body, parents may find it difficult to keep them at home. A variety of sporting and social activities will be more attractive than domestic interests. Any name will suit these dynamic children.

Thirty-ones Born in June (sixth month)

The 6 vibration which operates on the mental plane merges with the 3 to increase the mental orientation of these children. Their imaginative powers are supplemented by the reasoning and balancing attributes of the 6 vibration. The chapter on the sixth day of the month explains this personality in more detail. Children with this birth day will not allow their imaginations to run loose. In addition, these same attributes of the 6 will merge with the practicality of the 1 and 4 aspects of their nature. The end result will form a personality with realistic values. Uninhibited emotional expression may be lacking in these children. Love, loyalty, and attachment to home and family are all enhanced by the 6 vibration but these attributes will not be expressed in so many words or through outward demonstrations. Parents will not experience difficulty in getting these children to do their part in all domestic chores.

The 6 vibration also enhances the artistic talents inherent in all those born on the thirty-first day. It creates an increased appreciation of beauty in all things. Verbal effectiveness is also increased. These are well-adjusted children who can defend themselves through the powers of speech combined with logical and down-to-earth thought processes. It will not be easy to fob them off with unrealistic explanations or answers. They can be quite argumentative. As potentially brilliant students, they can undertake and succeed in any course of study they choose. In adulthood their range of opportunity is unlimited. They certainly profit from wise advice and encouragement; however, they are fundamentally self-sufficient personalities who fall back on their own mental and physical powers. Any name will suit these rational children.

Thirty-ones Born in July (seventh month)

The 7 vibration covering the month of July is responsible for artistic expression, manual dexterity, and down-to-earth values, but also for drawing out and activating spiritual nature. At an early stage of life, the degree and manner in which spiritualty is expressed, will depend largely on family beliefs. Independent views may arise later in life. Meanwhile, the nature-loving qualities of the 7 vibration will have an immediate effect on how these children view the world around them. The chapter on the seventh day of the month should be consulted for a better understanding of this vibratory force.

The 7 vibration also introduces a fair measure of elegance and poise which increases the attractiveness of these personalities. It reduces their egotistic and self-centered thoughts. This helps them move out of themselves to embrace wider perspectives. As this is a reserved and non-demonstrative force, what it does not provide is easier access to and demonstration of emotion. These children soon grow out of the need to be cuddled. As they grow older, they will not use touching as a means of communication., nor are they fond of being touched by others.

As the multiple talents generated from the thirty-first birth day are augmented by their birth month, these children hardly need a first name to provide additional talents. An outlet for emotional release can be obtained by a first name that reduces to the numbers 2 or 5. As these children are not confined to limited areas of self-expression, they are open to any course of study or any form of sport or hobby. They may not be as competitive as others born on the thirty-first day, but they achieve their ends through natural intelligence. Besides a name reducing to another 2 or 5, any other name will suit these clever children.

Thirty-ones Born in August (eighth month)

The 8 vibration as seen in the chapter on the eighth day of the month, is essentially one of control, organization, and power. Many high achievers have been backed by this force. Children with this birth day and birth month combination can reach this condition if given a proper upbringing.

These are children who, at an early age, expect to have their own way in most things. They will show instant resentment when they are justlflably checked by parents and elders. At the same time, they do not hesitate to exercise authority over children of their age group. They are unconsciously motivated by willpower and leadership talents, and consequently, not easy to discipline. They usually learn more through experience than by direct instructions. Their body language will be purposeful with early indications of maturity. Parents may rest assured that these children are, for the most part, capable of looking after themselves, as well as younger siblings placed in their charge. They assume responsibility with confidence. They could be a real asset to family stability, if handled properly. Any name will suit these competent children.

Thirty-ones Born in September (ninth month)

A wide opening of the mental plane is created in children born in the month of September. People influenced by the 9 vibration as the primary force, or as a secondary force, entertain thoughts outside of themselves into worldwide perspectives. Released in a good measure from ego-centered thinking, they develop the capacity to see a bigger picture of life. The chapter on the ninth day of the month will be of interest. Worldwide perspectives are accompanied by a humanitarian outlook.

As the 9 vibration in this birth day combination is a secondary force, its effects may take some time to emerge. (As a primary force, i.e. in the birth day itself, very early beginnings can be expected). One of the best features introduced by the 9 vibration is the ability to sense the needs of others. These children born on the thirty-first day can achieve a good balance between their own needs and their varied obligations toward others. They are more receptive to guidance than others born on the same day. The natural wisdom of the 9 vibration overcomes ego-centered resistance to advice and instruction. It reduces these children's fierce competitive spirit and, as a result, they are able to enjoy participation with others in whatever activity they choose, purely for the fun of it. Their extroverted nature is expanded, and so is their comfort zone, sociability, and popularity. Any name will suit these capable and wise children.

Thirty-ones Born in October (tenth month)

Please refer to the section on Thirty-ones born in January (first month). The zero in the tenth month does not introduce or take away any attributes of the 1 vibration.

Thirty-ones Born in November (eleventh month)

Please refer to the section on Thirty-ones born in January (first month). The force of the 1 vibration will be emphasized in this birth day and birth month combination due to its repetition.

Thirty-ones Born in December (twelfth month)

While attributes of the 1 vibration are strengthened by its repetition in the birth month, those of the 2 are also introduced. Please refer to the section on Thirty-ones born in January (first month) and in February (second month).